The Chivalrous Society

The Chivalrous Society

Georges Duby

Translated by Cynthia Postan

University of California Press
Berkeley and Los Angeles

UNIVERSITY OF CALIFORNIA PRESS
Berkeley and Los Angeles, California

© *Edward Arnold (Publishers) Ltd 1977*

ISBN 0–520–02813–9
Library of Congress Catalog Card Number: 74–81431

Printed in Great Britain

Contents

Abbreviations

B	*Cartulaire de l'église collégiale de Beaujeu*, edited by C. Guigue (Lyon, 1864).
Bull. Cl.	*Bullarium Sacri Ordinis Cluniacensis*, edited by P. Simon (Lyon, 1680).
C	A. Bernard and A. Bruel, *Recueil des chartes de l'abbaye de Cluny* (6 vols, Paris, 1870–1903).
GM	*L'Histoire de Guillaume le Maréchal*, edited by P. Meyer (Société de l'histoire de France, 3 vols, 1891–1901).
HE	Ordericus Vitalis, *Historia Ecclesiastica*, edited by A. Le Prévost and L. Delisle (Société de l'histoire de France, 5 vols, 1840–55).
H Gh	Lambert of Ardres, *Historia comitum Ghisnensium*, edited by H. Heller, MGH SS XXIV (Hanover, 1876).
M	*Cartulaire de Saint-Vincent de Mâcon*, edited by C. Ragut (Mâcon, 1864).
MGH	Monumenta Germaniae Historica
MGH SS	*Monumenta Germaniae Historica, Scriptores*, edited by G. H. Pertz and others (Hanover, 1826–1913).
P	*Cartulaire du prieuré de Paray-le-Monial*, edited by U. Chevalier (Paris, 1890).
PL	*Patrologia Cursus Completus, Series Latina*, edited by J. P. Migne (Paris, 1844–64).
SM	*Cartulaire du prieuré de Saint-Marcel-les-Chalon*, edited by M. and P. Canat de Chizy (Chalon, 1894).

Dates of documents quoted by number are given in square brackets.

Preface

The road I have travelled in my research will, I hope, be clearly revealed in the sequence of the articles assembled here. At the outset of my academic career I adopted the technique devised by Marc Bloch and attempted to describe within a limited territory, which also happened to possess an abundant documentation, the social structure known to us as feudal society whose outlines on the continent became apparent and gradually crystallized during the eleventh and twelfth centuries. The area I chose was, of course, the neighbourhood of the abbey of Cluny. By 1946 a preliminary study of judicial institutions had provided me with the tools with which to dissect the system and to isolate some of its more important manifestations. The method I chose—to reconstitute as far as possible within my limited framework the totality of social relations— proves that I had from the very beginning embraced the belief I was to assert twenty-five years later in my inaugural discourse to the Collège de France in 1970. This belief was that the historian of society must observe social relations in their entirety and allow for the inseparable nature of the various factors by which they are determined—the inter-relationship of economic activities, the institutional framework con-structed to maintain these immutable relations and the ideological propositions claiming to justify the rigour of the framework. From 1953 onwards, by enlarging my field of analysis to encompass western Europe, I undertook a systematic exploration of the material culture upon which the organization of this fundamentally agrarian society was based, and I am glad to be able to express here my gratitude to those British economic historians from whose work I have derived essential assistance. The study, here once more republished, of the economic mechanisms which linked together *seigneurie* and village society in the Provençal countryside at the beginning of the fourteenth century reflects the problems with which I was faced during this second period of my working life. However, in 1961 I turned my attention to other phenomena less easy to explain and too long left to historians of ideas, but which seemed to me more easily understood when based upon a better knowledge of the nature of the productive process. These phenomena concerned mental attitudes and all the ideological forms by which social behaviour was clothed and, for the most part, governed. Since then my investigations have been, and still are, concentrated within one period—the tenth, eleventh and twelfth centuries—and upon two topics. The first topic is systems of social classification—to begin with, those processes of classification, of necessity simplified, through which individuals attempt to place themselves in a relationship with others, and then the ideological models, the exemplary types, to which these processes give birth, as well as the systems of sanctions and rules which give this practical taxonomy its value and efficacity. My second line of investigation is into the patterns of kinship. In the latter field it seems necessary to begin by examining the social class in which the available sources, whether written or unwritten, make a coherent investigation possible. This class is, of course, that rank in society described in the documents of the period as 'princes' and 'knights'. My researches into these two topics had already begun while I was engaged on my first study of feudal society in the Mâconnais; thirty years later it is still proceeding through a process of revision, correction and slow progress on both the theoretical and the factual plane. Most of the articles presented in this collection bear witness to how far I have travelled, and I hope that they will elicit from my readers criticism and encouragement which may help me in my continuing labours.

Beaurecueil, September 1976

1

Medieval society

You have entrusted me not merely with the teaching of history of the middle ages, though such an act would have accorded perfectly with the traditions of this institution, but more specifically with the teaching of the history of medieval society.[1] I assume you have done so because it has seemed likely to you that a study of social relations might cast a fresh light on all the various elements that go to make up civilization as a whole. In addition I must also presume that, as the main purpose of the Collège de France is to teach science in the very process of being made, you have decided that the most urgent notions—those one can expect to yield the most up-to-date results—must be placed against the least perfectly defined perspectives of medieval history, in other words those of social history.

My audience may be surprised to hear me speak in this way about social history, standing as I do on the very spot where Lucien Febvre taught for so long and campaigned so vigorously for a new kind of history. We have all followed his battles with excitement and fascination and we may recall how much has already been accomplished, is being done at the present moment, and will be done in the future. For myself, I must also salute with gratitude and respect the memory of March Bloch, for it is to him I owe the discovery that we must always be looking beneath the dust of our documents and listening in the silence of our museums for man as he really was. However, we cannot ignore the fact—borne out, alas, by the arrangements and titles of countless pieces of research—that often social history still seems to be no more than an annexe, an appendage, dare I even say, the poor relation of economic history. For more than half a century the latter has indeed forged ahead to give a large body of prolific research life and content; it has conquered the wide open spaces and is at present, buttressed by recent developments in the archaeology of material culture, blazing fresh trails. It is all-triumphant, and by its very success it sweeps the history of society along in its train. For it is obvious that the study of social stratification and the relationships binding individuals or groups cannot be undertaken without first clearly understanding the organization

[1] An inaugural lecture at the Collège de France.

of production and the distribution of profits at any given moment.

However, we must be particularly on our guard in two respects. In the first place, historians of the medieval economy have not always avoided applying to their observation of the past economic concepts based on modern conditions, and these may be revealed in practice as both anachronistic and distorted. Thus, they have for long unconsciously accorded pride of place in their studies to commerce and the circulation of money without having precisely defined the role of money or the nature of exchange in a civilization which was as totally rural as the medieval west. (Some of the conclusions reached in ethnographical studies would surely have helped them here.) In the second place, and this is an even more important point, it would be wrong to think that we have taken the analysis of a society to its limits when, by examining censuses, surveys and the registers of *estimes*, we have been able to rank the heads of households in a hierarchy of wealth; when, by interpreting terms of leases or contracts of employment, we have seen how this worker or that suffered exploitation; when, through surveys made for tax purposes, we have laid bare the trends of demographic change. Indeed, the attitudes of individuals and groups of individuals to their own situation in society and the conduct these attitudes dictate are determined not so much by actual economic conditions as by the image in the minds of the individuals or groups. And the latter is, of course, never a faithful reflection of reality, but is affected by a complex play of factors. Thus, by putting social phenomena into the straightforward context of economic phenomena, we narrow drastically the field of enquiry, restrict the scope of the problem and prevent ourselves from forming a clear view of the essential dynamic.

In fact, from a very early stage, when economic history itself was in its beginnings, some scholars had found it necessary to complement the study of the material foundations of prehistoric societies with studies of rituals, beliefs, myths and other aspects of collective psychology by which individual behaviour is ruled and which order social relations just as directly and imperatively as economic facts do. In this way, that branch of history, which has been called rather inexactly the history of the mind, was born, although its progress was for long slow and hesitant. From these beginnings the younger humane sciences, such as social anthropology and semeiology (the study of symbols), have in recent years made rapid growth, and have lent us their methods and enlarged our aims. The vast fields they have opened up to scholars should be all the more attractive to medievalists since most of the documents of that period were written by churchmen, and therefore place much greater emphasis on spiritual matters than on economic realities; for, while throwing particular light on attitudes of mind, they provide few quantifiable facts susceptible to statistical manipulation. But there is a pitfall here for historians, which some have not been able to avoid. By allowing themselves to espouse the same point of view as their witnesses and by trying hard to separate the spiritual from the temporal, they have sometimes been led to ignore the concrete world and to place too much emphasis on attitudes of mind as compared to the material background by which these attitudes were determined. The history of attitudes of mind has thus unconsciously deviated in directions near to those of *Geistesgeschichte*.

Consequently, if we want social history to expand and gain its independence, we must set it on a path where the history of material civilization and the history of collective attitudes will converge. But first of all I think we have to postulate three principles of methodology. We have to start with the idea that man in society constitutes the ultimate object of historical research in which he is the leading protagonist. Social history is, in fact, all history. And since society is a single entity made up of economic, political and mental factors which cannot be separated except for the purposes of analysis, history draws upon all knowledge and all material, from whatever source. Obviously it should not be content with what emerges from written texts, either narrative or legal, which are intended merely to order the liturgy, to entertain, to point a moral or to make the transition from the real to the imaginary life. It is not even enough for us to reach out beyond the contents of the documents and to examine the formal constructions and try to reach a true understanding of the world of the men who wrote and used the manuscripts through the words and the arrangement of the vocables, figures and manner of calculation, the form of the discourse, or even the actual shape of the calligraphy. Social history has carefully to consider each relic of the past—the remains of tools and equipment unearthed on sites of excavations; all traces of former human settlement still visible on the face of the countryside or town; all that can be gleaned from the ground plan of a pilgrimage sanctuary, the composition of an illuminated manuscript, the rhythm of a Gregorian chant, or the universe reflected in the different manifestations of artistic creation. Because it is quite true, as Pierre Francastel has told us, that 'each society founding an economic and political order also creates a figurative order and simultaneously generates its own institutions, ideas, imagery and displays.'

Historians of society must, of course, make full use of all these sources, and must, for the convenience of research, begin by analysing phenomena at different levels. But they have to stop treating the history of society as the handmaid of the history of material civilization, or of power, or of ideas, for its true calling is one of synthesis. It has to gather together the results of enquiries conducted simultaneously in different fields and to unify them into a global vision. As Michelet has said, 'in order to rediscover the life of the past we have patiently to explore every path and to examine its every twist and turn.' But, he adds, 'we have also to weave our strands into a single web with loving care, and to connect the various parts so that, with one explosive movement, they fuse together into life itself.' Weaving the strands together means also recognizing the precise connections between the different threads.

This then is our second principle—to attempt to isolate the real connecting links which are contained in the heart of the larger whole; to reveal, for instance, how the pressure of economic forces can influence a scheme of ethics. The manner in which a striving for spiritual improvement could end in failure because of the way it reacted on a system of production is exemplified by the fate of those peculiar twelfth-century societies, the Cistercian abbeys. These fraternities wanted to set an example and were governed by a code of conduct six centuries old, the rule of Saint Benedict. The code was reinterpreted with the solicitude of total faith, so when the constitution of the new order was drawn up emphasis was laid on the need for poverty. Some reaction was, indeed, essential against the moral consequences of the affluence of the monks of Cluny, the most eminent Benedictine community of the age: their life of comfort and security based on the ownership of land appeared scandalous. But because the Cistericians refused to live off rents, insisted on gaining their daily bread by their own toil, chose to live in the wilderness among pasture and forest, and conformed to the archaic rule of life they had rashly adopted, they found themselves, in spite of their vow of poverty, in the forefront of economic activity. Over and above their own needs they produced wool, meat and iron which was in ever greater demand in the outside world. Economic forces therefore took an unforeseen revenge by making the apostles of poverty rich. No doubt they continued to live in the wilderness, faithful to their ideals, but in the eyes of those who only saw them at fairs making successful deals as traders and rounding off their estates at the expense of their neighbours, or in the eyes of those who, in the midst of growing prosperity, did not fare equally well, the men of God were certainly not poor. The Cistercians, then, ceased after a time to represent spiritual perfection and the world's respect was transferred to the men who, clad in sackcloth and owning nothing, walked barefoot in the outskirts of the cities.

But our investigations into these ramifications reveal that each motive force, even though depending on a link with other motive forces, nevertheless finds itself propelled forward by its own momentum. Even though they do not overlap, the forces are so closely connected that they are linked in a coherent system, each forward movement developing in its own way, but stimulated by the constantly changing sequence of outside events and by economic conditions and other influences of an even more profound nature moving with their own and slower rhythm. The difference in pace produces frequent discordances, time lags, attractions and sometimes total obstructions, all of which serve to tighten indiscriminately the springs capable of suddenly releasing violent changes. The system of justice is one example. If the system is fixed by written statutes it can evolve only with difficulty; but if it is preserved by no more than the collective memory it can change relatively easily. Nevertheless, in feudal times oral customs, although flexible, were not able to adjust themselves without a certain time lag to changes in the distribution of a power which was designed for a permanent control of social relations. Thus in the French *seigneuries* of the eleventh century, habits of speech, forms of justice and customary acts corresponding to them caused the survival for many decades of the cleavage between the descendants of slaves and labourers called free, although the public institutions which gave it birth were crumbling away. The differentials that these customs kept alive, and the prohibitions and exclusions which they permitted to continue for a time masked the evolution of economic forces. They slowed them down, held back population growth and created frustrations that helped the seeds of urban disturbances to germinate and the ferment of legal innovation to work. The very complexity of the social scene revealed so imperfectly by our discontinuous evidence leads us therefore to put forward one last methodological principle. The interaction of the forces of resistance and propulsion, the apparent interruptions thus provoked and the contradictions revealed must be analysed in minute detail. The static illusion of a coloured photograph produced at any given moment selected by the historian for his observation must be dissipated. It is only by picking out the connections and discordances from the scene viewed as a whole that we can attempt to construct a history of medieval society. I would now like to sketch out briefly the main outlines of this story.

There came a day when the chariots of the barbarians broke through the barrier of the Roman armies. There came a day when Sidonius Apollinaris was forced, to his disgust, to summon the Germanic chiefs to parley in the courtyard of his residence. In this way, an encounter between two societies with somewhat similar features inaugurated the middle ages. Rome still fascinated the barbarians; but in the west she presented no more than a crumbling façade. Indeed, for many years the repercussions of a prolonged demographic and economic decline had damaged and overstrained the network of cities and roads which the legions had thrown across the conquered provinces in order to hold them down and to protect the well-being of the small privileged classes in them. As the veneer of an urban and mercantile civilization peeled away from the rural and manorial substratum of pre-colonial times, the framework of the great estates peopled by bands of dependants tied to village headmen re-emerged. In the process of a slow osmosis, the actual barbarian invasions dated by historians appear as no more than especially turbulent episodes in a continuous evolution, during which the frontiers of the Empire lost their role as lines of demarcation. In their migrations the tribes probably brought with them some elements of their own culture—a less pervasive notion of liberty, a glorification of the military virtues, the art of making jewellery and a feeling for abstract design. They settled down in parts of the country where other traditions had survived—the consumption of bread and wine, the use of money and the employment of stone for building. Their leaders, acting against a backdrop of city palaces and amphitheatres, attempted to deck themselves out in the ostentatious finery of an expiring civilization. In any event the two societies, the invading and the native, were both rural, supported by slavery, dominated by a powerful aristocracy, and almost equally brutal in manners. Consequently they mixed without difficulty. The Christian church, anxious to gather into one faith all the peoples of the earth, hastened the fusion and the cross began to appear on Germanic tombs. But the church itself became more barbaric and countrified. Henceforth its outposts were to be monasteries, and in them were preserved no more than such fragments of Latin letters as would serve for its liturgy.

In the obscurity into which by the seventh century the wreck of classical culture had sunk, we may discern in the history of production and human settlement a few tenuous signs of a decisive reversal in the secular trend. From this point, then, we can trace the start of a slow growth, encouraged perhaps by the more favourable climatic changes in western Europe. But because the first stirring of growth took place against the primitive background of an economic system partly agrarian and partly military, the peasant clans found their only source of wealth in expeditions of plunder. In the process of the raids, and as a result of them, the bands of the best armed warriors consolidated into states founded on conquest. The most glorious of these political entities was the Carolingian Empire. But what was the reality of this empire? It was no more than glorified village settlement blown up into a universe which drew together in a series of concentric rings all the lands from the outer fringes of settlement to those of the sovereign himself. It stretched from the margin of impenetrable forests in which outlaws sought sanctuary, herds of swine rooted in autumn and huntsmen ventured, and included the clearings where the starving peasants struggled to grow the food they were forced to bring to the residences of the gentry—the men trained in combat, whom the king, their warlord, led each springtime further afield on raiding sorties. This concentric organization was linked together by a chain of personal obedience forged in the inner heart of family groups and households and in the bands of fighting men. The chain depended on a complex play of dues and obligations which Carolingian legislation claimed to institutionalize. But clustered around the person of the sovereign were the monks and clergy whose attitudes to a large extent disguised the reality of social relations. They were the heirs of Roman culture, and just as they urged Charlemagne to transport antique columns from Italy to help build his chapel at Aix, so also they endeavoured to rebuild a political edifice based on the remnants of Roman culture which turned out to be in fact no more than a re-assembly of the debris of the old. They attempted to persuade the king that he was Caesar's successor and that his mission therefore was to preside over the rebirth of the Empire and the Roman order. Taking their inspiration from both Bible and classical literature they set themselves the singular task of constructing an all-encompassing society. And so successful were they in their efforts that this society was for centuries able to maintain its place in collective consciousness.

This society's shape was also a concentric one. As it was felt to be the earthly reflection of the only true reality, the kingdom of God, it was conceived to be permanent, for it was a part of the divine purpose in which the only advance was by a spiritual road leading mankind to the last judgment. Alone at the centre was the king, the Lord's anointed, representative of the one God, presiding over the destiny of all Christianity and charged with the duty of leading it to salvation. As Augustus, the Prince of Peace, he was obliged to spread the faith by chastising evildoers and by forcing baptism on pagans beyond the frontiers. His other duty was to reduce, or at least to halt, the expansion of the Jewish community, a hard core of spiritual opposition which, though rejected, was still full of vitality. As he was the guarantor of the established order, so also was he the appointed protector of the church and of the poor who were threatened by the forces of evil and the assaults of the mighty.

This account reflects sufficiently accurately some of the tendencies of contemporary reality—the missionary zeal, the pushing back of frontiers which from the beginning of the ninth century turned military expeditions into hazardous and barely profitable undertakings and, most of all, the increasing pressure of the great estate which absorbed and yoked the few peasants who were still independent. The picture as painted by the intellectuals of the church is thus revealed as a complete contrast to the very framework of power that it was intended to reflect and justify. The wish to make the king a peaceful ruler had in fact the immediate effect of loosening his hold over the powerful nobles whom he controlled best when they were assembled for war and the division of spoils. The wish to moralize about the royal function, to impose duties on the king, and to range him on the side of the poor, was to set him in direct opposition to an aristocracy which was becoming more and more aggressive and whose power was being reinforced, without it realizing it, by changes taking place in the rural economy. But no sooner was the idealized picture of the social structure clarified and, as in the reign of Louis the Pious, beginning to affect the ruler's consciousness, than other forces gathered to encompass the ruin of the great Empire. The political structure implanted by the Carolingian colonization in the new lands of Germania was to survive for many years to come; further afield, in the savage world of Slav and Scandinavian, foundations were being laid of an organization of powers similar to the one which two centuries earlier had been sketched out by the ancestors of Charlemagne. But in southern and western Gaul and in Lombardy, the most advanced regions, the king's authority was by the beginning of the tenth century crumbling away; the high level of cultural achievement was for a time brought down with it. The shaft of bright light thrown by the renaissance of the written word was followed by a darkness in the court of the Frankish rulers which plunged their social relations into obscurity and seemed to interrupt the march of history.

The break was an artificial one, however; barely discernible among the shadows, population continued to grow and agrarian technique to improve, thus strengthening the everyday life which was not to be found in the king's court, nor in the heavens above, nor on the earth beneath, but rather in the manor. The manor was the focal point of a power rooted in the soil of the countryside and contained within the narrow perspective of a totally rural world and it could not be directed from a distance. The fragmentation of royal power allowed the lords of field and forest to dominate their men more completely at an ever deeper level. Their castles, the centres of local defence, became the only places of refuge for a people terrorized by the latest incursions of pillaging hordes, and their new-found function of protection gave them the means to appropriate a yet larger share of the constantly increasing produce of the soil. Thus the frontiers of two clearly defined classes were drawn—on the one hand the lords, and on the other the peasants. Meanwhile, competition for profits between the lords themselves ruptured the common interest which had until then bound together the aristocracy of laymen and churchmen. Now they were to be opponents and rivals.

So for its part the church had joined the ranks of the lords: it had become rich. The ensuing cultural revival about the year 1000 favoured the formulation of a new set of mental attitudes. It was once more the work of the clergy and monks and appeared in the event to be no more than a reworking of the Carolingian original. Indeed, it held kingship to be fundamental. 'A single being who makes the thunder reigns in the kingdom of heaven,' one of these intellectuals affirms; 'it is therefore only natural that below him a single being should also rule the earth.' But the authority of the sovereign was henceforth to be intangible, manifest in real life only by a display of supernatural power. The system, like its prototype, rested upon the idea of peace, relying on an ultra-conservative concept of social stratification, confirming and foreshadowing the order of relationships in the celestial Jerusalem. It proposed a triangular organization with three orders—three stable, strictly defined, social categories, each invested with a particular function. In the first rank were the men of prayer, united to form the church; this, in its reforming zeal, tried to distinguish itself ever more clearly from the laity by invoking the superiority of the spiritual over the temporal power, and sought a closer cohesion by offering clerks the monastic code. The order next in rank consisted of the warriors whose duty it was to defend all the people, and whose mission, like that of the clergy, justified their right to be supported by the labour of others. Last of all, in total subjection, came the peasants, burdened with endless toil because they were charged with the duty of feeding the other two orders of humanity.

A straightforward model of this kind, perpetuated for so long by its very simplicity, presents three different aspects. In the first place it reflects certain changes in social relationships arising from progress in material civilization and certain changes in political relations. Thus, by welding all country dwellers into one homogeneous class, it brought about under the pressure of manorial cultivation the gradual disappearance in private jurisdiction of the last relics of slavery. It also brings even more clearly into the open a triple antagonism between three related aspects of domination—the economic domination of lords over their labourers; the political domination of warriors over unarmed men;

and the spiritual domination that the Church wished to extend over the laity. But in another way, of course, the model tended to make the antagonisms less blatant. This it did by relying on the notion of service reinforced by personal obedience which it claimed was the basis of the social order. The men who devised the notion of service through obedience had taken Saint Paul's precept that 'the body is a whole with many members, which in spite of their plurality, form but one body.' To their way of thinking, therefore, each of the three orders of society had to play its part in maintaining the status quo in a world which was ordered by divine dispensation and was consequently unalterable. But thereby—and this was the model's third aspect—it was brought face to face with concrete reality, that is the pursuit and acceleration of the economic changes occurring in the last years of the eleventh century. Agricultural growth did indeed take place and increased in speed: wastes and marshes were retreating everywhere before the cultivated fields and vineyards and new villages were springing up. And because agriculture expanded into virgin soil with accumulated reserves of fertility, yields did not fall off and the volume of output constantly increased. As growth was taking place under a manorial system of cultivation where the condition of labourers was at the lowest level, the larger part of the surplus went to the lords, and thereby stimulated their inclination towards luxury. To satisfy new demands, groups of specialists, masons, vinedressers, craftsmen and merchants, emerged from the mass of peasants and the resultant quickening of the exchanges of money and of goods encouraged a rebirth of towns. All over Europe new suburbs grew up around the ancient towns, and *bourgades* appeared where roads and waterways intersected. By the end of the twelfth century the civilization of the west had experienced a fundamental metamorphosis: based for centuries on the countryside, it was from now on to be dominated by the existence of towns, and all wealth, power and creativity was to emanate from urban activities.

Such profound upheavals obviously helped to disorganize the system of relationships which was intended to perpetuate the model of the three orders, although it was conceivable that for a time spiritual harmony could have been restored by the Crusaders' armies, marching to the end of the world to recapture Our Lord's tomb. Disturbances there were and they were manifest on three levels. To begin with, material progress began to complicate the social stratification by arousing within each social category increasingly acute antagonisms. Within the church itself the renewal of urban life brought out into the open the divergence, hitherto concealed, between monastic society, identified with country life, and the society of the secular church centred on the cathedrals. The latter was pulsating with vitality and was to produce many of the leaders of a new era. The increasing circulation and exchange of money reinforced the power of the state and helped to widen within the warrior class the gap between the majority, possessing no more than their land and living humble village existences, and a small and shrinking group, in whose hands were concentrated the reins of power from which they derived ever greater profit.

Finally, the economic condition of the labouring classes showed divergent tendencies. The greater mobility of landholding raised some richer peasants above the general level, while the pressure of population fragmented inheritances and multiplied the numbers of landless villagers in need of any job that would keep them alive. In the suburbs of the towns, there was an even sharper contrast between the groups of craftsmen and small shopkeepers on the one hand and the great merchant adventurers on the other.

In the second place, material progress had a profound influence on the ordering of social relations. The latter had up to that time operated mainly in a vertical direction through the hierarchy of authority and subordination. Now, cutting across this arrangement, appeared horizontal connections which brought about the association of equals, such as religious brotherhoods or the inhabitants of rural parishes combining in defence of common interests. In the towns there emerged communes or gilds, companies of armed men and groups of masters and scholars in the vicinity of the episcopal seats. Lastly, the economic forces encouraged personal initiative, stretched the ancient bonds of family, household and great estate, spread widely the hope of personal advancement and imprinted on people's minds an all-pervading sensation of progress. This accentuated several new antagonisms. The latter sprang not only from the opposition between old social categories whose dividing lines were gradually becoming blurred, or between the various strata within all classes, which caused growth while at the same time it helped to break them down; but they also ranged whole generations against each other. The older generation, content with the existing order and anxious to preserve it unchanged, henceforth found itself opposed by a younger generation who saw before it a future rich in prospects for those individuals with the spirit of adventure and initiative. Among these were students competing in scholastic disputations, bachelor knights-errant seeking fortune and glory in tournaments and adventure, and the sons of peasants hoping to find liberty and greater freedom of action in the newly colonized wastelands. But the true inspirers of the great forward drive of the economy and the real architects of progress were those servants of the great magnates who promoted their master's interests while also building up their own fortunes, and those merchants who met at the fairs, changed money on the bridges and lent it out at interest.

By the second half of the twelfth century we can discern various ideas emerging which attempted to embody and justify these social innovations. Those responsible were mostly in the privileged group, the clergy in holy orders, who continued to be the guardians of learning: for while both moralists and preachers were attempting to construct a system of ethics appropriate to the separate professional 'estates' they had distinguished, the problem of poverty was becoming urgent and was creating a spirit of soul-searching among Christians. Within the orthodox as well as the heretical sects, the 'haves' were becoming increasingly aware that the only act of salvation capable of compensating for the prosperity which they felt to be sinful was to divest themselves of their wealth. But charity towards the sick, the homeless and the wretched who dwelt on the outskirts of the towns was accompanied by a growing contempt for the poor who were held to be themselves responsible for their miserable state and were considered a danger to society. Imperceptibly the notion became current that the poor of all sorts, not only lepers but also the able-bodied indigent, ought to be herded together and excluded from society.

In the decades before and after the year 1300 several clear breaks in continuity occurred. One such break came in the economic field, when a long period of growth was followed by a period of decline, in which the most obvious feature almost everywhere in Europe was a demographic collapse. There was another break in the cultural field with a sudden vulgarization of Christianity. The shift from clerical to lay influence, and the introduction of new values and images, turned Christianity into a popular religion. In fact the main centres of the creative impulse were gradually removed from the patronage of the church and came to reside in the courts of princes. Finally, one even more decisive break with the past occurred in the raw materials of history. The historian's sources become suddenly both much more plentiful and largely non-ecclesiastical in provenance. Thus, by making use of notaries' registers and tax records, by analysing the themes of paintings that had become largely realistic and concerned to portray real life, and by examining the abundant objects dug up by archaeologists which for the first time reveal the atmosphere of the interior of a peasant's hut, the plan of a village, the organization of an estate, or the tools to be found in a craftsman's workshop, it is possible to uncover economic reality and to lay bare, with the help of some quantitative data, the mechanics of growth and decline. The documents also reveal for the first time an array of symbols, ornamentation and emblems which in contemporary eyes marked the distinction between social ranks. Lastly, this documentation throws a direct light on a section of society which had never before been observed except through a distorting glass formed by the judgment of the clergy and the nobility—the only witnesses up to now available to us. For the first time ever our sources reveal the humble folk as they really were. All these breaks in continuity have effectively cut a swathe through the traditions of medieval historiography and nowhere is this more apparent than in France. The result has been to isolate the fourteenth and fifteenth centuries from earlier ones. Is this change of emphasis also valid for the history of societies? Does it not risk introducing fallacious discontinuities into this field?

It so happens that for many years—in France as also in most other European countries—the two last centuries of the middle ages have been the period chosen for the most active research and have produced the most illuminating discoveries. This is why we can see more or less clearly the way in which Europe was decimated by the great epidemics of 1348, and are familiar with the business affairs of the merchants of Toulouse or the bankers of Genoa. And even if country life is less well understood than town life, at least we have some idea today of the relations between lords and peasants in the Bordelais or the midlands of England, and of the sort of life led by men in the region of Senlis, and by the knights of Namurois or the Ile de France. But just because our sources are so very abundant and the methods of medievalists themselves are so like those of craftsmen, they cannot be speedily exploited; the studies so far completed are generally confined within the framework of small provinces, individual cities or, an even more restricted field, selected social classes within individual cities. But the very multiplicity of these studies, their widely separated impact, and their often excessively narrow area, prevent us from easily taking a general view. It is true that recent progress in historical knowledge has allowed us to correct the conclusions of older attempts at synthesis. We no longer speak of the great changes which occurred in European history during the fourteenth century as a 'crisis' and we may now dispense with the romantic notions which, excited by the sounds of battle, the overfull charnel houses and the macabre atmosphere of religious art, show the middle ages as a whole ending in a aura of slump, withdrawal and uncertainty, and which neglect all those currents of vitality that caused great expansive enterprises and the wonderful outpourings of a reborn aesthetic in many different localities. But we have to go even further and combine in a single stream the material enriched by so much historical analysis and attempt to grasp the significance of some major events. One phenomenon in particular claims our attention because it seems so characteristic of the age. I refer, of course, to the mass outbreaks of violence, the series of popular revolts and agitations which convulsed the lower ranks of society and which spread in the course of the fourteenth century from one end of Europe to the other. All over the place peasants rose, tools in hand, pillaged the habitations of the nobles and massacred the agents of the princes. Here and there in the suburbs of the towns, bands of craftsmen rioted and, like the Ciompi in Florence, claimed the right to share in communal government. One preliminary question mark is raised by movements of such amplitude continuing over so long a period. Were the later middle ages the only times to have experienced such commotions? Were not the thirteenth, and even the twelfth, centuries similarly shaken? And did equally violent tensions persist between the masses and their lords, although the evidence for them has not perhaps been examined with sufficient enthusiasm, and still lies concealed? And when we seek to isolate the motives which provoked the troubles in earlier periods, we look first at economic conditions because the new documentation available to us means that economic history dominates social history in this period even more imperatively. But in doing so we notice that men like Jacques du Beauvaisis and Wat Tyler's English mob were not recruited from the very poor and that the pauper class was not always attracted to the movements of protest. We may therefore ask ourselves: what precisely were the germs of conflict which originated in the organization of the productive process? Political history, also well served by the nature of the sources, supplies part of the answer. It encourages us to see in these uprisings a reaction to the increasing weight of the state apparatus and the pressure of taxation. However, to reach conclusions which satisfy us completely we have obviously to delve more deeply into mental attitudes. We must search for links between the origins of the troubles and the systems of beliefs and myths which governed popular consciousness and which in this period become apparent for the first time. We must ask ourselves if these movements were not also set in motion by the millenary yearnings of a still unsophisticated religion, or more simply by the process of education which accompanied the slow popularization of Christianity through the sermons of the wandering friars and the theatre, both of which were powerful means of instructing the masses. The study of religious attitudes, the activities of the brotherhoods and sects and also oral traditions and iconographic themes must all be called upon to shed light on these aspects of social history. But it is as well to recognize that among all the elements that the desired synthesis should assemble, those emerging from history of the collective mind still appear the most uncertain and the least studied. This leads us to conclude that the progress of the history of society depends henceforth on the progress of the history of the mind. But it immediately raises another question, perhaps the most important of all, with which historians today are preoccupied. How can we combine the history of people's minds with the rest of historical research?

It is my fervent wish that the chair to which I have been elevated should become a permanent place for meeting and reflection on this aspect of history. Indeed, it seems to me that the study of the middle ages provides peculiarly favourable conditions because economic theory is perhaps less directly relevant to it than it is to more recent times, and also because the period is sufficiently far removed for the historian to have a better perspective of modes of thought and resulting behaviour. In fact, of course, anyone wishing to understand societies of the past must make a determined effort to liberate himself from the pressure of his own mental attitudes. I have just pointed out how difficult it is to free oneself from current views of economics in order to be able to see the economies of former times in their true perspective. It is even harder not to carry over into our observation of the attitudes of other ages reflections of our own times. And this is what makes the history of collective psychology, and the ethics and concepts of the world upon which it is based, such an intractable subject. It is hard enough that the phenomena of the mind should be embedded in mechanisms far more subtle than those set in motion by the material framework of life: they are not responsive to any of the measurements we dispose of at the present moment and their very lack of substance makes them intangible. What makes history of this kind all the more difficult is that different levels of culture coexist in society and that close interactions develop between them: they are bound together by movements of which the strongest are those that cause models fashioned for elites to become gradually involved in deeper and wider circles, and thereby to become distorted. The dividing lines between the cultural strata are blurred and shifting and they seldom coincide exactly with those defining the economic conditions. In the last resort history of this kind is difficult because man's mental images and behaviour in the past are never perceived except through the medium of languages, many of which have become confused and sometimes totally lost, while others have a history peculiar to themselves. In this development the signs which make up these languages are generally little modified; by gradually taking on a new sense they combine with the movement of the collective mind, but such semantic shifts are not easily observed by those nearest to them. Yet history of this kind has somehow to be written. The only scientific way of doing so is to throw overboard the principle that perceptions, knowledge, affective reactions, dreams and fantasies; rites, legal maxims and customs; the amalgam of received ideas adhering to individual awareness from which even intelligent beings wishing to be totally independent never quite succeed in disassociating themselves; and the half jumbled, half logical view of the world which infuses men's actions, desires and negations in their mutual relations, are isolated elements. Instead we must accept that they are all closely united into one coherent structure. Furthermore, we must admit that such a structure can never be viewed in isolation from any other edifice which influences it and which it influences in return. Progress in the history of ideas, and consequently in social history, without which the former cannot exist, must therefore depend upon our using the most effective tools and methodology available to historians of today. I mean of course that we need to analyse concurrently and with equal energy the material world in its ecological and economic aspects, the political structure, and finally the ideological superstructure. This is because there are facts widely separated in time and apparently totally unconnected which may prove in effect to be interdependent: facts of this sort might be, on the one hand, the almost imperceptible climatic changes that encouraged the spread of cultivation on the fringes of the Merovingian forests and, on the other, the decision made by Paolo Uccello and his patrons in the early days of the Renaissance to crystallize the tumultuous events of the victory of San Romana in a geometric and nocturnal universe. To make our way as best we can through this jungle of articulations and resonances would mean to advance painfully, patiently or devotedly towards an understanding of that historical whole which is the history of society and, in pursuit of Michelet's dream, to try to grasp it 'in one stupendous movement which would become life itself'.

2

The evolution of judicial institutions

Burgundy in the tenth and eleventh centuries

I

Among the many historical studies of medieval legal institutions are to be found detailed descriptions of the administration of justice in Carolingian times. A large number of official documents, discussed and commented upon by generations of historians, gives us a perfectly clear idea of the competence and functioning of the various public courts of justice and enables us to define the limited sectors of society which were subject to private jurisdiction. The picture can be supplemented by equally advanced studies of judicial institutions during the classic feudal period; these, quite rightly, stress the purely private character then taken by justice, as well as the complex and confused state of the seigneurial jurisdictions, and the contrast between the brutal and summary punishments inflicted upon ordinary folk and the weak enforcement of judgments against nobles. In the twelfth century private settlements were sufficiently numerous to prove the existence of institutions which were later to be described by professional jurists. However, the period connecting these two well known stages is usually left in the shadows. We cannot tell at all clearly how, in the course of the tenth and the eleventh centuries, the simple and coherent Carolingian system gave way to a confused conception of the judicial function entirely at the mercy of personal relations and domestic considerations. This gap is very serious. The historian of law who cannot follow the continuous development of the institutions he is studying is tempted to pass over the obscure period and to link judicial practices of the twelfth century directly with their organization in the eighth century. For instance, the origin of the feudal notion of high and low justice is commonly sought in the precise distinction between *causae majores* and *causae minores* in the time of Charlemagne. Moreover, as we know that the history of judicial institutions can throw a vivid light on the history of society as a whole,[1] it is particularly to be regretted that our know-

[1] M. Bloch, *Feudal Society* (translated by L. A. Manyon, London, 1961), pp. 359ff.

ledge of that part of the early middle ages when feudal society was establishing itself should be so vague.

Unfortunately, in France the documents of the eleventh, and especially the tenth, centuries are too few for us to entertain the hope that we can completely dispel the obscurity. However, there are some highly useful studies, covering a limited geographical area, which show that for at least some regions, such as Flanders and Anjou, research can produce solid results of very great interest. Among the provinces in which documentation for this kind of study is most serviceable, southern Burgundy takes pride of place: in fact the cartularies of the church of Mâcon and the abbey of Cluny provide an abundant and very complete collection of tenth- and eleventh-century deeds. Some scholars have already thought of using them to study the administration of justice at this time, but it seems to me that their work needs supplementing.[2] In the following pages, therefore I have myself attempted to take up the historical thread of judicial institutions in the region served by the documents from Mâcon and Cluny.[3] For this purpose I propose to make use of additional material from the monastic archives of Tournus and Saint Rigaud and the early charters of La Ferté Abbey, as well as from the cartularies of the priory of Paray-le-Monial and the collegiate church of Beaujeu.

The essential aim of my study is to date the stages of development with the greatest possible precision. For this purpose I shall take what seems the most reliable path, in other words a study of the judicial assemblies whose fate we know most about. These will be, to begin with, the count's courts, followed by the private courts which dispensed justice in the name of the church at Mâcon and the abbey of Cluny. Only then, armed with the experience thus gained, shall we attempt to penetrate into the much more obscure domain of other seigneurial jurisdictions.

It seems well established that the count's courts in southern Burgundy stemmed directly from the ancient Carolingian *mallus publicus*, the character of which had gradually changed.[4] There are plenty of docu-

[2] A. Deléage did not include justice in his study *La Vie rurale en Bourgogne jusqu'au début du XIe siècle* (Mâcon, 1941). Ch. Seignobos, in *Le Régime féodal en Bourgogne jusqu'en 1360* (Paris, 1882), described the burdens of justice borne by humble people, and F.-L. Ganshof in 'Administration de la justice dans la région bourguignonne de la fin du Xe au début du XIIIe siècle', *Revue historique* cxxxv (1920), pp. 193–218, described the judicial institutions used by the upper classes; but this was in a wider context and neither author gave a very precise chronology. However, F.-L. Ganshof's 'Contribution à l'étude des origines des cours féodales en France', *Revue historique de droit français et étranger* (1928), pp. 644–65, is outstanding.

[3] The geographical region forming the background to the present study mainly comprises the Mâconnais and Clunisois, with the addition of Beaujolais, Charollais, southern Chalonnais and the Bresse side of the river Saône. Within this area my earlier studies have given me a detailed knowledge of the local seigneurial families which has been of considerable assistance in my task of investigating the problems of judicial institutions.

[4] This conclusion emerges from Ganshof's study 'Origines des cours féodales' and I can do no more than agree with him. However, B. Althoffer in *Les Scabins* (unpublished legal thesis, Nancy, 1938), pp. 141–4, considers that a feudal court had existed alongside the moribund *mallus* from the tenth century onwards and had in the end supplanted it, but I am not convinced by his arguments.

ments to enlighten us about the court of the counts of Chalon and, above all, about the court at Mâcon, making it possible to follow closely the transformation which simultaneously affected, during the tenth and eleventh centuries, the composition, functioning and competence of the assemblies.

The social position of the persons who, during the course of two centuries, took their place alongside the count to assist him in his judicial functions will provide a deep insight into the way in which the sessions of the count's court evolved in Carolingian times. F.-L. Ganshof's conclusions, in particular, are based on the composition of the court. According to him, the *boni homines*, the *scabini*, disappeared by the middle of the tenth century and henceforth the regular assessors were to be men owing allegiance to the count. Thus it was at this point that the ancient *mallus publicus* was transformed into a feudal court.[5] It is certain that about the year 940 the vocabulary changed;[6] this phenomenon, however, can be related to the new favour which the term *fidelis* found with the scribes of Mâcon at this time, and continued to enjoy until the first decades of the eleventh century.[7] Whatever the exact meaning of the word, it is certain that the personal relationship it expressed united the count and the usual assessors of his court well before that time.[8] The regular adoption of this new epithet proves that although the relationship came to the forefront, there was no change in personnel. The members of the judicial court belonged, as before, to the same social category. The count's lieges were not in fact, as F.-L. Ganshof supposed,[9] humble armed servants forced by the count to come and take their place at his court at a time when the numbers of free independent men who could have fulfilled the role of *scabini* dwindled. The Nardouins, the Rathiers, the Roclens, the Garoux, were all well known in other contexts.[10] They were the most considerable men of the region,

[5] Ganshof, 'Origines des cours féodales', p. 650.

[6] Between 943 and 964 there is a particularly large number of documents. Out of fourteen explicit entries, five still mention the *mallus publicus* (C 632, 764, 1100, 1179; M 186); two mention *scabini* (C 799, 1179); one *boni homines* (C 1179); and eight the count's liegemen (C 644, 719, 799, 856, 1034, 1087; M 156, 186). It is quite clear that when the *mallus* is mentioned there is no question of lieges and, in C 799, the *scabini* are in opposition to the lieges.

[7] I have studied this change in the language of the charters in *La Société aux XIe et XIIe siècles dans la région mâconnaise* (Paris, 1953), pp. 230ff. For the meaning of the term, cf. F. Lot, *Fidèles ou vassaux?* (Paris, 1904), p. 249 and A. Dumas, 'Encore la question: fidèles ou vassaux?', *Revue historique de droit français et étranger* (1920) pp. 186–9.

[8] From the beginning of the tenth century some *boni homines* of the classic *mallus* were the count's vassals; Gondoury, Letard and Gilard, present at the count's court (M 501 [928]) are elsewhere described as liegemen (C276 [926]).

[9] Ganshof, 'Origines des cours féodales', p. 661: 'those . . . whom he had established in the city of Mâcon or its immediate neighbourhood, or indeed even some aspiring knights who lived nearby'.

[10] I cannot hope to give references to all the numerous documents through which I have been able to identify the individuals who will appear in the course of this study or to indicate their place in the social scale. I must ask for the reader's indulgence in this respect. Nardouin—viscount—was the forebear of several castellan lineages; Rathier and his son Thibert were the forebears of the sires of Bâgé in Bresse; Roclen and Garoux were ancestors of the castellans of Brancion; as for Evrard, who belonged to an important

the direct ancestors of the twelfth-century *domini*. Well provided with allods, they probably did not refuse to avail themselves of other benefices as well, but their dependence upon the count did not imply household service. If they continued to attend the judicial sessions of the count's court with the same zeal and assiduity, it may have been (although there is no proof) because their relationship with the count entailed some obligation; but mainly it was because the essential nature of the court had not changed and its social importance remained the same. At the end of the tenth century the count's tribunal was still, like the ancient *mallus* of which it was the descendant, the normal rallying point of the entire landed aristocracy of the countryside. The real change took place in the first years of the eleventh century, when the attractions of the count's court suddenly and definitively declined.[11] At that point the descendants of the magnates who had in the tenth century regularly assisted the count to dispense justice stopped appearing at the assemblies. They came only if one of the parties happened to be closely connected with them, or if the property in dispute was situated in the territory which they were at that time trying to dominate.[12] When these periodical reunions which had made the count the true focal point of local society came to an end, the drift towards dispersal of those powers which the court itself represented was accelerated. But more than anything it was the dispersal of the homogeneous group of top-ranking assessors that struck the gravest blow at the judicial powers of the count. The count's court was no longer able to maintain its leading role: it had lost its character of superior justice in men's eyes. It is true that, about the year 1100, we sometimes observe the *proceres patriae*[13] gathering round the count on the occasion of some solemn sitting of the court. But these reunions, occurring very occasionally at this period, disappeared completely in subsequent years. In 1097 Humbert of Beaujeu was still, as his ancestors had been, the distinguished assessor of the count's *curia*, but some thirty years later, his son, Guichard, being of the same rank as the counts, was to arbitrate in their quarrel with the bishop.[14] By the time of the first crusade the men called *domini* were completely and utterly disconnected from the judicial court of the counts of Mâcon.[15]

lineage, see Abbé M. Chaume, 'Féodaux mâconnais: les premiers possesseurs de la roche de Solutré', *Annales de Bourgogne* (1937), 280–93.

[11] There was a new change in vocabulary in the first years of the tenth century: the term *fidelis* went out of fashion (still used in C 2406 [997–1007]); the emphasis was now put on the social distinction of the assessors: *nobiles viri* (C 2719 [1019]; 3342 [1050–65]), *nobiles seniores* (C 2992 [1049–65]), *nobiles homines* (C 2552 [1002]), *milites* (C 2406, 2552). This should not surprise us for it was the precise moment when, as we shall see, attending the count's court and participating in its judgments became by itself enough to distinguish the members of the upper class. I have studied the true social significance of these different terms in detail in *La Société mâconnaise*: I do not think that, in Burgundian sources, they have the meaning attributed to them by A. Guillermoz in his *Essai sur les origines de la noblesse en France* (Paris, 1902).

[12] Oury, son of Thibert and sire of Bâgé, attended when Bresse affairs were in question (M 96 [1018–30]; 464 [1018–30]).   [13] C 3726 [1096].   [14] M 590 [1126–43].

[15] The much scarcer documents concerning the court at Chalon confirm these conclusions.

Henceforth, the *curia* consisted essentially of two elements. Members of the count's family, his son, the countess[16] and his officials, especially the provost of Mâcon, formed the permanent nucleus which gave the tribunal a wholly private, almost family, character. Around this nucleus a highly variable group came together on occasions, made up of the relations, friends and neighbours of the confronting parties.[17] These assessors were fortunate people, who were only occasionally connected with the count by a relationship of dependence. The count's court was, unlike the classic feudal court, not a regular meeting of vassals;[18] it was a fortuitous assembly of two coherent and mutually opposed groups representing the adversaries. Between them, the count surrounded by his own people no longer played the part of judge, but acted as an arbiter and conciliator.

Indeed, by the last years of the eleventh century, the count was no longer capable of putting the decisions of his court into effect.[19] He attempted to obtain from the two parties an agreement satisfactory to both; and we can see his peace-making interventions multiplying.[20] But by insisting on suitable guarantees, the count revealed just how far he himself was doubtful of the effectiveness of his mediation.[21] The way in which the deeds recording the verdicts of the *curia* were drawn up also bear witness to the gradual decay of the count's jurisdiction. Until about 1020 the entries remain faithful to the old formulae,[22] but from the middle of the tenth century the first signs of change appear. Little by little they turn into deeds of personal obligation signed by the convicted person and confirmed by those attending the proceedings.[23] The solemn oath binding all descendants,[24] the curses and spiritual threats[25] and the moral participation of the witnesses, were all extra sanctions invoked, presumably, because the judicial decision did not by itself provide a

[16] C 2552; M 464.

[17] 'venerunt . . . ipse Hugo cum propinquis et amicis et senioribus suis' (M 10 [1074–78]).

[18] See C 2552 [1002] (lawsuit between Cluny and Maieul, a clerk). Milon was perhaps a member of the count's retinue; but this was certainly not the case with Guibert, Rainaud, Arlier and Engeaume. They were middling lords in the valley of the Grosne, who held fiefs from Cluny and were neighbours and perhaps relatives of Maieul. When the count himself was a litigant, the count's court was normally composed of vassals. See C 3841 [1106]. Robert of Bresse-sur-Grosne (M 589) and Robert l'Enchaîné (see M 589 and 590) were, I am sure, the count's feoffees.

[19] The restitution imposed by count Thibaud on Bernard de l'Ile was never enforced (C 3651 [c. 1040]). After the verdict given in Cluny's favour by the count of Mâcon (C 3726 [1096]), an appeal to the pope and threats of ecclesiastical sanctions were needed to force the abbot of Tournus to conform to it, and even then he did not perform more than half the sentence.

[20] Beginning of the eleventh century: 'tam potestate quam blanda suasione fecerunt ei vuerpitionem facere' (C 2406 [1002]); end of eleventh century, the count gives his judgment: 'causa equitatis et concordie' (M 10 [1074–8]). However, the most active part of the proceedings were the debates between those present; the count was content to preside: 'presidente comite . . . dum eadem res communi omnium consilio juste examinis finem expeteret . . . judicio definitum est', in the words of Humbert of Beaujeu, 'et cunctorum presentium'.

[21] C 2848 [nd, about 1040], C 3726: 'datis insuper pro confirmatione in manu comitis ab utraque partis obsidibus'.

[22] C 2719 [1019]; M 96 [1018–30].

[23] C 1249 [968–78]; 2406.

[24] C 1249 [968–78]; 2406.

[25] C 2406, 2719, 2906 [c. 1030].

sufficient certainty of enforcement. By the first years of the eleventh century the transformation was complete: the entries were regularly reinforced by formal declarations of renunciation[26] or else, more often, replaced by deeds of gift,[27] and contain a record of facts in which the beneficiaries of the sentence drew attention to the efforts they had to make in order to obtain satisfaction and made careful note of the names of witnesses who may be called upon one day as sureties.[28] Finally, about the year 1100 all meetings of the count's court ended with treaties by which the adversaries engaged to keep peace with each other during a fixed period,[29] or else agreed upon reciprocal compensation guaranteed by the signatures of relations and friends.[30] In the tenth century a notary drew up an account of the case which was kept in the records of the beneficiary, for whom alone it was of positive value if and when it was contested. A hundred years later the count's advice expedited the conclusion of an agreement of which he was not even a guarantor.[31] It is easy to chart what had happened in the interval. The former superior jurisdiction had been transformed into a court of arbitration selected by the plaintiffs for purely private reasons because of its location or personal links. It was used in preference to other agencies of arbitration by members of the knightly class most in the public eye: this was all it owed to its official origins.

The competence of the count's court had undergone a transformation analogous to the one that had affected its composition and functioning. We cannot, it is true, find any great change in the nature of the cases that were brought before it. As in the case of the Carolingian *mallus*, the essential task of the count's court in the eleventh century was to pronounce on lawsuits brought before it concerning patrimonies, contested inheritances,[32] recovery by families of lands that had been the subject of former gifts[33] or straightforward usurpations.[34] About the year 1000 there appeared the first complaints against the imposition of unjust customs upon the lands of others.[35] On the other hand, the geographical coverage of the count's tribunal had changed considerably. It was not that the memory of the territorial boundaries where the count had once exercised his high judicial functions was lost; their extent, which embraced the entire region in which we are interested, still lived in men's memories at the end of the eleventh century, or at least it lived in

[26] C 2407, entry, and C 2552, restitution. C 2992, entry, and C 3322 [1050–65], statement drawn up by the condemned man mentioning the witnesses and particularly the indemnity (100 sous), received 'ut hec vuerpitio firma et stabilis permaneat'.

[27] C 2848 and 2905 [*c.* 1040] and M 424.

[28] C 3726, 3841 [1106]; SM 105 [*c.* 1090].

[29] SM 107 [1093]. After a judgment given by the court of the counts of Chalon, the knight Boniface gave a pledge to the monks of Saint-Marcel: 'non capiam in eo quicquam per violentiam per tres annos. Inde mitto fidejussores F. de R. et S. militem, et de tribus annis in antea scienter rapinam non faciam, neque ego neque aliquis de meis meo consensu; et si factum est, reddam caput et legem'. The counts agreed to give no more than their support in the event of a violation of the agreement: 'et si noluerit tenere, ego Gaufredus et Guido, comites, adjutores sumus per fidem sine enganno'.

[30] M 10.   [31] *Ibid.*   [32] *Ibid.*   [33] SM 105, 107.   [34] C 3276.

[35] First reference: C 2406, 2552 [1002]; then: C 2905, 2906, 3841; M 464.

the memory of those scribes who referred to it in locating the deeds they drew up.[36] But the framework had for some time ceased to correspond to anything significant. The zone of influence of the count's jurisdiction, irrespective of its former boundaries, extended, according to the count's personality, over more or less of the immediate neighbourhood of the customary seat of the tribunal. The distinguishing feature of the court of the counts of Mâcon was that it always met, as the ancient *mallus* had done, within the walls of the city.[37] It had lost all contact with the western part of the ancient *pagus*.[38] In exchange its field of activity developed greatly in that part of Bresse near at hand which had never, so it seems, known any true administrative organization and through which passed the road frequently taken by the counts when visiting their family estates at the foot of the Juras.[39] On the other hand, the *curia* of Chalon made itself felt over a much more extensive area; in fact it followed the count on his frequent travels and could assemble in one of the castles he owned in the region of Autun or Chalon, or sometimes even beneath some village elm tree.[40] Its influence, when presided over by such lively personalities as Count Hugh or Count Theobald in the first half of the eleventh century, could spill over the region of Cluny and encroach on the ordinary clientele of the court of Mâcon.[41] Attached to his person, and varying according to his individual qualities and the extent of his prestige, the count's judicial powers were, in the eleventh century, private attributes, no longer preserving any trace of the ancient public function from which they had sprung.

What sorts of men were subject at this period to the count's court? Had the latter become a purely feudal court of justice, only frequented by

[36] On these limits see Abbé M. Chaume, *Les Origines du duché de Bourgogne* II, *Géographie historique*, part 3, pp. 821, 985–9, 1023–7; maps pp. 832, 1000, 1088.

[37] Out of twenty-nine known sessions, only one took place outside Mâcon, at Lons-le-Saunier (M 589, end of eleventh century) at a time when the count's dynasty was split between the possessions in Revermont and the county; it was felt necessary, moreover, to repeat the pleas when the count returned to the city.

[38] The last known intervention in these regions dates from about 960 (M 420, *Liciaco, in pago Dunensi*, Saint-Martin-de-Lixy (canton Chauffailes)). Later, the influence of the Mâcon court did not extend to the west beyond Cluny; it must be admitted, however, that we know very little about the more westerly districts.

[39] Sermoyer (canton Pont-de-Vaux), M 96; Crottet, Chavagny-sur-Veyle (canton Pont-de-Veyle), M 464. But the sire of Bâgé, who was in the process of becoming *dominus Brixiae*, was always present.

[40] Out of six known sessions, only one was held at Chalon, another at Charolles, and one at Besornay (commune Saint-Vincent-des-Prés, canton Cluny). Castles belonging to the count of Chalon were Charolles (C 1249); Sigy-le-Châtel (canton Saint-Gengoux, C 1794); Mont-Saint-Vincent (P 194). It may be that the contrast between the preference shown by the Mâcon court for the location of the city and the itinerant habits of the Chalon court reveal a profound difference in the way of life. It is a well known fact that more than one of the frontiers dividing the traditions of the north from those of the Midi pass between Mâcon and Chalon. On the itinerant courts of the north see Ganshof, 'Origines des cours féodales', p. 202 (Burgundy) and, by the same author, 'Die Rechtssprechungen des gräflichen Hofgerichtes in Flandern', *Zeitschrift der Savigny Stiftung, G.A.* (1938), p. 167 (Flanders); on the sedentary courts of the Midi see F. Kiener, *Verfassungsgeschichte der Provence* (Leipzig, 1900).

[41] At Besornay for possessions situated at Courzy (commune Sainte-Cécile, canton Cluny), and at Curtil-sous-Buffières (canton Cluny, C 2848); for possessions situated at Ameugny (canton Cluny, C 2906).

vassals who applied to their lord so that he could settle in his court the disputes that divided them? To be complete our enquiry must attempt an answer to this last question. Our field of investigation is unfortunately somewhat limited; save for a very few exceptions we know only those lawsuits in which the ecclesiastical establishments were engaged; for them recourse to the count was normal within the limits which we shall define later. But the origin of our documents condemns us to remain ignorant of the behaviour of laymen. Were the knights whom we see pleading before the count's tribunal the usual clients of this court? Would they have presented themselves before it had not the abbot or bishop, who was their adversary, taken the initiative to place the affair before the count? It is impossible to be sure and, consequently, to lay down precisely the sections of society for whom the count appeared as the normal arbiter of justice. We shall, nevertheless, attempt to discover the exact social position of those laymen who, at grips with churchmen, defended their rights before him. Out of the fourteen people brought to our notice by the tenth-century documents, eleven can be identified.[42] They were all important lords, the equal of those gathered around the count and forming his court; sometimes indeed they were the customary assessors of the tribunal itself.[43] Some of them were known to have been his liegemen.[44] But it should be noted that, exactly contrary to what happened with the assessors, entries of judgments never put their emphasis on the personal relation with the count.[45] We may, therefore, conclude that no obvious connection can be established between the grading of the count's men and their submission to his jurisdiction. Furthermore, some of them, and we can be certain of this, had stood in no relationship of any kind to him. We can assert this in particular in the case of the lord Airoard, who is referred to in charter 1179 of the Cluny collection and who we know quite well from other contexts. It was the place of a lord in society that, it seems, usually made him answerable to the count's jurisdiction. In the following century the editors of the deeds never mention any kind of personal dependence; in at least one particular case obviously no bond existed between the count and the knight he was judging;[46] but in other cases it is not possible to be sure. On the other hand, what is certain is that the social position of the men who subjected themselves to the count's jurisdiction was becoming at that period less elevated. As they had ceased to take their place at court, the greatest lords of the region henceforth escaped from the count's jurisdiction, despite the bonds of fealty that until recently they had not concealed. All the plaintiffs we can identify from 1030 onwards belong

[42] The heirs of the priest Alard (C 632, 634, 719, 764) were members of an important lineage (see Chaume, 'Féodaux mâconnais'); similarly, the members of the Garoux family, castellans of Brancion (C 856, 1087); for Rathier (C 1037), see above note 11, p. 18.

[43] This was the case of Rainaud, Gilard and Rathier.

[44] Rathier (see C 644, 764, etc.) and Gilard (C 276) were, we know, the count's liegemen.

[45] Except in M 420, a complaint by the canons of Saint-Vincent against the count's liegemen.

[46] Guichard of Minciaco was perhaps the count of Mâcon's man, his justiciary in C 2992 and 3342, but he certainly had no relationship with the count of Chalon who had settled the dispute in which he was the opponent of the abbey of Cluny (C 2848).

to the directly inferior class of *milites*.[47] In spite of the vagueness of our information, we may conclude that at the end of the eleventh century the count's courts were not simply feudal courts suited only for settling the disputes between members of a vassal group. The men who now presented themselves before the courts were not bound to be the count's men. The remaining clientele of knights was quite extensive, but after the first years of the eleventh century the count's court had ceased to attract the more important lords, owners of castles, who, as we shall see, were at this moment extending their own independent jurisdictions at the expense of those of the count.

We are now able to be more precise about the development of the count's judicial powers after the end of the eleventh century. Throughout the tenth century the count's court had preserved the essential character of the Carolingian public assembly of which it was the direct extension. It was the regular meeting place of the most important freemen of the county around the superior judge whose main task was always to resolve the disputes between the greatest landlords. The first thirty years of the eleventh century saw a complete transformation. The local aristocracy ceased to provide the count with the regular personnel for his tribunal, and was no longer prepared to submit to his judgments. The bonds of fealty which linked the count with the most important lords, whose growing social importance since 950 had been underlined by the wording of the deeds, were no longer sufficient to bind them. This demonstrates, in particular, that in legal matters the strength of a vassal's obligations at this period should not be exaggerated.[48] The consequences of this development had been decisive; it was solely responsible for the count's court losing its official and superior character. It is true the court was not thereby reduced to the simple role of feudal jurisdiction; it still continued to attract, within an area depending on the activity of the count, men belonging to the knightly class, even if they had no links of vassalage with the count. But its task henceforth was reduced to arbitration and, except by the vague remembrance of its origins, it can no longer be distinguished from the other private courts whose sway had increased at the very same moment that the count's court lost its prestige.

[47] Nine out of the ten lay plaintiffs in the eleventh century are known. Some other people of note are to be found during the first thirty years of the century: Tessa of Brancion and her son, a future bishop (C 2719 [1019]), and Bernard de la Chapelle, nephew of Airoard (C 2905 [c. 1030]). All the rest were knights of lesser importance: the sons of Audin, forebears of the knightly family of Cluny (C 1989); Maieul Pouverel (C 2406, 2552); the sons of Josseran of Merzé (C 2848, 2992, 3342); Hugh Saint-Nizier (M. 10); similarly, Bernard de l'Ile (C 3651); Letaud of Ameugny (C 2906); Boniface of Saint-Marcel (SM 105, 107), judged by the count of Chalon.

[48] On the limits that must be set to the judicial powers exercised over his vassal by the Carolingian lord, see A. Beaudoin, 'Etude sur les origines du régime féodal, la recommandation et la justice seigneuriale', *Annales de l'enseignement supérieur de Grenoble* (1889); N. Ferrand, 'Origines des justices féodales', *Le Moyen Age* (1921); F.-L. Ganshof, 'La juridiction du seigneur sur son vassal à l'épôque carolingienne', *Revue de l'université de Bruxelles* XXVIII (1921–2) and, also, H. Mitteis, *Lehnrecht und Staatsgewalt* (Weimar, 1933), p. 36.

Everyone is agreed in regarding the privileges of immunity granted by the Carolingian sovereigns as one of the obvious origins of private jurisdiction in the feudal epoch. Within the area of our research all the great religious establishments—the church at Mâcon, the abbeys of Tournus, Saint-Marcel-lès-Chalon, even Cluny itself—preserved in their archives the solemn diplomas which gave them this privilege.[49] Several forgeries,[50] probably dating from the eleventh century, reveal the importance that was attached at that period to royal grants, always thought of as the most reliable justification for judicial autonomy. But the rights that flowed legally from such rights of justice were, nevertheless, limited in extent as well as in power.[51] Yet at the end of the eleventh century, some of the immune churches appeared to have been in possession of much wider powers of jurisdiction than those emanating from the particular privileges granted by royal diploma. Other origins must therefore be sought. We shall attempt to enquire into the background of the jurisdiction wielded by Saint Vincent of Mâcon and Saint Peter of Cluny, about which we have fortunately a great deal of material.

At the end of the eleventh century the lords of the church at Mâcon disposed of rights of justice over the men and lands of Saint Vincent which must be considered as a natural development of the original immunity.[52] But we know very little about how far and in what way these rights were exercised at that period. We know no more than that the disagreements between the lords of Saint Vincent and the officials of the manor were settled before the chapter[53] and also before mixed assemblies at which lay friends of the provost were present.[54] We can also guess that, the episcopal and canonical revenues being strictly separate, the bishop and the chapter each had their autonomous jurisdiction over their patrimony. Similarly, each obedientiary canon would have owned all the rights of justice over the lands and men pertaining to his office.[55]

The bishop, however, possessed judicial powers that spilled over a

---

[49] Mâcon: diploma of Pepin (M 66 [743]), replacing ancient concessions which had been lost and renewed by Louis the Pious (M 65 [815]). Tournus: diploma of Charles the Bald delivered at the time of the installation of the monks of Saint-Philibert (in P. Juénin, *Histoire de l'abbaye de Tournus, Preuves*, p. 91 [875]. Saint-Marcel: diploma of Charlemagne (SM 3 [779]), and two forgeries, expressly directed against the duke of Burgundy and the count of Chalon, obviously concocted during the second half of the eleventh century.

[50] SM 1 and 2.

[51] On the jurisdiction of the holder of immunity see M. Kroell, *L'Immunité franque* (Paris, 1910), pp. 208ff and 322ff.

[52] M 589: 'episcopum autem et canonicos habere homines suos, domos, terras, possessiones, clausuras, integre et pure [sine omni] comitale consuetudine preter clamorem sicut dictum est'.

[53] M 567 [1096–1124], agreement with Landry of Montceau, forester.

[54] M 555 [1096–1124], agreement with the provost of Montgouin, before the bishop and chapter, and the priests and knights of the locality.

[55] Agreement with Ogier of Saint-Cyr (canton Bâgé, department of Ain), M 598 [1096–1120] 'et si circa decimam male aliquia egerit, in curia decani arrationatus respondeat'. In the twelfth century the powers of the obedientiary are seen very clearly (see M 632 [1162–84]).

wider area than the rather limited estates of Saint Vincent. Some of the powers came from his position in the ecclesiastical hierarchy. At the end of the eleventh century his exclusive competence was recognized in all cases concerning his clergy. Furthermore, since the formation of the institutions of peace, he was charged with judging all infractions of the peace and the truce and all violations of places of asylum.[56] In 1100 he alone was charged with this to the exclusion of any intervention by lay judges or, expressly, by the count's tribunal. In this field his jurisdiction, so it seems, had gained ground, for in the mid-eleventh century offences of *fractio pacis* had still been subject jointly to the temporal and spiritual justice.[57] This totally independent jurisdiction, exceptionally widespread and, as we can see, peculiarly prone to indefinite extension, was in fact exercised easily not only over churchmen but also over all laymen who so wished.

But we may also ask ourselves whether the competence of the epis-copal court, as we see it functioning during the eleventh century, had not another, civil and public, origin of the same nature as the count's own jurisdiction. No document formally mentions the division of the official judicial function between count and bishop,[58] but quite often in the tenth century we see the bishop presiding, by the side of the count or his representative, over certain sessions of the count's tribunal.[59] These sessions were in no way distinguished from others, either by the form of the assembly which was always described as *mallus publicus*,[60] or by the character of the cases at issue, or by the personal status of the plain-tiffs.[61] Was the presence of the prelate purely honorific? We might think so since we never find the bishop's or his followers' signatures at the end of the report alongside those of the count and his lay assessors. And yet the entries emphasize so insistently the equality of the two presidents and especially their common position in relation to the assessors who were their lieges[62] that the bishop seems in fact to have participated in the official jurisdiction of the count. However, if the two powers of the region, both temporal and spiritual, were in fact associated according to

[56] M 589 (end eleventh century): 'ad episcopum pertinere justicias integre de christiani-tate et treva et pace et cimiteriis; et clericis; et justicia clericorum plenarie quibuscumque rebus accusentur; et rebus ecclesiasticis'. On the usual competence of the bishop for offences of *fractio pacis*, see G. Molinié, *L'Organisation judiciaire militaire et financière des associations de la paix: étude sure la paix et la trêve de Dieu dans le midi et le centre de la France* (Toulouse, 1912), pp. 42ff, taken up again by L. Huberti, *Die Friedensordnungen in Frankreich* (Ansbach, 1892).

[57] See Saint Odilon's letter to the Italian bishops [1041] (*Recueil des historiens* XI, p. 516) and its interpretation by Molinié, *L'Organisation judiciaire*, p. 48.

[58] At the end of the eleventh century, however, the bishop exercised, conjointly with the count, certain rights which seem to have proceeded from the *regalia*; see M 589.

[59] C 632 [943], 764 [950], 856 [953], 2719 [1019]. M 409 [971–86].

[60] C 632, 764.

[61] The presence of the bishop is sometimes explained when the episcopal rights were being debated (M 409: complaint against the former bishop) and by his relationship to the defendant (C 2719: Tessa de Brancion, sister of the former bishop and mother of the future bishop).

[62] C 856; M 420 [971–86]: 'testificavit comes et domnus episcopus et ceteri fidelium illorum'.

the spirit of Carolingian legislation, only one single court of justice, the *mallus*, need have existed in the city right up to the last years of the tenth century. But from that time on, when the count's court showed its first signs of decay, we can see an autonomous episcopal court gradually hiving off. To begin with, in the count's absence, the bishop and chapter, surrounded by the customary assessors of the *mallus*, themselves settled the disputes which concerned them;[63] by then the role of the churchmen gradually became more important.[64] Finally, by the first years of the eleventh century the change was complete; an independent episcopal tribunal functioned regularly.[65] Presided over by the bishop, it was usually held in the cloister and was composed of canons[66] joined by a few laymen.[67] He alone directed all the business of the church of Mâcon which from then on was never to be taken before the count's court.[68] Right up to the end of the century, we cannot see him called upon to settle any other disputes. If this was not rooted in the origin of our evidence, we might think that for a certain period the bishop's court had had its essential function confined to the defence of Saint Vincent's patrimony against attacks from outside. This function could have meant nothing more than the extension into the outside world of the jurisdiction of the immunity, favoured by the decay of the count's court and strengthened by the degree of sovereignty that the bishop had been able to draw from his long attendance at public assemblies. Moreover, some at least of the plaintiffs who presented themselves before the episcopal court were manifestly bound to Saint Vincent by possession of leaseholdings in *precaria* or of fiefs or by personal relations,[69] it seems that some rights of justice of a feudal nature were part of these jurisdictional powers. In any case, the bishop's jurisdiction was adequate, during the entire eleventh century, for his essential tasks, since he settled all the business in which the interests of the church were at issue. But from about 1095 onwards, the bishop's court, which had until then continued to expand at the expense of the count's court, itself weakened. While increasingly being chosen by a growing number of plaintiffs to arbitrate in cases that did not directly concern it,[70] it was at the same

---

[63] M 243 [c. 960].

[64] M 376 [968–71]; the inquest and decision were the act of the bishop and canons: 'diu inter se requirentes non invenerunt juste aut recte tenere posse'.

[65] M 31 [1062–72], 434 [nd, mid-eleventh century], 548 [1074–1108], 504 [1096–1124]; C 3707 [c. 1100], 3868 [1107].   [66] M 374, 434, 31, 548; C 3797.

[67] M 376, 548 (knight of the locality, provosts and humble people).

[68] M 156, 186, 204, 282, 284, 292, 409, 420, 426. The last judgment by the count in a dispute between Saint Vincent and some laymen; M 16 [1018–30].

[69] Maieul of Vinzelles, holder of lease in *precaria* (M 30); Hugh Burdin, holder of a lease in *precaria* (M 31); as for M 548, it was a property in a lawsuit which was an ancient benefice. On the other hand, Robert of Chaintré (M 504) did not seem to have been a member of the church's clientele.

[70] It was chosen by the monks of Cluny (C 3797, 3868, 3951 [c. 1120]), by the church of Beaujeu (B 29 [1095, 1120]); the bishop's court did not seem always capable or desirous of fulfilling this role (C 3868). For the bishop of Autun, see P 218 [end of eleventh century]; for the archbishop of Lyons, C 3333. This power of arbitration extended beyond the diocese: C 3920 [1115], a dispute between Cluny and the sire of Brancion over property in the diocese in Chalon: 'de quibus controversis, in examinationem Eduensis, episcopi d.

time no longer capable of preventing its own enemies from coming before it to question the rights of Saint Vincent. On the one hand the bishops undertook their ancient function of conciliator and continued to extend it; on the other, although spiritual threats and ecclesiastical weapons provided them with a means of constraint not at the disposal of lay tribunals,[71] the bishops and canons were themselves obliged to seek arbitrators for their own suits. Often it was the count,[72] but sometimes a private person.[73]

The history of the judicial powers of the bishop of Mâcon unfolds in three stages. In the tenth century, the bishop was a lord of an immunity and as such enjoyed rights of justice over men and property in the patrimony of the church. He was associated with the count in presiding over the *mallus*, and thereby shared in its superior judicial functions. Then, at the end of the century, the bishop gradually detached himself from the public court and surrounded himself with an independent judicial assembly and with a clientele which grew quickly at the expense of the count's court. The knights who happened to be in dispute with the clergy, or mixed up in affairs touching upon institutions of peace, or contesting the rights of Saint Vincent, or connected with the church by feudal ties, were normally subject to the bishop's court which was at one and the same time a Christian court, a court of immunity and a court of vassalage. Finally, by the last years of the eleventh century, the episcopal court, like that of the count, lost its power. Its judgments gave way to agreements which often invoked the intervention of outsiders. On the other hand, because of his position, the bishop was most frequently chosen as arbiter, and his exercise of the jurisdiction of arbitration soon became very active.

An even larger quantity of documents enables us to take our researches further in connection with the jurisdiction dispensed by the abbey of Cluny. As a foundation of later date the monastery had not benefited from any classical privileges of immunity, but it had in fact almost immediately been placed in a position like that of neighbouring churches. The privileged status of the property forming the original gift, the strict stipulations of the foundation charter, and the authority of William the Pious over the *judices publici* of the region, established, without any express mention being necessary, the constitution of an autonomous judicial organization, extending at least over the estates nearest to the monastery. This state of affairs was formalized by a diploma of King Lothair giving the monks protection from any judicial intervention, although the actual territorial limits of the protection were left rather vague.[74] We have no information about what powers

abbas Poncius et predictus Bernardus se posuerunt'. Here again, we cannot be sure whether the laymen came before the court spontaneously or not.

[71] M 548: 'cum de hec injuria canonicis . . . justiciam recusabat, aliquamdiu anathematis vinculo strictus . . . in judicium . . . venit'.

[72] M 10 [1074–8].

[73] M 30 [1060–1108]; a dispute between Saint Vincent and Maieul of Vinzelles; the arbiters were the neighbouring lords, Aimon of Laisé and Oury of Montpont.

[74] C 980 [995]: 'decernimus quoque, et nostra regia institutione sanccimus, ut in primis

were spawned by this immunity before the last years of the eleventh century. At this time justice seemed essentially personal and covered all the men of Saint Peter, *tam interioribus quam exterioribus*.[75] When the latter were in dispute with the dependants of other lords, Cluny attempted to preserve its jurisdiction over them by imposing limits to the enforcement of reprisals on opposing lords and by obliging them to lodge their complaint before its own court.[76] The abbey's judicial powers were exercised by deans who watched over the functioning of the individual estates making up the apostle's patrimony. The powers, both civil and criminal, were completely in their hands,[77] and were certainly vigorously exercised since there was no distinction between the profits of justice and the other revenues of the estates. Luckily a fragment of an account drawn up at the beginning of the twelfth century has been preserved which lists the cash income collected by the dean of Chevignes.[78] Among sums emanating from various sources, such as *chevage*, money rents, or harvest sales, we find, after a reference to an offence, a list of names followed by the amount of fines.[79] There is nothing to help us discover what form the judicial activities of the deans took: we do not know what part the officers of the estate played in its administration, nor whether there were any peasant assemblies who shared in the judgments. Neither do we know how far this patrimonial jurisdiction extended to men who did not directly depend upon the Cluniac lordship. We can discern the manner in which justice was dispensed only when it concerned the upper ranks of manorial society when the status of the men subject to justice required the use of the more important judicial organs. There was the case of the prosecution of two provosts of the deaneries of Cluny and Berzé-la-Ville[80] who had exceeded the rights attached to their functions. The solemn nature of the judicial assembly presided over by the abbot[81] in which the knightly clients of the abbey were brought together[82] lends an air of importance to the social position of the officials who were at that time very much in the ascendant. But the harshness of the sentence which condemned the culprits to total confiscation of their property, fiefs and allods, and

castrum monasterii omnimodo sit immune et sub ditione corum libere constitutum, nullusque, intra gium ejus vel extra, quamlibet judiciariam exerceat potestatem contra voluntatem ipsorum.'

[75] C 3821 [1103–4].

[76] C 3324 [c. 1060]: agreement between Walter of Berzé and Cluny: 'ut si aliquis ex hominibus illorum sibi vel suis aliquam intulerit calumpniam vel molestiam, nullam vindictam accipiat quosque se per spatium XL dierum proclamet. Si infra hoc terminum non sibi justiciam fecerint tunc ipse per se talem vindictam sumat, ut non plus accipiat, se sciente, quantum sua causa valuit.'

[77] C 3821.

[78] Chevignes, commune Prissé, canton south Mâcon, C 3790. Peculiarities of proper names and the condition of the Cluniac possessions in the Solutré region enable this text to be dated about the year 1100.

[79] 'De quo etiam molendinum nostrum frangerent et multa mala faciunt.'

[80] C 3666 [1093], 3685 [1095].

[81] C 3666.

[82] C 3685: Lambert Deschaux, Geoffrey of Cluny, Ansoud of Bled and Hugh Burdin, important knights.

which handed both them and their families over to the mercy of the lords[83] was characteristic of a punishment a master would mete out to his dishonest man. On the other hand, the wealth of precautions taken to guarantee the execution of the sentence and the gracious restitution of the greater part of the confiscated property,[84] suggest that we should not exaggerate the effectiveness of the territorial justice the abbot could wield over his more highly placed dependants at the end of the eleventh century.[85]

However, the judicial powers of the monks of Cluny did not owe their strength solely to the guarantees of immunity possessed by the monastery since its foundation. Over and above this estate justice, they evolved on one side a jurisdiction of peace, and on the other side definite judicial rights originally intended to defend the patrimony against external forces and to ensure peace within the group of the abbey's vassals. These powers were capable of much greater extension, and revealed themselves for the first time at the end of the tenth century just when rights of a similar kind were gathered in the hands of the bishop of Mâcon. This was of course at the precise moment when the count's court was declining.

In 994, by decisions taken at the Council of Anse[86] which was the first manifestation of the religious movement associated with the institutions of the peace in the Saône valley, the monastery of Cluny was shrouded in a special rule of peace which gave it protection from all forms of violence. The administration of the ecclesiastical penalties with which violators of this peace were threatened was confided to the monks themselves.[87] This was the point of departure for a jurisdiction extending over all crimes and acts of violence committed within the protected territory; spiritual penalties were also to be accompanied by worldly punishment. The traditional fine of 600 sous that, since the Carolingian epoch, had followed violations of the immunity,[88] was soon considered to be the penalty that Cluny had the right to demand.[89] To begin with, judgment on infractions of the peace seems to have belonged jointly to the abbey and the secular jurisdiction, that is the count's court. Gilbert and Orné, who gave two *courtils* to Cluny *in emendationem . . . propter locum quem violavimus*[90] had, it seems, been condemned for the

---

[83] C 3666, 3685: 'judicatum est ut tam feodum quam alodium suum et omnem censum et se et filios suos redderet in misericordiam fratrum et se deinceps nullatenus intromitteret nisi quantum et misericordia fratrum concederet'.

[84] C 3666: 'Ipse D. cum filiis suis sacramentum fecit.' C 3685: remission of sureties.

[85] See the judicial practices of the English abbots of Ramsey in W. O. Ault, *Private Jurisdiction in England* (New Haven, 1923), p. 56.

[86] C 2255 [994].

[87] 'Violatores anathemata maranatha dampnantur, nisi resipuerint et poenitententiam egerint, aut ab abbatibus sanctissimi loci Cluniensis vel a fratribus ipsius loci absoluti quandoque fuerint'.

[88] See Kroell, *L'Immunité franque*, p. 234; J. Flach, *Les Origines de l'ancienne France* (Paris, 1886) II, p. 162; see also the clauses of the diploma of immunity granted to Tournus, Juénin, *Tournus, Preuves*, p. 91. On the jurisdiction exercised over the right of asylum see P. Timbal Duclaux de Martin, *Le Droit d'asile* (unpublished law thesis, Paris, 1939), p. 169.

[89] C 2848 [1023].   [90] C 2296 [995].

same act by the count's court.[91] In 1041 Saint Odilon, in the letter he sent to the Italian bishops about propagating the truce of God, seemed to consider quite usual an intervention on the part of the lay justiciary upon whom fell the burden of inflicting the worldly punishment.[92] But at the beginning of the eleventh century we see the abbey inflicting heavy customary fines on its own. In 1023 Josseran of Merzé, having slain a knight before the monastery gate, was brought by his friends to submit himself to the prior's justice; he was compelled to donate several pieces of land, to renounce the benefice that he held from Saint Peter and to pay the 600 sous.[93] The lords of Cluny charged thus with maintaining peace in the immediate surroundings of the monastic buildings, in fact exercised their peace-keeping duty over a much wider range. Many of the donations to make amends for various acts of violence[94] were certainly the final penitences of repentant sinners,[95] or else indemnities intended to make good some damage; however, there are traces of judgments imposed by the monks in order to put an end to private feuds and to guarantee by the threat of a pecuniary fine the continued observance of a pardon.[96] It might be thought that, in a field so difficult to demarcate, the monks had abstracted from the normal jurisdiction of the bishop all the offences of *fractio pacis*, and that, from the mid-eleventh century, they and not the count regularly inflicted secular punishments. But adjudication over offences such as these was only one part of the activity of the prior's judicial court.

The existence of the latter court is revealed for the first time in the last years of the tenth century when it was already in regular operation.[97] It was usually held at Cluny, but it sometimes took place at the neighbouring castle of Lourdon,[98] or at a deanery—Berzé in particular where Saint Hugh chose to live.[99] It was the prior who usually presided, [100] and the abbot seldom attended.[101] It comprised the whole chapter when the case was an exceptional one,[102] but was ordinarily composed of six or seven monks, probably specialists since they were nearly always the same men, who were joined by an exactly equivalent number of laymen. These assessors[103] could sometimes be priests[104] or humble men,[105] but in most of the cases known to us they were petty lords living in the immediate vicinity of the abbey. Many, perhaps all, were bound to Cluny by feudal ties. We can be quite sure that, out of

[91] C 1989 (Gilbert and Orné were the sons of Audin who was the subject of this entry).

[92] See above, note 57, p. 25.

[93] C 2848, followed by C 2784, which gives the date.

[94] C 1951 (burning of a church), 2290 (theft of cattle), 2464 (mutilation).

[95] C 1951, preamble to C 2464.

[96] C 2889 [1032–48]. Gilbert and his son give up their revenge for the death of a brother and give guarantees: 'ut nec nos nec ullus homo sit in damnum contra alium hominem pro morte fratris nostri: sin alias unusquisque solvat solidos C'. C 594 [nd]: 'omnia ista perdonaverunt pro amore Dei et S. Petri, et per cujus culpam jam amplius fuerit remotum, sexaginta solidos emendet.'

[97] C 1723 [986].   [98] C 594.   [99] C 3821.

[100] C 594, 1723, 1759, 1821, 1851, 1887, 1965, 2090, 2508, 2848, 2975, 3178, 3262.

[101] C 1855, 1978, 2086, 3666, 3821; P 130, 207.   [102] C 2852.

[103] *Seculares* (C 2090), *judices* (3865), *milites* (1821, 3262), *nobiles viri* (1723, 2508).

[104] C 2090; P 207.   [105] C 3666; P 207.

about twenty individuals who can be identified at the beginning of the eleventh century, at least six held *precaria* leases from the abbey.[106] Later, it was their descendants who themselves held the apostle's lands in fief.[107] In any case, they were as a rule very close conections of the parties in the case; they were always the peers of the defendant and, when he was himself a man of humble condition and of no great account, his friends or at any rate his neighbours.[108] These were the relationships which determined their presence. Thus, the court of Cluny, whenever we observe it assembling, was a mixed court; supporters in equal numbers of both parties met together in the presence of the prior with the monks representing the interests of Saint Peter. As we have already seen, the court of the counts of Mâcon presented a similar appearance when it become a court of arbitration.

The assembly was solely occupied with the defence of the abbey's patrimony except in cases directly concerned with the jurisdiction of peace. At any rate we have no evidence of any more extensive areas of activity. The local lords appeared before this court when they were in conflict with the rectors of the monastery on matters concerning lands or serfs,[109] when they laid claim to the possessions of their lineage,[110] or when there was disagreement about customs unjustly levied.[111] However, all cases of this kind, either because of their content or because of the status of the persons involved, should normally have pertained to the count's jurisdiction. How had they escaped the latter and come to be judged in this private court which could not even, as could the episcopal court, claim to have in any part originated in the public powers of justice? Never exercised except when the rights of Saint Peter were questioned, the judicial powers could have been merely the extension of the normal jurisdiction of a holder of an immunity. To begin with, the monks had had legal competence in all the disputes in which they themselves were implicated; then, as we have seen, they had attempted to attract all complaints from without directed against the actions of their dependants.[112] They had thus been led naturally to claim all the lawsuits which could be of interest to the whole of their lordship. But we cannot conclude on the sole evidence of our documents that the court of Cluny had never judged any other cases; the archives of the abbey were not intended to preserve the record of sentences not directly concerning the patrimony. It is, therefore, just possible that the Cluniac jurisdiction also extended over purely lay cases. One fact might justify this supposition. The prior's justice was feudal justice, and we have already

---

[106] See C 2549 for Audin, C 2389 for Guibert, C 1837 for Grimon, C 2422 for Constantin, and C 2296 for Gilbert and Orné.

[107] Geoffrey and Ouroy of Cluny, brothers of Sologny, Hugh Burdin, Lambert Deschaux; see C 3262, 3666, 3685, 3821, 3828.

[108] Among others, C 1821: Engeaume, Sequin and Constantin belonged to the lineage of the Merzé brothers who were judged; C 3821, the lords of Les Dombes who accompanied Humbert of Châtillon.

[109] C 1723, 1759, 1821, 1887, 1965, 1978, 2086, 2975, 2794, 3868.

[110] C 2090, 2508, 3178, 3821.

[111] C 2852, 3862.   [112] See above, note 76, p. 28.

pointed out how most of the time the feudal ties of dependence were linked to the latter by the laymen who took part in the judicial functions of the lords of Cluny. This fact comes out even more clearly where the men subject to the justice were concerned. The form of words in the deeds in which for the first time the activity of the Cluny court is revealed is itself most significant, for the lay plaintiffs are regularly presented in them as *vassi*.[113] This evidence is supported by what we can gather of the nineteen persons whom we can identify: for four of them precise identification is unfortunately impossible, and for seven others we have not been able to discover any formal proof of the precise feudal tie—they were merely close neighbours of the monastery who were in constant touch with the monks and who came, when needed, to sit alongside them at the sittings of the assembly. But at least six men certainly held leases in *precaria* or fiefs from Cluny,[114] and only the remaining two were greater lords who had no feudal ties whatsoever with the abbey.[115] Lastly, we know of some sessions in the eleventh century in which the judicial assembly of Cluny unquestionably bore all the characteristics of a feudal court. In 1064, composed of enfeoffed knights of the monastery, it forced Lambert Deschaux to give up the fief he had held after his father and which had given rise to a long dispute.[116] In 1072, in order to recover his fief which the abbot had confiscated, Geoffrey of Saint Nizier had to renounce his claims before the prior, four monks and three vassals of whom the aforesaid Lambert was one.[117]

So far as the abbey of Cluny was concerned we can now see the directions in which the purely private jurisdiction developed. Based on the lord's rights and reinforced by the immunity, the rights of justice came to be exercised over all men of Saint Peter, no matter where they resided. This manorial justice was one of a personal nature, and tended therefore to spread beyond the rather tenuous bounds of the landed property itself. The feudal justice exercised over vassals when they were in direct conflict with their lord was also a personal justice, but it could range outside the group of vassals and deal with disagreements between Cluny and members of the knightly class, whatever were their relations to the monastery. Lastly Cluny exercised the jurisdiction of peace, which encompassed all criminals whoever they were, but was of course restricted to a limited territorial domain.[118]

Justice over vassals and justice of peace was confined to freemen of a higher class normally answerable to the count's tribunal. To begin with these two classes of justice were subject to the count's jurisdiction, the latter because the monks originally imposed on violators of the peace

---

[113] C. 1723 [986], 1759 [987–96], 1852 [990], 1885 [990]. The term *vassus* was used by the Mâcon scribes for a rather short period, more precisely between 980 and 990 (see M 410 [981–6]).

[114] Airoard (C 1759), holder of a *precaria* (C 1528); Josseran and Lambert of Merzé (C 1821), holders of benefices (C 2296); Maieul, a clerk (C 2508), benefice holder [941]; Achard of Merzé (C 2975), feoffee (C 3221); Hugh of Bussières (C 3262), feoffee (C 3400).

[115] C 2852, 3821.   [116] C 3400.   [117] C 3503.

[118] These three kinds of justice are to be found in thirteenth-century England in the hands of the monks of Ramsey (see Ault, *Private Jurisdiction in England*).

spiritual penalties accompanied by secular sanctions; the former because, as we have pointed out in connection with the count's justice, a vassal's ties did not, at the beginning of the eleventh century, impose upon him an imperative obligation to submit to the justice of his lord. Also, until the mid-eleventh century, many lawsuits, even those between Cluny and their precarists or their vassals, were taken by the monks to the courts of the counts of Mâcon and Chalon,[119] or else were submitted to the arbitration of the bishop if the latter should have had any influence over the monastery's adversaries.[120] Sometimes, when the first sentence pronounced by the Cluny court could not be executed, an appeal was made to the count,[121] which shows how relatively ineffective the Cluniacs' own justice was when applied to vassals.

However, about the year 1050 the Cluny court became completely independent; from then onwards, the monks no longer lodged their complaints with the count's court unless it was a matter of a direct difference with the count himself.[122] The reason for this must be sought in the weakening of the secular justice. It was not that with the passage of time Cluny became capable of enforcing respect for its rights against the encroachments of its neighbours.[123] On the contrary, an increasing number of cases escaped its grasp even though they concerned it directly. The lords of Saint Peter found themselves obliged either to appear before their opponents, or to settle with them out of court;[124] alternatively, they had to submit the case for conciliation by the bishop,[125] or, even more often, bring it to an assembly of arbitrators meeting specially for the purpose.[126] Such a refusal to accept the prior's jurisdiction came not only from powerful lords like Bernard Gros or the Enchainés brothers,[127] but also from obscure knights[128] and even former provosts.[129] The only thing that mattered in the society of that time was the extent to which the abbey's justice could be evaded, in the same way

---

[119] C 1989 [993–1020], 2407 and 2552 [1002], 2906 [c. 1030]; Guichard, son of the vassal Josseran of Merzé, was condemned by the court of Mâcon (C 2992, 3342 [c. 1050]) and of Chalon (C 2848).

[120] C 2719 [1019], 2870 [1031–59].

[121] The count's decisions of 1002 (C 2407, 2552) came after the first judgment of the clerk Maieul (C 2508).

[122] C 3841 [1106].

[123] The change in the form of the entries, which runs parallel to the change in the acts of the count, confirms this impression: to the impersonal entries at the end of the tenth century (C 1978, 2086, 2508, 3171, 3262), already replaced by charters of gift which were sometimes added to the act of judgment (C 2090, 1852, 1965), soon came mention of guarantees, curses (C 1978, 2090, 3821, 3975), solemn oaths (C 3666; P 207), etc. The mention of compensation granted with increasing frequency by Cluny (C 1978, 2090, etc.) gave these deeds the appearance of a contract; judgments were replaced by agreements.

[124] C 3822 [1103–4]: a dispute with certain knights of the castles of Brancion and Sennecey, whose fathers were still subject to the decisions of the Cluniac court, ' Jussu itaque ejusdem venerandi patris, d. L, Cluniacensis ville decanus et d. A., Lordoni decanus . . . ad placitum in Brancedunensi et Seneciacensi castro convenerunt.'

[125] C 3797, 3868, 3920.   [126] C 333, 3577, 3951.

[127] C 3333, the Enchainés brothers, descendants of one of the most powerful families in the region and, at that time, castellans of Montmerle. C 3420, Bernard Gros, castellan of Uxelles and Brancion.

[128] C 3868.   [129] C 3951.

as the abbey tried to evade the bishop's justice or the count's justice. The gradual disappearance of all legal constraints over the class of lords was in the course of the eleventh century a generally accepted fact.

The ecclesiastical lordships, provided with privileges of immunity, were not the only ones to have acquired extensive jurisdiction to the detriment of the count's power. Throughout the tenth century, it is true, the only courts to appear alongside the public organs of judicial administration were the ecclesiastical ones. But in the early years of the eleventh century, at the moment when, as we know, the count's powers were waning, we see for the first time laymen wielding a private jurisdiction. In 1016, Pope Benedict VIII drew the attention of all powerful men who had received from God the duty of defending the faithful and pointed out to them a number of serious usurpations committed at the expense of the abbey of Cluny. He turned first to the counts of Mâcon and Chalon as the official representatives of the secular power, but then also to the powerful family of Viscount Guigue, to Oury de Bagé, to Arnould of Bourbon-Lancy, and to all other strong men of the region.[130] From the early years of the eleventh century some *optimates*, though apparently few in number, were thus deemed capable of meting out temporal punishment to the spoliators of the monks in the same way as the count. One hundred years later, when the first slightly more precise evidence about lords' justice appears, the lay possessors of the rights of justice were still few, but we can see more clearly what their position in society was: they were all *domini*, or in the words of the period, holders of castles.[131] The judicial powers which they dispensed can be thought of as emanating from these fortresses[132] which, though also still few in number,[133] were in the eyes of contemporaries clothed with a distinctly public character.[134] At the end of the eleventh century, these castles that originally

[130] *Bull. Cl.*, pp. 6 and 7; 'illustribus viris d. Wigoni vicecomiti et frati ejus d. Willemo d. quoque Odulrico et d. Ansedeo et ceteris principibus et optimatibus totius Burgundie'.

[131] C 3744 [1100]: agreement between Cluny and Roland Bressan, castellan of Berzé: 'si alius quilibet homo quem ipse Rollannus justiciare aut per suum habere possit, aut constringere'. C 3896 [1106]: agreement with Bernard Gros, castellan of Uxelles and Brancion: 'si quisquam de meis hominibus effregerit aut aliquis homo quem ego in jus decere possim'.

[132] See Bloch, *Feudal Society*, p. 372. H. Janeau, 'les Institutions du Dauphiné au moyen âge: les agents locaux de la primitive justice comtale (XIe–XIIe siècle)', *Annales de l'université de Grenoble, section Lettres-Droit* (1943), pp. 74–5.

[133] The following is a brief provisional list of the castles in the neighbourhood of Cluny which are known to have existed before the twelfth century: Lourdon (C 34 [888]); Brancion (C 405 [932]); suin (C 675 [945]); Mont-Saint-Vincent (C 761 [950]); Charolles (C 1249 [968–77]); Berzé (C 1810 [989]); Uxelles (C 3475 [1074]); Sennecey (C 3822 [1103–4]); Bâgé (Juénin, *Tournus, Preuves*, p. 130 [1075]); Chaumont (commune, Saint-Bennet-de-Joux, P 87 [end eleventh century]).

[134] I agree with R. Aubenas, 'Les Chateaux forts du Xe et XIe siècles, *Revue historique de droit français et étranger* (1938), pp. 548–86; see also A. Deléage, 'Les Forteresses de la Bourgogne franque' in *Annales de Bourgogne* (1931), pp. 168–8 and *Les Origines des châtellenies en Charollais* (La Physiophile, Monceau-les-Mines, 1937). See the precautions taken at the Council of Anse in order to protect the public peace against the building of private castles (C 2255); there are similar prescriptions in a diploma of King Robert (C 2800 [1027]).

were no more than the favourite seats for the count's courts, and subsequently of other private judicial assemblies,[135] came to confer on their owners, the sires of Brancion, Berzé, Bâgé, Beaujeu, and some others, a certain jurisdiction over the surrounding territory. By the time of Saint Hugh, we begin to see court sittings at the castle arbitrate in competition with the count's and the ecclesiastical courts over disputes between the lords.[136] But these castellan lords, whose judicial functions grew up at the beginning of the eleventh century, were direct descendants of those very great men who had in the preceding period sat on the count's tribunal. The connection between their independent jurisdictions and their abandoning of the count's assembly thus clearly manifests itself.

An analysis of the judicial powers of the castellans and research into the origin of their powers are not made any easier by the fact that documents earlier than the twelfth century are scarce and widely dispersed, and that we are sometimes compelled to be content with hypotheses. To begin with it does not seem as if we need assume that the basis of these rights of privilege were similar, even when usurped, to those which the ecclesiastical establishments enjoyed. Nor need we assume them to have been similar to the patrimony of some castellans which, having been composed of properties of fiscal origin,[137] escaped ordinary jurisdiction because of that. On the contrary, it should be taken that the basic legal powers—the ones which allowed the jurisdiction of the *dominus* to spread well beyond the boundaries of his landlordship and to enjoy, about the year 1100, an influence equal to the count's—came, in ways we cannot exactly trace, from the appropriation of certain functions of public origin. Indeed, it is possible on the one hand to think the castellans were the heirs of the jurisdiction exercised in Carolingian times by the inferior agents of the count and, on the other hand, to consider these rights as accretions to the general powers of the *districtio* centring on the fortresses, whose original purpose had been to maintain public peace.

A study of the fate of those public judicial powers directly exercised by the Carolingian count appears to support the first of these hypotheses. It should be noted first of all that in our region there had not been any usurpation of the title of count—not at the extremities of the vast *pagus* of Autun and not even in that part of Bresse which totally escaped the control of the count of Lyons.[138] No lord had thus attempted, by adopting

---

[135] Meetings for arbitration always took place in the open air (C 3577, 3726, *in saltu sive foresta*; M 548); but sittings of the courts, when they did not take place in the city, were situated most frequently in a castle, either belonging to the count (see above, note 41, p. 21) or in private hands; Lourdon (C 594); Sanvingnes (P 76); Huchon (P 166); Brancion and Sennecey (C 3822).   [136] See P 166.

[137] In particular, some lands owned by the Garoux, castellans of Brancion, in the tenth century came from the same source as the original patrimony of Cluny Abbey, William the Pious having divided his personal estates in western Clunisois between his vassal and Abbot Bernon.

[138] The old historians of Bresse, for instance, Guichenon, *Histoire de Bresse* (Lyons, 1650), p. 40, followed by the compilers of the eighteenth century, endowed the sires of Bâgé with the title of count; but their opinion was based upon a genealogical confusion. As for *Ildinus comes* of the *Bull. Cl.*, p. 6, it was the result of misreading (see C).

an official title, to add the prestige of a public power to the jurisdiction which he had been able to establish for his own profit. In other parts of the country the dignity of viscount had been able to serve as the foundation of judicial powers of wide scope. But the tenth-century viscount of Mâcon had never emerged from his subordinate position. He helped the count in his judicial functions, sat alongside him and was charged in his absence with presiding over the *mallus publicus*; but he exercised no independent judicial activity. Nonetheless, the office which quickly established him among the great families,[139] conferred upon him a particular aptitude for the exercise of the rights of justice. In the bull issued by Benedict VIII, Viscount Guigue was named immediately after the count. In the first years of the eleventh century, the viscount, like other great assessors, freed himself from the count's tribunal and made the castles he owned into the principal centre of his activities.[140] The Blanc family, who were destined to keep the title until its disappearance,[141] were established on their allods around the *castrum* of Montmelard and no longer appear in the Saône valley.[142] They would later create an important lordship in the western part of the former *pagus* and gradually attach themselves to the Loire region where in the eleventh century they enjoyed extensive judicial powers. Of these powers we unfortunately know nothing, except that they mainly resulted from the concentration of the jurisdiction of many *vicariae* in their hands.[143]

In fact it was essentially through the absorption of the former *vicariae* that the castellans established rights of civil justice over the rural population of the district. The vicarial assemblies were still actively functioning in southern Burgundy throughout the entire tenth century, and we are adequately informed about the role they were called upon to play.[144] A rural assembly of this kind which was held in a corner of the village church was made up of the freemen of the place,[145] people in humble circumstances,[146] presided over by the *vicarius* who, it appears, was not himself a member of the superior class of society.[147] The three

[139] Walter [*c.* 940–60] succeeded his father, Maieul [930–40], see Chaume, 'Féodaux mâconnais'. Guigue succeeded his father-in-law Nardouin (C 1179 [964]).

[140] The last reference to the viscount in his role of assessor: M 96 [1018–30].

[141] C 2992 [1037].

[142] The identification made by Ganshof ('Origines des cours féodales', p. 210, note 15), *Archimbaldi cognomento Nigelli* = Archibald le Blanc, is erroneous: the reference is to a knightly family of Bresse.

[143] Artaud le Blanc was the lord of the *vicarii* of Montmelard (Archives of Saône-et-Loire, H 142/2 [1067]); Hugh le Blanc gave the chapel of Saint-André-de-Villars near Charlieu to Saint Peter of Mâcon with the *vicaria*; the right formed part of the *vicecomitatus* (*Nécrologe de Saint-Pierre-de-Mâcon*, edited by C. Guigue, p. 51 [1096]).

[144] C 1524 [980], 2391 [997], 2591 [1004]. The court in M 426 [968–71], in spite of the title of *vicarius* given to the president (an important lord, one of the most assiduous frequenters of the *mallus*), was a session of the count's court, presided over in the count's and viscount's absence by one of the principal assessors who took the title of vicar.

[145] C 1524, *scabinei*; C 2391, *boni homines*.

[146] After fairly exhaustive researches, I have the impression of knowing, at least by name, all the lords of any note, forebears of the knights of feudal times, living about the year 1000 in the region of Château (canton Cluny), where the vicarial assembly of C 2591 was held. None of them were present at it.

[147] There was no president for C 2391.

cases known to us in the records, faithfully drawn up by the country scribe according to the ancient formulae, were concerned to settle law suits about allods. The competence of these courts at the end of the tenth century did not appear to be essentially different from that of the count's tribunal. Contrary to current opinion which remains faithful to notions based on the evidence of the capitularies of the classical period,[148] I myself think that all civil cases, even the most important ones, were normally subject to the jurisdiction of the *vicarius*. The fundamental difference between the respective competencies of the vicarial courts and county courts lay in the clientele; the *vicarius* and his court attendants (*scabini*) dealt with disputes between freemen of modest condition, living within a narrow geographical ambit,[149] and excluded members of the upper class who were answerable to the count's court. The relationship between these two courts was similar to that between the hundred and the shire courts in England.

In 1004 a vicarial court was still functioning in two places lying to the south-west of Cluny.[150] At the same moment only twenty kilometres away, within the zone of influence of the castle of Uxelles, the *vicaria* was no more than a custom levied to the castellan's profit on the lands of the territory. Josseran, ancestor of the Gros family who were, in the twelfth century, the count's equals, held from the monks of Cluny certain rights incumbent upon the lands and the men of the deanery of Saint Hippolyte which he had inherited from his parents. Among these rights the *vicaria* (the equivalent on the continent of the view of the frankpledge) figures prominently.[151] In the first years of the eleventh century, which quite clearly appear as the decisive years in the evolution of judicial institutions, the most powerful lay lords—those who held castles—took over judicial assemblies concerned with the affairs of humble folk in the surrounding villages.

What were the consequences of the appropriation? First the *vicarius* became an official[152] of the lord who rarely kept the title for himself.[153] As in Lyonnais, Anjou, Poitou, Limousin and elsewhere,[154] the eleventh

---

[148] See particularly E. Chenon, *Histoire générale du droit français public et privé* I (Paris, 1926), p. 222, and the texts cited in the note on p. 243.

[149] The three entries we have at our disposal relate to judgments made at Prissé (C 1521), Château (C 2591), and Nogent-sous-Brancion (C 2391). The geographical notion of the *vicaria* was still used in deeds at the end of the eleventh century (M 50 [1060–1108]). If these indications really correspond to the jurisdiction of the judicial assemblies, then in the Mâconnais these were very small. See Chaume, *Origines du duché de Bourgogne*, p. 1027, list of *vicariae*.

[150] C 2591.

[151] C 2943 [997–1027] Uxelles (commune Bissy-sur-Uxelles, canton Saint-Gengoux), Saint-Hippolyte (commune Malay, same canton).

[152] Archives of Saône-et-Loire, H 142/2.

[153] Landry Gros, grandson of Josseran, at the height of his power, was still called *vicarius de Branceduno* (C 3914 [nd, end eleventh century]).

[154] On the *vicarius*, see F. Lot, 'La *vicaria* et le *vicarius*', *Nouvelle revue historique de droit* (1893); in Anjou: L. Halphen, 'Prévôts et voyers au Xe siècles; région angevine', *Le Moyen Age* (1902), p. 319; in Poitou: M. Garaud, *Essai sur les institutions judiciaires de Poitou sous le gouvernement des comtes independants: 902–1137* (Poitiers, 1910), pp. 149–51; in Lyonnais: M. David, *Le Patrimoine foncier de l'église de Lyon de 984 à 1267* (Lyon, 1942), pp. 203ff; in Limousin it can be guessed from the documents used by G.

century *vicarius* was no more than a humble dependant administering justice over the radius of the former *vicaria* in the name of his master and, above all else, collecting its profits. This was the second consequence which was not indeed peculiar to our region: when judicial powers became private rights, they were considered a source of income by the lords who held them. Under the same name of *vicaria* the lords levied a lucrative revenue over the whole area covered by their rights.[155] The *vicaria* held by Hugh le Blanc in the district of Charlieu is an example;[156] and so, even more obviously, is the *servitium vichariale* levied on two manses given to the abbey of Saint Rigaud by the *vicarii* of Montmelard.[157] Thus the vicarial courts had not simply disappeared because the number of freemen in the countryside was diminishing; the vitality of the examples known to us about the year 1000 prevents us from assuming that. But, eclipsed by the private powers of the castellans who had confiscated them for their own profit, they cease to appear. What we know about the *vicarius* and the *vicaria* in feudal times[158] encourages us to give our conclusion a more general significance, which has still to be tested by the results of other regional enquiries.

In any event, public vicarial courts at the beginning of the eleventh century had completely disappeared in southern Burgundy; only the use of the word *vicaria* in its geographical sense remained for a little time longer. Nor had the institution survived in areas where the count retained a presence—and these, it should be noted, were only where he preserved the disposal of castles. The count had also probably taken over the lower public jurisdictions, but he does not seem to have preserved the *vicarii*. His usual agents were provosts, members of his household who make their appearance in the first years of the eleventh century.[159] They were installed either in the city or in one of the count's castles,[160] and were remunerated by fiefs that they added to their own allods[161] and by a share in the profits of justice.[162] Their office was probably hereditary,[163] which allowed them to rise rapidly; by the beginning of the twelfth century they were persons of importance.[164] The time when

Tenant de la Tour, *L'Homme et la terre de Charlemagne à saint Louis* (Paris, 1942), pp. 521–8.

[155] On the sense of the word *vicaria*, see Lot, 'Vicaria', p. 283, Garaud, *Institutions judiciaires de Poitou*, p. 32; in Lorraine the term *centena* underwent a similar semantic change: Ch.-E. Perrin, 'Sur le sens du mot *centena* dans les chartes lorraines du moyen âge', *Bulletin Ducange* v (1929–30). Deléage, *Vie rurale en Bourgogne*, p. 534, has noted the change, but it was not quite complete by 1050.

[156] See above, note 143, p. 36.   [157] *Ibid.*

[158] See the general enquiry in Lot, 'Vicaria'.

[159] P 194. Provosts also replaced *vicarii* in other regions of the realm: Tenant de la Tour, *L'Homme et la terre*, p. 519; Garaud, *Institutions judiciaires de Poitou*, p. 155; Halphen, 'Prévôts et voyers', p. 319; Angevin provosts appeared at the same time.

[160] Mâcon: C 2992 [1049–65]; M 589 [1096–1124]; Mont-Saint-Vincent: P 194 [c. 1030]; Charolles: P 44, 45, 46 [second half eleventh century].

[161] For the provosts of Charolles in particular: P 44, 45, 46.

[162] P 194.   [163] P 44, 45, 46.

[164] Evrard, lay provost of Mâcon was perhaps the father of the knight, Humbert (C 2861, 2969); the provosts of Charolles were *milites* (see Halphen, 'Prévôts et voyers', p. 307, for the form of the provost of Angers).

those who were the furthest away would break all ties constraining them and would dispense justice to their own advantage can be foreseen.

In the same territory over which they exercised the rights of jurisdiction in civil cases originating in the rights of *vicarii*, castellans possessed all criminal justice because they were masters of castles. If we admit, following Hirsch,[165] that the prosecution of crime belonged by right to the Carolingian *vicarius*, then possession of these rights can be explained simply because vicarial courts had been appropriated. But I think, as do some other scholars,[166] that blood justice was really constituted when the movements of peace attempted to replace private settlement through vengeance or agreement, by severe punishment for acts of violence. But when about the year 1000 the institutions of peace were established in southern Burgundy, the vicarial courts had already, for the most part, been taken over by the castellans. On the other hand the castle which, because of its military function, was the seat of a special kind of peace, appeared well placed to serve as the main support of the secular powers charged with supporting the clergy's attempts to enforce the peace. At this time also the defection of the principal assessors, now ensconced in their fortresses, had considerably weakened the count's jurisdiction. This could explain why the count did not, as in other provinces, keep the monopoly of blood justice.[167] He obviously exercised it himself in the territorial domain where he had maintained his prestige. After the discovery of a crime committed in 1030 in the neighbourhood of Mâcon, Raoul Glaber, a first-hand witness, tells us that the facts were reported to the count, and it was he who, after an enquiry, seized the culprit and had him burned.[168] Similarly, at the beginning of the twelfth century the right to punish adultery and robbery in the city and its surroundings belonged solely to the count.[169] He also exercised this right in a wider area over all men who, because of their social position, did not accept submission to the castellans' justice. But locally the latter punished, without any opposition, all crimes committed by lesser folk within the limits of the protected area (*salvamentum*).

The *salvamentum* was the territory in which the castellan had the basic duty to defend the peace, whether it was threatened from without or whether it was broken by certain offences inside the territory itself. This function, called *custodia* or *vuarda*,[170] conferred special rights of

---

[165] H. Hirsch, *Die hohe Gerichtsbarkeit im deutschen Mittelalter* (Prague, 1922) I, chapters 1 and 6.

[166] Hirsch, *Gerichtsbarkeit*, p. 198. Bloch, *Feudal Society*, pp. 365ff.

[167] See blood justice, the monopoly of the counts of Flanders, Ganshof, 'Rechtssprechungen', p. 170.

[168] Raoul Glaber, *Histoires*, edited by M. Prou (Paris, 1886) IV, p. 2: 'ad quam (civitatem) veniens, quod compererat Ottoni comiti ceterisque civibus indicavit qui protinus mittentes viros quamplurimos qui rei veritatem inquirerent, pergentesque velocius, repererunt illum crudelissimum . . . quem deducentes ad civitatem, in quodam horreo religatum ad stipitem, ut ipsi postmodem consepeximus, igne comburerunt.'

[169] M 589: 'ad comiten pertinere adulteros latrones publicos'.

[170] We must distinguish between this particular and territorial guardianship and the general guardianship over all the property of a church which is investigated by N. Didier, *La Garde des églises au XIIIe siècle* (Grenoble, 1927). On this distinction see David,

justice on the guardian. He was the judge in the case of disputes with outsiders about property situated within the protected area;[171] to him fell punishment of all misdeeds.[172] In a region where the *advocati* (laymen whom the Carolingian rulers placed under the ecclesiastical immunities in order to exercise the power of restraint) never rose above the subordinate role of judicial representatives and where, in the mid-tenth century, the term as well as the idea of such an office (*advocatio*) disappeared,[173] the church lords, in spite of the rights conferred on them by the immunity and the place they occupied in the framework of the institutions of peace, were bound to submit to the superior rights of the guardian lord. They did this willingly enough when it was a question of their peripheral possessions, but reluctantly for those nearer at hand. The only possessions to escape completely were those lying in the immediate neighbourhood of the ecclesiastical establishments.[174] The guardianship was either expressly conceded.[175] or else was rudely imposed by the castellan, unless it had already existed on lands brought into the patrimony of the monks by gift. Originally this right always belonged to the master of the castle (the count when he himself held the fortress),[176] a private owner[177] who added it to the *vicaria*,[178] or else the direct heirs of the castellans.[179] But, because of the phenomenon I have already mentioned, the term describing the function tended mainly to reflect the material rewards attached to it;[180] and the term *vuarda* generally referred to the customs that the guardian lord levied on the

Patrimoine foncier, pp. 174ff. There is nothing to be learned from the chapter devoted to this institution by G. de Valous, *Le Monachisme clunisien*, (Paris, 1935) II, pp. 142ff.

[171] It was not as general guardian of the abbey of Cluny that the count of Mâcon judged the dispute between this monastery and the abbey of Tournus, but as special guardian of the property under litigation, a function that he owed to his personal possessions in the lower valley of the Seille (C 3726): 'cujus custodie possessio jam dicta noscitur delegata'. For another opinion see Didier, *Garde des églises*, p. 233.

[172] C 3821: *vuardam et malefactorum justiciam*. See Didier, *Garde des églises*, p. 228.

[173] The *advocati* of the tenth century represented the interests of the ecclesiastical establishments before the count's court (M 284 [888–98]; C 764 [950], 799 [951]), sometimes playing the part of champion in the judicial combat (M 282 [936–54]). Exceptionally the count, when, if need be, he fulfilled this function, took the title (M 156 [936–54]). Called *actores* at a certain period (C 856 [953], 1037 [957], 1100 [961]), they then disappeared completely. On this point, the geographical limits given by F. Senn, *L'Institution des avoueries ecclésiastiques en France* (Paris, 1903), p. 104, should be corrected.

[174] C 3821.

[175] Saint Maieul gave to Humbert of Beaujeu the guardianship over certain Cluniac obedientiaries (C 889 [954–65]) 'commendo . . . ad custodiendum et defendendum a malis et perversis hominibus . . . ita tamen ut pauperibus nostris reddas quae eis tulisti.'

[176] The count of Chalon had the *salvamentum* around his castle of Mont-Saint-Vincent (P 194 [c. 1030]).

[177] The sire of Beaujeu: (C 884; M 476 [1031–60]); the sire of Digoine (P 179); Oury of Bâgé (the service he levied on the obedience of Perronne seems to have been the salary for his function of guardian).

[178] The sire of Brancion (C 3920 [1115]); Landry and Bernard Gros possessed the *salvamentum* in the same villages as their grandfather Josseran had held the *vicaria* (C 3073 [1070]).

[179] Stephen of Neublans, heir to the Garoux, ancient castellans of Brancion, claimed *vuardam* and *salvamentum* over a valley close to the castle (C 3737 [1100]).

[180] See Didier, *Garde des églises*, p. 16.

territory of the ward. Like the vicarial courts, the wardship attached to certain lands followed their fate; by the mid-eleventh century, partitions of inheritance, alienations and infeudations had all detached the *custodia* from the castle and we find it fragmented in the patrimony of middle-ranking lords;[181] but the castellan, even if he had sometimes alienated the rents by which he was remunerated, alone exercised the function.

Blood justice, guardianship and the vicarial courts thus formed the sum of the judicial powers that extended over all the territories subjected to the castle's influence. This territorial justice used to include completely the personal rights of justice claimed by other lords over their dependants residing inside the territories of the protected area.[182] Before the twelfth century we have, it is true, no evidence of the exercise by lesser lay lords of any kind of jurisdiction. The small lordship, highly fragmented,[183] and without any integral entity, could not in any case have provided an effective framework for judicial administration. Free tenants, formerly subject to the justice of the vicarial courts, probably continued to submit to the judgments handed down by the private *vicarius*, who also extended his jurisdiction over serfs. Until the end of the eleventh century, justice over humble folk was thus heavily concentrated in the hands of a few local strong men. But in the twelfth century these lucrative rights based on land began to be regularly considered as dependent upon land ownership. Regular references in deeds of sale and donation to rights of justice are from this time onwards evidence of the fact.[184] Henceforward these rights followed the course of landed property and were parcelled up.

The castle also became the normal seat of the feudal court. The *milites castri*, all those freemen belonging to the class who lived within reach of the castle, normally made up the court when, in the tenth century, the count, during his stay in the fortress, dispensed justice.[185] Bound to the private owner of the castle by military ties, they continued to come together periodically and to judge at these meetings the disputes arising within the group of vassals. But these courts of knights appeared to be the normal tribunal for the lordly class of the entire region and attracted all those who had formerly been subject to the count's courts. At the end of the eleventh century some of these assemblies, particularly those in Western Burgundy, in districts such as Charollais, and around Brionne

[181] C 2944 [c. 1050], guardianship over a wood; C 3640 [nd], *salvamentum* over two manses; M 27: *per consuetudinem salvamenti;* C 3085 [c. 1050]): Guichard of Chaselles gave up 'de omnibus malis consuetudinibus quas ipse et antecessores ejus inmitterant in omnibus terris que in eorum videbantur esse custodia'.

[182] Extension of the rights of superior justice over the landlordships of churches: C 2846 [978–1039], 2943 [999–1027].

[183] See Deléage, *Vie rurale en Bourgogne.*

[184] It is in this sense that the justice can be considered as depending on the property. See Seignobos, *Régime féodal en Bourgogne*, p. 242, who notes the point without explaining it and states that the judicial rights of landlords are never referred to before the twelfth century.

[185] The count of Chalon was surrounded by the *seniores viros Carelle castri* (C 1249 [968–78]).

and Autun, which escaped the regular influence of the counts, played this part unrestrictedly.[186]

In the eleventh century, the castle was therefore the fundamental element in the judicial organization. The area over which the count's justice extended depended on the number of castles in his possession. The lords of the church also enjoyed the special powers of immunity and their jurisdiction of the peace to the extent that these rights were strengthened by the ownership of a fortress.[187] The judicial power of the castellan extended over all classes in society: as defender of the peace he could take action over all 'body' subjects linked most intimately to their lord. After the *vicarius* had become his agent, he had become the normal fount of justice for the smaller freemen; and finally, the ties of vassalage had allowed him to form a court of knights through which his verdicts were accepted by the lords of the locality. By the tenth century the administration of justice had been divided into superimposed but water-tight compartments whose arrangement corresponded to the main lines of social demarcation—justice of the master over his *servi*, of local vicarial assemblies over the lower class of freemen, of the count's *mallus* over the magnates of the county. In the eleventh century this vertical structure gave way to a geographical juxtaposition; but whatever the local arrangements were, the castellan claimed justice over all the inhabitants of the territory under his control. However, it must be admitted that as society evolved the event with the most significant consequences was the appropriation of the vicarial justice. Free peasants, who formed the clientele of these assemblies at village level, found themselves subjected to the justice of a lord strictly enforced by officials all the more efficient and enterprising because its pursuit provided an indefinitely elastic profit for the *dominus*. Losing all contact with the official organs of the public justice, confused with the non-free before the lord's jurisdiction and in the rules of law which flowed from it, they too became dependants of the territorial lordship formed around the castle. For all such men, who were after all the greater proportion of country people, a very detailed judicial organization existed.[188] Members of the upper class, lords of middling rank and *milites*, answerable to the count's court, did not fall under the jurisdiction of the castellan when the latter appropriated the vicarial courts. They continued normally to depend on the only jurisdiction which had kept its public character. This unique fact was enough to set them apart and to be the reason why they could be considered as the only true freemen. But, as the count's court lost its power, they were simultaneously sought after by prelates' tribunals of arbitration, by feudal courts answerable to the lord of their fief, and by meetings of their peers held in the neighbouring castle. For

---

[186] P 166 [*c.* 1080], the *curia* of the sire of Semur, at the castle of Huchon, comprised all the knights of the locality.

[187] Hence the importance of the ownership by the monks of Cluny of the neighbouring castle of Lourdon.

[188] See L. Halphen, 'les Institutions judiciaires en France aux XIe siècle, région angevine', *Revue historique* LXXVIII (1901), p. 304; Garaud, *Institutions judiciaires de Poitou*, p. 144.

all practical purposes they became beyond the law because manifestly none of these organs possessed the power to put them under forcible constraint. By the end of the eleventh century no judicial institution remained capable of enforcing the peace over the knightly class.[189]

A well defined judicial structure that actively and efficiently controlled the mass of lesser folk on the one hand; an inconsistent and utterly powerless jurisdiction over the aristocracy on the other: the contrast was complete. It was the consequence of a significant event in the early years of the eleventh century—the establishment of the justice of the castellanies. The early years of the twelfth century marked one further stage in the evolution of judicial institutions. After about sixty years of spontaneous growth the need for organization was apparent. The rights which had developed on parallel lines had begun to compete and had to be defined. At the same time, the defects of institutions established at random had to be supplemented by new forms. These two aspects of the administration of justice were now so utterly different when they applied to labourers or to knights that they must be looked at and analysed.

II

The lord who exercised justice over humble people considered it primarily as a source of profit and therefore strove to extend his jurisdiction over the greatest possible number of people. However, in this he was soon faced by competitors who were either persons exercising in neighbouring localities rights similar to his own, or else claimed within his own territory other rights which enabled them to dispute his. The first rules which attempted to end this competition, by defining precisely the reciprocal rights of dispensers of justice, appeared in southern Burgundy at the end of the eleventh century. It was the beginning of a lengthy process which continued throughout the twelfth century and which finally formed the hierarchical structure of classic feudal justice with its superimposed levels of high, middle and low courts.

It was above all necessary to regulate relations between the territorial justice of castellans and the personal justice claimed over dependants by men who owned lordships sufficiently important for them to dispense justice and who had, moreover, solid judicial traditions as well as the necessary means to combat local judges. Around the millennium only the great churches were in that position. In any case it was they alone who have left traces of their struggles against lay holders of justice—struggles all the more bitter for the reforming notions which had made the encroachments of the laity seem even more intolerable.

The first settlement we know about in the context of our researches regulated the respective judicial rights of an ecclesiastical lordship and

---

[189] Halphen, 'Institutions judiciaires', p. 282; Garaud, *Institutions judiciaires de Poitou*, p. 41; Ganshof, 'Origines des cours féodales', p. 197.

a lord who held its guardianship. It dates from 1103,[190] and takes the form of a treaty between the abbey of Cluny and Humbert of Chatillon who had recently inherited the 'guardian' rights possessed by his father-in-law over the deanery of Chaveyriat in Bresse.[191] It was to be a return to the original state of affairs as recalled in the evidence of a friend of the deceased, a knight of the locality, *prudens homo ac plenus dierum*. By virtue of his right of guardianship, the castellan normally possessed the *malefactorum justicia*, but his exercise of it was to be somewhat narrowly restricted: the lay lord was to have no right of jurisdiction over the men of Saint Peter whether or not they sat on Cluniac lands; if he intervened to punish any crimes they might have committed, this was only to be done at the express request of the dean and on condition that the profits of justice were shared. Lastly, although the 'guardian' could exercise full rights of justice over strangers in the market at Chaveyriat, he had to pay half the profits to the monks.[192] Very like the classic settlements between ecclesiastical lords and lay *advocati*,[193] this agreement was weighted in favour of the patrimonial jurisdiction of the lord over his men which in this instance prevailed. The castellan was to be no more than the occasional executor of punitive sentences remunerated by an indemnity over all those men of the rival lordship who were scattered up and down the territory subject to his influence.[194]

The second statute, contemporary with the first,[195] drew a line between the competing rights of the count and the bishop of Mâcon within and around the city itself. A mixed commission, composed of two ecclesiastical dignitaries, a knight of the count's retinue and inhabitants of the town who were perhaps the count's or the bishop's officials, did no more than confirm the customary arrangement. Otherwise the independence of the bishop's jurisdiction was recognized over all Christian cases, such as breaches of the peace, truce, places of asylum, or cases in which the clergy were implicated. Outside this reserved area, a boundary was drawn between the general repressive powers of the count and the jurisdiction claimed for Saint Vincent over all the dependencies of the landlordship. The count alone had the right to punish all public crimes as soon as they were committed, no matter who was the culprit; in less serious cases, the bishop and canons possessed rights of

[190] In Burgundy the movement seems to have been relatively late; in Lorraine settlements regulating the judicial rights of the *advocati* began about the year 1050; see Ch.-E. Perrin, *Recherches sur la seigneurie rurale en Lorraine d'après les plus anciens censiers* (Strasburg, 1935), p. 118, note 1.

[191] Châtillon-sur-Chalaronne, department of Ain; Chaveyriat (same canton).

[192] C 3821.

[193] See Perrin, *Recherches sur la seigneurie rurale*, p. 676; Flach, *Origines de l'ancienne france* I, 182–3.

[194] All these rights were normally held by the guardian lord, see Didier, *Garde des églises*, p. 237; Senn, *L'Institution des avoueries*, p. 124; R. Laprat, 'Avoué', *Dictionnaire d'histoire et géographie écclesiastique* (Paris, 1931) V, col. 1232.

[195] M 89 [1096–1124]. The settlement took place on the accession of Count Renaud of the junior branch from Franche-Comté. The bishop was the brother of the same Humbert of Châtillon who concluded at the same time a similar agreement with the monks of Cluny about the guardianship (*vuarda*) of Chaveyriat.

justice over their own men and their property. However, the count reserved the right to intervene and to collect fines if the church's men had made their complaint to him, but in this case he could act only in order to make restitution to the victim and his lord. Lastly, in the event of a dispute between the count's men and Saint Vincent's men the count's town provost was to preside on neutral territory, at a crossroads, over a joint meeting where the dispute was to be settled once for all *per rectum et concordiam*. Here, even though this was the very heart of lordship, personal jurisdiction and the jurisdiction of estate lordship had gained little ground from territorial justice. The superior position of the count as rival is probably sufficient to explain this. Justice in the patrimony of Saint Vincent was on two levels: the inferior justice was administered by officials of the landlord, the superior justice was in the hands of the count who was always to be apprised of the most serious crimes and, when necessary, of other cases which could be brought before him. Finally, there was always an effort to settle amicably disagreements between the men of the two lordships and to prevent suits developing into disputes between the two lords themselves.

These two agreements—the only ones for this period to come down to us—show under what conditions the distribution of the rights of justice was parcelled out. According to the strength at his disposal and the cohesion of his estate, and according to whether his property was located far or near from the centre of the lordship, the ecclesiastical lord kept his rights of patrimonial justice, reserving at his discretion the power of the territorial lord for use in more serious cases. He retained the less important cases while the castellan imposed his jurisdiction over crimes and intervened every time the inferior justice failed to satisfy the dependants of the lordship; or else (this alternative, however, could leave no trace in the church archives) the dispenser of justice in a castle held the entire rights of justice over the scattered portions of the estate and over individual men dispersed in distant lordships.

Perhaps we should also date to the first years of the twelfth century those early settlements which, at the lowest level of society, were equally responsible for creating a hierarchy analogous to the judicial powers. At this time some lords began, it seems to grant to members of the most advanced communities living within their lordship the right to settle their small disputes to their own satisfaction. When, about the year 1160, Abbot Stephen drew up the good customs of the 'bourg' of Cluny with the help of recollections of the oldest inhabitants of the town, he attributed the first attempt to do so to Saint Hugh.[196] Even if this were no more than a respectful reference to the memory of an eminent predecessor, the community of burgesses of Cluny had by the year 1100 begun to enjoy a certain judicial autonomy.[197] While the monastic lords reserved for themselves the main criminal violations of the peace of the town, as well as the possibility of intervening in cases raised by formal

[196] C 4205 [1161–72].
[197] The maturity of the burgesses of Cluny showed itself in other ways from the early years of the twelfth century onwards (see C 3874, etc.).

complaints, the settlement of lesser misdemeanours[198] and the policing of the disruptive elements in the population were left to the burgesses by a twelfth-century charter.[199] Between the rights of this privileged group of dependants and those of the superior dispenser of justice a hierarchy was established which corresponds exactly to the one which superimposed the castellan's jurisdiction upon the landlords.

The hierarchy was exactly the same as that current in the thirteenth century when 'high' and 'low' justices were differentiated. The notion of separate justices, therefore, had begun to appear in the last years of the eleventh century; furthermore the manner in which the distinction grew up shows that judicial powers identical in essence and origin could, according to particular circumstances, confer either high or low justice. The rights of those holding a superior justice could as easily have developed from the private justice of an immunity reinforced by a pacifying mission of a spiritual kind (as in the case of the monks at Chaveyriat or Cluny) as from ancient public powers of jurisdiction passed on by inheritance (such as those assembled directly by the count of Mâcon, or indirectly by the guardian lord through the *salvamentum*). The superimposed layers were the result of the various rival justice holders in the same territory competing for and disputing over the profits of fines and confiscations. The rights of the more powerful holders thus overbore those of the weaker ones who, even if their powers were not completely extinguished, retained no more than the inferior justice.

The value the lords attached to possessing the lucrative rights of jurisdiction over humble people, the superimposition of different kinds of justice always poised to intervene, leaves us in no doubt about the activity of the lords in administering justice and the efficiency of their actions. Law and order were harshly enforced over the lower classes. But at the end of the eleventh century, as we have seen, there were no judicial institutions capable of fulfilling a similar role for the upper ranks of society. Regular tribunals to judge knights did not exist and there was no power to force them to fulfil the verdicts of peace.

Chroniclers describing at great length the conflicts of the lords, the pessimistic phraseology of preambles to charters, the sombre mood of moralistic writings by Saint Odilon and Peter the Venerable, even the wording of the liturgy, all combine to draw a dismal picture of the lay lords of their period. Faithfully adhering to this evidence, historians have always portrayed the eleventh century as a violent time when the strongest and most audacious individuals were able to impose their will at the expense of the weaker lords, including the men of the church.[200] Violence and usurpation are the motives most frequently invoked to explain the transformation of landownership and indeed of an entire society. This alone would suggest that we should look more closely to discover how far and by what means, in the absence of any regular

---

[198] C 4205, §v.   [199] C 4205, §xviii.   [200] Bloch, *Feudal Society*, pp. 410ff.

administration, the conditions indispensable for the maintenance of an organized society were secured in the face of lordly rivalries. Personal safety had to be achieved by repressing violence and the security of property by settling quarrels over ownership; these two aspects of society were accepted by men of those days as clearly distinct and they must be examined in turn.

The documents at our disposal are only occasionally able to give us information about acts of violence and how they were punished. Nevertheless, what they do allow us to assume is that, in the Mâconnais as elsewhere,[201] the normal reaction in face of damage or injury was still, as it had been in the eleventh century and long before that, a private matter. Kinsfolk, lord and vassals sought retribution from the culprit in the name of the victim. The matter was concluded with the payment of compensation. Our information on lords is confined to the indemnities in the form of land which, in cases of homicide, the family generally gave later on to God for the repose of the soul of the dead man.[202] These arrangements were not prompted by threats of reprisals alone, for we can see powerful lords paying much humbler persons fines for the death of their kinsmen.[203] We should not, therefore, underestimate the influence of moral considerations, especially on the deathbed,[204] and it should not prevent us from believing that such moral obligations were already a deterrent to wrongdoing. But just how much of a deterrent? The problem of the respective influence of Christian teaching and the *inimicus veritatis* upon the behaviour of eleventh-century knights is unfortunately an insoluble one.

Around the millennium, at the moment when the decay of the count's court began to be apparent, the movement of peace entered the Saône valley.[205] At Anse in 995,[206] at Verdun-sur-le-Doubs in 1016,[207] and again at Anse in 1025,[208] ecclesiastical assemblies gathered together the good intentions of lay lords and obliged them on oath to accept certain restrictions on their violent deeds; in addition the assemblies insisted on the special peace radiating from the ecclesiastical headquarters.[209] These requirements gave birth, as we have seen, to the special jurisdictions exercised by the great churches. By undertaking to put a speedy

[201] See Halphen, 'Institutions judiciaires', p. 296; Janeau, 'Institutions du Dauphiné', p. 76.

[202] C 2946 [beginning eleventh century]; p 173 [c. 1033].

[203] C 3125 [nd, beginning eleventh century]; Bernard, a lord in a very small way, gave a piece of land which came to him from Audin, castellan of Berzé, a man of some importance: 'quod dedit mihi Ildinus, pro nece fratris mei Malguini, ut cum Domini absolvit'.

[204] C 310 [nd, beginning eleventh century], 1931 [993]. 2464 [997].

[205] On the introduction of the institutions of peace into Burgundy see R. Poupardin, *Le Royaume de Bourgogne (888–1038)* (Paris, 1907), pp. 302ff.

[206] C 2255. On the true nature of this council, see Poupardin, *Royaume de Bourgogne*, p. 302.

[207] Text published by G. Valat, *Poursuite privée et composition pécuniaire dans l'ancienne Bourgogne* (Paris, 1897), p. 82.

[208] See G. de Manteyer, 'Les Origines de la maison de Savoie, la paix en Viennois (Anse, 17 juin 1025)', *Bulletin de la société statistique de l'Isère* (1904).

[209] C 2255; pact of Verdun 'ecclesiam nullo modo infringam; atria ecclesiae non infringam'.

end to private feuds through the payment of compensation, and then making these agreements respected by the threat of a heavy fine which, originally, punished those who had violated the *salvitas* (a zone specially protected by the peace of God),[210] bishops and abbots at least tried to underwrite by guarantees the individual vengeance which was virtually the only means available. Just how far their efforts were successful in this direction we cannot guess.

In fact the most obvious consequence of the movement of peace was the demarcation of places of asylum. Around the ecclesiastical buildings, the privileged areas were rapidly built over by peasants coming to put themselves under their protection.[211] At the end of the eleventh century, the boundaries of these safe areas were defined by a series of acts. The popes, solicitous for those establishments that were particularly dear to them, or else on the occasion of a particular visit, established privileges which, by their spirit, succeeded in freeing the churches from secular interference. The most important of these pontifical acts was the one which Urban II promulgated in favour of Cluny at the end of his stay in the abbey in 1095.[212] Remembering the time when, as Prior Odo, his main task had been to combat the encroachments of laymen, the pope fixed in minute detail the territorial limits inside which nobody could commit an act of violence, particularly an act of homicide or mutilation,[213] and where rectors of the monastery could pronounce excommunication in order to force transgressors to pay the fines.[214] At the same time, Urban II laid down prescriptions of a like kind in favour of the cloister of Saint Vincent of Mâcon, and Calixtus II also set up a *salvitas* around the monastery of Tournus.[215] The novelty of the privileges, which in fact did no more than give sanction to an ancient practice, lay in the precise definition of the territory. According to a custom which appeared widespread, crosses were erected that indicated to all comers the boundaries of the asylum. This is one more proof of how necessary it was felt at that time to fix precisely the frontiers of the different jurisdictions. The aim of the express ban on all killings and mutilations within the 'peace' was perhaps to reserve for the ecclesiastical lords the exercise of the superior justice near the church. In this way,

[210] C 2889 [1032–48]; see above, note 96, p. 30.

[211] P 22, 17, 167 (but in general these safe areas (*salvitae*), like the churches which they surrounded, were owned by laymen: P 18, 19, 21, 22, 25, 132, 150, 162. 167). See Timbal, *Droit d'asile*, p. 170. C 3674 [1094].

[212] *Bull. Cl.*, p. 25.

[213] 'Huis loco . . . quosdam certos limites immunitatis de securilatis circum circa undique assignare . . . infra quos terminos nullus homo, cujuscumque conditionis ac potestatis umquam invasionem aliquam grandam vel parvam, aut incendium aut praedam aut rapinam facere, aut hominem rapere, vel per iram ferire, aut, quod multo gravius est, homicidium perpetrare vel truncationem membrorum hominis ullatenus audeat.' This was within a radius of about 4 kilometres.

[214] Excommunication was strictly enforced against anyone who deliberately infringed the prescriptions and who 'congrua satisfactione non emendaverit. . . . Excommunicatus pro banno fracto ubi emendationem congruam faceret absolvatur.'

[215] M 514 [1096]; Tournus: Juénin, *Tournus, Preuves*, p. 148 [1120] and p. 149; the forged diploma of Saint-Marcel-lès-Chalon. probably drawn up at the same time, granted the right of asylum within a radius of 2000 paces (Sm 1).

the heart of the lordship was to be protected against all the pretensions of neighbouring dispensers of justice.[216] Nevertheless, the fact that the date of the pontifical privilege granting total protection to the cloister of the church of Mâcon was earlier than that of the agreement already mentioned between Saint Vincent and the count, by which the exercise of blood justice was left to the latter without restriction, prevents us from concluding that all these attempts were crowned with success. The main hope was that by establishing ecclesiastical safe areas a more peaceful atmosphere around religious foundations would be created. At the beginning of the twelfth century the practice was widespread,[217] each new foundation being preceded by a strictly defined *bannus* with privileges protecting the consecrated cross.[218]

Outside these islands of peace, men whose status enabled them to escape the brutal punishments of holders of blood justice could only be arraigned through moral sanctions. The constant resort to compensation, the fear of ecclesiastical displeasure, fidelity to certain oaths or, more usually, to the prescriptions of the Gospel were the only restraints on their excesses. The practical result of obligations of this kind is difficult to assess; our sources, apart from empty phrases, give us no precise information. One fact alone may be significant. To die a violent death in a markedly unfavourable spiritual state was considered to be a signal misfortune,[219] and deeds of gift intended to ransom souls in peril hardly ever fail to mention this fact. But, apart from the four references to compensation (see above p. 30, notes 93, 96, and p. 47, note 203) which all belong to the early years of the eleventh century, any mention of murder in the charters is extremely rare.[220] This is not enough to justify a conclusion, but, taken with the general impression gained from reading the texts, it suggests that some limitation on violence operated at the end of the eleventh century.

We are, on the other hand, perfectly informed about what went on concerning property rights, although we only know the squabbles of the greatest lords of the church and are ignorant of the means available to the small lay lords for resisting the encroachments of the neighbouring great lords. Within this field we can define precisely enough the place which the *justicia* (which in Raoul Glaber's view was, above all else, the maintenance of an equitable distribution of property[221]) occupied in the upper ranks of society in the last years of the eleventh century in the absence of any organized jurisdiction.

[216] See Flach, *Origines de l'ancienne france* I, p. 180; Timbal, *Droit d'asile*, p. 152 (after Seeliger).

[217] See documents published by Flach, *Origines de l'ancienne france* I, pp. 173ff.

[218] Foundation of La Ferté Abbey: 'sicut opportunum fuit designaverunt fixis crucibus. In qua postea designatione sicut duo episcopi diffinierunt in dedicatione ipsius loci ... bannum statuerunt quos si quis fratrum ... possessionem ... ullo modo infringeret, excommunicationi in perpetuum subjaceret' (Archives of Saône-et-Loire, H 24, 1).

[219] C 3435 [*c.* 1080] 'pro remedio anime filii mei karissimi B ... qui in ultimo vite exitu, heu pro dolor! morte subitanea preventus est.'

[220] P 17 [nd]; 13 [1090], 24 [1090]. C 3412 [1067], 2937 [1040], 588 [nd].

[221] Raoul Glaber, *Histoires* I, p. 2 (edited by M. Prou, p. 3), 'subsistens atque immobilis collocatio recte distributionis'.

Disputes about property were extremely frequent since there were many potent threats to ownership. On the one hand the prevailing idea of collective participation in the enjoyment of property meant that individual alienations were contested: to the endless claims by families[222] were added those of vassals or feudal lords.[223] On the other hand, the growth of the territorial domination of the *domini* superimposed upon landlordship provoked passionate controversy about the legitimacy of certain customs[224] or even outright usurpation.[225]

If the victim was not powerful enough for recourse to the *vindicta* to give him satisfaction, he had, in order to defend his rights, to attempt to deal directly with his adversary.[226] If this proved impossible, he carried his complaint before one of the superior courts, either county, episcopal or feudal, which might have some influence with the usurper; in particular it was usual to claim justice from the lord under whose protection the contested property lay.[227] But it was often difficult to persuade a court of its competence to settle a conflict between lords because, unlike the lucrative jurisdiction over lesser folk, the court's action could only bring problems in its wake.[228] More important still, none of these courts was capable of imposing the decision on the condemned party unless the latter had formally accepted beforehand to submit himself to its judgment.[229] A prior agreement to decide which tribunal would settle the difference was thus indispensable. At the end of the eleventh century, lords were no longer subject to the jurisdiction of particular courts, but were free to make their own choice of judge.[230] In cases when the affair dragged on too long, perhaps after a first judgment remained without effect,[231] in face of general reprobation towards the man who refused to discuss his rights publicly,[232] or after intervention by relatives, friends

---

[222] See preamble to C 3149; for example, Odo, a knight of the junior branch of the lineage of the sires of Berzé, gave a mill to Cluny about 1070 which, however, formed part of his sister's dowry; the latter's son bought back his rights (C 3301); then it was the turn of Odo's brother (C 3504: 'licet jam laudasset ipsum donum tamen illico calumpniam fratribus cluniacensibus intulit et usque finem vite sue calumniam inferre non destitit. In fine vero vite sue recordatus quod injuste calumniam faciebat de ipso molendino pro remedio anime sue donum quod frater suus fecerat bono animo laudavit et filio sou Garulfo laudare fecit'); finally Cluny had again to contest the pretensions of the chief of the lineage and his son and to silence them with a heavy indemnity.

[223] C 3806; P 64, 87, 152; claims against the holding of property under concession beyond the legal term became much rarer, since the number of *precaria* and fiefs conceded for a limited time rapidly decreased: still, however, in M 26 [1074–96], and 547 [1106].

[224] C 2997, 3065, 3150, 3262, 3367, 3503, 3841; M 4.

[225] See the Enchaînés family, castellans of Montmerle (C 3314. 3333, 3654); the Gros family of Brancion (C 3340, 3926, 3929); the Bâgé family (M 587); the castellan of Sennecey (SM 79); the sires of Bourbon-Lancy (P 115–54) or of Digoine (P 178, 159); the Deschaux family who, at this time, installed themselves in the castle of La Bussière (C 3829).

[226] SM 101 [end eleventh century]; P 154 [end eleventh century].

[227] C 3726, see above, note 171, p. 40.

[228] C 3868; SM 105; see Ganshof, 'Origines des cours féodales', p. 198.

[229] C 3868; see Ganshof, 'Origines des cours féodales', p. 197; Janeau, Institutions du Dauphiné, p. 76; 'the very act of presenting oneself for justice was then evidence of a real desire to come to an agreement.'

[230] Ganshof, 'Origines des cours féodales', pp. 210–11.

[231] C 3868.   [232] See the attitude of Audin in *Bull. Cl.*, p. 6.

and vassals,[233] and even by intermediaries who did not object to having their palms greased,[234] a man would finally agree to let a court of arbitration decide. When it had been agreed that the matter should be put before the regular court of the count, castellan or, more often, bishop, the friends of both parties came forward in equal numbers to form the tribunal. But, frequently, the role of conciliator was confided to a private individual, usually an ecclesiastic,[235] or else to an assembly brought together for the purpose and made up of intimates of plaintiff and defendant, or of their allies.[236] Not only the great castellans[237] but, increasingly, less prominent people—like the former provost of Solutré recently embroiled in the narrow bonds of estate justice[238]—demanded that a special meeting of an assembly should judge their case.

Before the arbiters, it was the plaintiff's business to provide proof of his right.[239] Among the proofs of a mystical character, only the judicial combat and the purge by oath were currently in use in the tenth century. They were still considered adequate and were put forward by knights[240] and also by canons[241] to justify their behaviour. But in Burgundy recourse to such antiquated procedures seems to have been exceptional and, in fact, in the only two late eleventh-century documents in which they were mentioned, they are seen as being preferred to other methods, and it may be asked whether this preference should be considered appropriate only to ecclesiastics.[242] The inquest, on the other hand, enjoyed such great favour once again from the last years of the eleventh century that it must be compared with the widely adopted processes of arbitration. The evidence of elderly people knowing the custom was gathered,[243] also that of neighbours who could speak of the long peaceful ownership of estates.[244] Information also came from witnesses to previous transactions, preserved in memory who considered their evidence to be inherited testimony orally transmitted from father to son.[245] But in

[233] *consilio amicorum* (C 3868; M 554); *a suis magnatibus commonitus* (P 154).

[234] C 3034, 3758, 3874; P 154.

[235] C 3760, 3868 (on Archibald le Blanc, see above, note 142, p. 36); M 598.

[236] C 3951; M 30.

[237] The Enchaînés, C 3577; the sire of Beaujeu, C 3577; Bernard Gros, C 3920.

[238] For valuable evidence on the emancipation of provosts, see judgments passed by Cluny, probably with due form and care, although harshly, on its provosts twenty years earlier. [239] C 3920 [1115], 3951 [beginning twelfth century].

[240] M 434.

[241] M 30; before the claims of a knight, the canons of Saint Vincent 'venerunt ad placitum parati per sacramentum ei campionem sic probare et sic facere de illis terris sicut judicatum fuit'; the church's repugnance for these lawsuits was generally admitted. See A. Esmein, *Cours élémentaire d'histoire du droit français* (14th edn, Paris, 1921), p. 279.

[242] See Ganshof, 'Origines des cours féodales', p. 205, note 6; in other regions it was the opposite, the judicial combat was preferred and even one-sided ordeals (Halphen, 'Institutions judiciaires', pp. 291–3; Esmein, *Cours élémentaire*, p. 261; Chenon, *Histoire générale du droit*, p. 673; Bloch, *Feudal Society*, p. 360). [243] C 3841.

[244] M 567 [1096–1124]; C 3920, 3726: 'testifactus est publice quidam de hominibus S. Petri ... XXXa et uno annis se vidisse easdem res absque legali calumnia cluniacenses monachos tenuisse.'

[245] C 3577: 'coastantibus multis et maxime P. de V. qui hujus doni testis fidelis et idoneis extitit quamdiu vixit, quique moriens hujusmodi testimonium filio suo B. sepius inculcavit, precipiens ei adtencius ut si ita res poposcisset, etiam jurejrando hoc affirmaret'; a subsequent lawsuit was then settled on the evidence of the son.

spite of promises to bear true witness in case of dispute, sometimes formally expressed,[246] the inquest provided an adequate guarantee only if the witnesses were neither forgetful, fearful nor false.[247]

However, recourse to the written deed was in the twelfth century, as in the tenth and the eleventh centuries, the commonest means of proof; the care of archivists and editors of cartularies,[248] the fear of fire,[249] even the formulae of charters, all bear witness to the importance that was attached to this kind of guarantee. If there was no written trace of a transaction then all claims could be allowed.[250] Was the use of writing equally widespread in lay society? It certainly was in the tenth century, when the existence of many village notaries, the appearance in Cluny archives of files compiled by laymen to safeguard their rights, and references here and there to deeds passing between laymen, all give abundant proof.[251] But by the end of the eleventh century this type of evidence had almost disappeared,[252] and as this may be almost entirely a result of changes in our documentation, the question cannot be settled one way or another. What is certain, at least, is that the laity at that period recognized the value of the written deed; the reason why usurpers endeavoured first of all to destroy all documents was because they were in no doubt about the force of their title.[253]

The marked preference for written proof and for the inquest—in this field Burgundy was clearly ahead of other regions—conferred a certain degree of superiority on legitimate owners in disputes; but as adjudicators did not possess any power of constraint, they could do no more than advise agreement and, at most, promise their support to the party whom they had judged to be in the right.[254] Very often their verdict was not implemented. Moreover, even if the usurper's claim was without foundation, he would not consent to abandon it except on condition that the rights were shared, or at least that he should receive an

---

[246] C 3744 [1100].

[247] C 3920: 'de muliere H. dicit A. quod L. dedit eam et homines Bernardi nominat qui hec sciant, illi negant.'

[248] If the Cluny archives after Saint Hugh's time ceased to be well ordered, the magnificent pancartes at La Ferté bear witness to the care taken by the Cistercians in the twelfth century.

[249] The evidence of the Tournus chronicle describes the fire of 1080, 'librorum non minima perdition, cum chartis testamentalibus magno pondere argenti acquisitis' (Juénin, *Tournus, Preuves*, p. 23), echoes the complaints of M 66 over four centuries.

[250] Landry Gros laid claim to the descendants of a female serf given earlier by his father, 'et ideo eos requirebam, qui patris datum nesciebam, et ipsi monachi de hoc dono se cartam habere nesciebant.' In the end he gave up his claim 'accepi . . . quinquaginta solidos . . . cum . . . cartam se habere nescirent; nam si scirent, nihil utique mihi dedissent.'

[251] C 430 [935], 856, 1296, 1312 [972], 2552 [1102].

[252] Some deeds passing between laymen in C 3755 [c. 1096]; it should be pointed out that these were townsmen.

[253] C 2844 [c. 1080], 'a quibus . . . ablata fuit ista terra . . . et, quod pejus est, carta legalis descripta ab ipsis igne exusta.'

[254] SM 107; arbiters were often content to put into the hands of the victim the sureties deposited by the condemned man before the judgment (C 3868), but they were sometimes themselves guarantors of the peace (C 3760: 'promiserunt ut per fidam adjuvarent ipsi Odonoi, si hoc placitum H. non teneret').

indemnity.[255] Behind each agreement we can guess at financial transactions preceding it and the offer of a gift was the simplest way of getting rid of an adversary.[256] For some lords, to quibble and then to settle for a quick renunciation, seems to have been a way of life.[257] Also, in order to avoid the often considerable expense of going to law, a man would attempt to activate a whole host of previous warrants of title which, coming into play automatically, would make it unnecessary for him to follow it up by putting in train an inefficient process of plea.

To begin with, the ancient warrants were becoming more numerous and weighty. At the end of the eleventh century material on moral obligations accumulated on the occasion of each agreement and each transaction. The sanctions which would fall upon a possible violator were made explicit; fines[258] as well as damages[259] which soon became important,[260] and also the traditional curses of anathema or excommunication; solemn oaths of renunciation,[261] and even aid against possible assaults by a third party[262] also came to be required. Further still, there was an attempt to establish between the two parties a spiritual communion that would be a surety for their good faith;[263] and the gestures that were performed in these matters sometimes even led to the ceremony of homage,[264] considered to be the most reliable way of preventing future differences. Finally, there was an endeavour to impose on an individual the constraint of an entire group made responsible for his behaviour. The ancient practice by which the contracting party was obliged to provide sureties became even more widespread as regular courts became weaker.[265] Henceforth, the practice of sureties became a regular one: chosen from among the natural relations of the party, kinsfolk, friends or vassals,[266] but usually of a sufficiently high rank for them to be more influential,[267] they had also in the event of a breakdown

---

[255] See Halphen, 'Institutions judiciaires', p. 294; Garaud, *Institutions judiciaires de Poitou*, p. 129; Ganshof, 'Origines des cours féodales', p. 215.

[256] C. 2736; around 1020 the monks of Cluny, wishing to regain possession of their lordships of Amberieu-en-Dombes and Jully-lès-Buxy 'aurique et argenti ac palliorum diversas species offerentes illis qui eas a suis antecessoribus . . . injuste usurpatas susceperunt.'

[257] Lebaud of Digoine and his repeated claims upon the possessions of the priory of Paray are a good example of this (P 64, 66, 152, 159, 178).

[258] C 3653 'ut si hoc donum calumpniatum fuerit ab ullo homine, ut ipsi emendent sexagenta solidos'; C 3868, a fine which seems to be symbolic 'auri libram monachis exsolvat.'

[259] SM 107 'reddam caput et legem'.   [260] C 3726, 3744, 3896; P 207.

[261] C 3666, 3703, 3744, 3868, 3951, 3891; M 560, 586, 587; P 207.

[262] C 3744, *fidelis adjutor*, C 3017 [end eleventh century].

[263] P 130, 'ut deinceps sint fideles et amici'.

[264] The embrace: M 4, 26, 456. SM 105; the gesture in C 3874 is already very close to the ceremonial of homage. Geoffrey of Berzé abandoned his claims and before Saint Hugh 'jam dicto patri junctis manibus se commendavit ac insuper sancto Petro sibi fidelitatem super sanctas furavit reliquias, adstantibus et conlaudantibus suis parvulis duobus filiis . . . quos etiam supradicto patri commendavit' (C 3324). On homage as a means of contracting obligations see G. Platon, 'L'Hommage comme moyen de contracter des obligations privées', *Revue générale du droit et de la législation* (1902); see Mitteis, *Lehnrecht*, p. 483.

[265] C 2018.

[266] C 2593, *parentibus nostris, vicinis nostris et amicis nostris*; C 2848: six guarantors—brother, nephew, feudal lord and three allies.   [267] C 3685.

themselves to pay a fine[268] or to give the injured party the less precise help they had promised on their honour.[269]

But a new kind of process (first mentioned in 1093[270]) appeared in southern Burgundy in the last years of the eleventh century and soon became general. Its advantage was that, in the event of an agreement being broken, the delinquent was automatically put into the hands of the injured party and was forced to come to a quick understanding. A lord who submitted to this obligation was indeed pledged as soon as the break in the peace became known, or after a stated interval,[271] to repair the damage as soon as possible or to put himself as a surety at the disposition of the opposing party and to remain so until restitution was made.[272] But what made the guarantee more efficacious was that the obligation extended to a whole group of people; if the contracting party were to violate the agreement all his sureties immediately became hostages for the same period of time. The participants pledged themselves, sometimes individually,[273] to surrender at a given place, usually a fortress or a castle,[274] and not to leave the specified boundaries unless they had obtained a truce or some event should put their life in danger.[275] If one of them should no longer be able to fulfil his function, either by dying, entering a monastery, or departing on a pilgrimage, the two parties were to choose a replacement of equivalent social rank.[276] Relations and friends were the usual sureties,[277] but the group of sureties who shared the responsibility for the great castellans generally came from the customary satellite knights of the castle.[278] In the case of a failure on the part of a lord, the entire vassal household would gather around him, charged with giving him good advice.

The guarantees used at the end of the eleventh century, to make up for the absence of any judicial organ capable of enforcing the law in disputes between lords about land and to expedite equitable agreements, relied (as did the institutions of peace) on sacred oaths and on the participation of the group surrounding each party to the contract. The maintenance of order thus rested solely on personal obligations. And, at a higher level,

---

[268] C 2848, 2889, 3653.   [269] C 3760.   [270] C 3666.

[271] C 3666, 3744, 3896: fourteen days; P 207: one month; C 3703: forty days.

[272] C 3774 [1100] 'juravit . . . ut si umquam faceret forfactum S. Petro . . . in illa terra . . . ingenio ejus aut assensu ejus infra quatuordecim dies post submonitionem . . . aut summam tolti per capitale reddat, aut in prehensione semet ipsum intro Cluniacum conducat et inde nulla ratione exeat, nisi licentia . . . induciatus et ad terminum induciarum iterum se in prehensione Clunacum conducat et hoc tamdiu faciat donec summam tolti ad integrum reddat.'

[273] One of these individual obligations has been preserved in C 3784.

[274] Cluny (C 3744, 3896; P 207); Mâcon (M 560); Uxelles (C 3784); Beaujeu (M 586); Charolles (P 207).

[275] C 3784, 'exeam si ignis incendio villa cremari ceperit'.

[276] M 586; C 3744, *ejusdem valentie.*

[277] M 560, the hostages were members of the lineage of H. Geoffrey.

[278] C 3784: all the petty knights, clients of the Gros family around Bernard the castellan; M 586: vassals of the Beaujeu family; C 3744: agreement between Cluny and Roland Bressan sire of Berzé, fifteen hostages were given—ten for Roland who were lords from Les Dombes and southern Bresse, his country of birth; five for his son who were knights of the locality.

the power able to provide the supreme guarantee of public peace was no more than an extension of spiritual authority—first, that of the pope, the ultimate recourse of the churches,[279] and then that of the king of France who, reappearing in the role of judge of the peace in 1119, took the abbey of Cluny and its possessions under his superior protection.[280] The royal act was entirely symbolic; nearly a century was to pass before the king intervened efficiently and regularly in the Mâconnais to contain the turbulent behaviour of the knights. Were moral considerations, then, alone sufficient to guarantee respect for the rights of everyone? There is obvious doubt on this point. Nevertheless, ecclesiastical establishments, thanks to their financial standing and to the prestige with which they were surrounded, were always able to resist satisfactorily the pressures of their lay neighbours. There is no instance in our region of a church not being able eventually to assert its rights, as frequently happened at the same period in western provinces.[281] We know nothing about what happened in disputes between lay lords, but we may assume that in spite of everything the use of wealth and, more particularly, constraints of a moral kind could, to a certain extent, impose limits on the untrammelled use of force.

From the foregoing study we can draw certain conclusions which are valid for southern Burgundy even though they still require further research in other regions before they can be applied more widely.

The decisive transformation of judicial institutions took place between the years 1000 and 1030. Throughout the whole of the tenth century, the organization characteristic of the early middle ages had preserved its essential form: in each county a superior court presided over by the count surrounded by the highest personages of the region functioned for the use of members of the aristocracy, while lawsuits concerning freemen of inferior rank were judged in local assemblies brought together by the *vicarius*. So far as the nature of the cases was concerned there was no difference between the competence of the count's courts and the courts of popular assembly. The only distinction was in the status of the litigants: the fact that *causae majorum* were reserved for the central assembly and *causae minorum* were left to the village courts meant that the distinction corresponded more with reality than did the contrast between *causae majores* and *causae minores* in the capitularies of the classical Carolingian epoch. Outside these public institutions the lords of immunities fulfilled the function of *vicarius*[282] within their estates and the master disposed of corrective powers over his *servi*.

But in the first thirty years of the eleventh century all this underwent a change. Public judicial institutions suddenly collapsed, and there

---

[279] C 3726.
[280] C 3943 'manutenere, deffendere et custodire sicut res proprias; vim et violentiam removere; damna et injuria facere emendari promittimus et tenemur.'
[281] Halphen, 'Institutions judiciaires', p. 299.
[282] H. Brunner, *Deutsche Rechtsgeschichte* (2nd edn, Leipzig, 1928) II, 302.

appeared a new and essential factor, whose significance extended far beyond the organization of justice and influenced the whole tenor of rural society (as Deléage has clearly shown[283]). This factor was the castle which assumed an enormous importance at this period. The men who owned castles, still few in number, first of all deserted the *mallus comtal* and thereby caused it to lose most of its prestige, then captured the judicial powers of the *vicarii* for their own profit and finally turned these ancient local assemblies of freemen into instruments of private domination. Henceforth, the castle became in the eleventh century the focal point for all the judicial powers extending over the territory subject to its influence, and the knightly courts which came under its wing disputed with the count's court the authority over the settlement of differences between lords. The administration of justice was thus fragmented into small, local, self-contained units.

Neither the lower courts nor the count himself were able to resist the all-pervading pressure. Why should this have been so? The justices of vicarial courts were probably incapable of enforcing the regular execution of their verdicts;[284] on the other hand, the real power of constraint depended on the castle, and litigants were able to accept without difficulty the new and very efficient jurisdiction. But the count should have been able to oppose the excessive growth of the judicial powers of the castellans, who were, after all, his own men, and to maintain the vicarial assemblies by lending them the support of his strength,[285] or at least to reserve for his own tribunal (as did, for example, the counts of Flanders).[286] the exclusive jurisdiction over crimes and cases in which knights were implicated. Was his failure caused by impotence or lack of interest? Nothing could have been further from this. It is tempting to look for the reason for inaction in the personal attitudes of certain princes: for instance, one of them, Otto-William, embroiled in schemes of far-reaching application, could not be bothered with the petty affairs of his Mâconnais county. But the phenomenon was too widespread to be explained by such private reasons, and researches in other directions, such as into the real significance of the obligations of vassals at this period, or into the family life of the upper ranks of society, might allow us to uncover the true reasons for the eclipse of the counts' judicial powers in most French provinces.

But personal justice, born of the private jurisdiction which bound the serf closely to his master and of the economic relations which united the lord and his tenants, profited from the disappearance of public justice and developed apace while remaining at the same time overlaid by the territorial justice of the castle. The relationship of these essentially different justices remains to be defined. Thus, the end of the eleventh century, when the first adjustments between competing jurisdictions

[283] Deléage, *Vie rurale en Bourgogne*, pp. 622ff., pp. 49–63.

[284] See H. Cam, 'Suitors and *scabini*', *Liberties and Communities in medieval England* (Cambridge, 1944).

[285] F.-L. Ganshoff, *Recherches sur les tribunaux de Châtellenie en Flandre avant le milieu du XIIe siècle* (Ghent, 1932), p. 84.   [286] *Ibid.*, p. 60.

took place, marks a new stage in the development of judicial institutions. It was then that the hierarchy was established which, by superimposing a superior justice over limited rights of jurisdiction, formed one of the most characteristic features of medieval judicial administration. The notion of a higher justice was therefore late in appearing; its basis was essentially blood justice—the power to punish the particularly serious crimes which, singled out by the movements of peace, were not themselves defined until the first years of the eleventh century. Consequently, it is not possible to relate the notion of higher justice with those early medieval judicial institutions which, at the time when it emerged, were either no longer in existence or were on the point of disappearing. To uncover its origins we cannot hark back to the distinction, long since effaced, between *causae majores* and *causae minores*.[287] What we know about the decay of the count's jurisdiction prevents us from concluding that the higher justice was one of the count's privileges subsequently given away or usurped; and we cannot attribute its exercise to simple *vicarii* who were no longer anything but agents of the lords.[288] Nor, conversely, is it possible to make it into a right held in common by all lords and to assume, as has been done,[289] that every public justice originated from global jurisdictions gradually despoiled of their superior prerogatives by invading particular jurisdictions. At the moment when blood justice emerged, the castle, source of a superior *districtio*,[290] was alone qualified to be its seat. But the castle was still an exceptional phenomenon in the rural landscape. Therefore, higher justice originated in the privilege of some lords who were castellans and, alongside them, certain great ecclesiastical establishments who were the spiritual protectors of the sacred peace.

Finally, I have always considered the transformation of judicial institutions to be only one aspect of the general evolution of society. Tenth-century institutions had reflected the social structure of the times: both *nobiles* and freemen of inferior status were answerable to distinct public jurisdictions; only the humblest dependants were abandoned to private disciplinary powers. The substitution of private jurisdictions for the inferior public assemblies at the beginning of the eleventh century corresponds to a new cleavage in society; humble but free peasants, by ceasing to come together in the vicarial courts, lost one of the essential attributes of their liberty. Confounded henceforth with former serfs and, like them, subject to increasingly heavy burdens, they came to be, in the territorial lordship established around the castle, the 'boors', the yokels, the *homines expletabiles* of the classical feudal epoch. Only the *milites*, who were considerable enough to be, in the year 1000,

[287] Chenon, *Histoire générale du droit* I, pp. 244ff; F. Olivier-Martin, *Précis d'histoire du droit français* (4th edn, Paris, 1945), p. 104.

[288] Hirsch, *Gerichtsbarkeit*; A. Gasser, *Enstehung und Ausbildung der Landeshoheit im Gebiete der schweizer. Eidgenossenschaft* (Leipzig, 1930); see E. Champeaux, 'Nouvelles Théories sur les justices du moyen âge,' in *Revue historique de droit français et etranger* (1935).

[289] By Génestal, cited by Champeaux in 'Nouvelles théories', p. 109.

[290] Bloch, *Feudal Society*, p. 400.

directly answerable to the justice of the count, could pass as truly free; they were already real nobles and one of their de facto privileges was the absence of any judicial constraint. Moral obligations and the persuasion of their peers were all that could impose a limit to their violence and greed.

3

Lineage, nobility and knighthood

The Mâconnais in the twelfth century—a revision

It is more than twenty years since I finished my study of society in the Mâcon region during the eleventh and twelfth centuries. A reissue of my book has made me wish to revise its contents on several points, and on one in particular. I was at the time deeply influenced by Marc Bloch's ideas, and it seemed to me that throughout the eleventh century in southern Burgundy knighthood was emerging as an increasingly distinct section of a much less well defined class, denominated before the year 1000 as the nobility. The relationship between knighthood and nobility has been seen in a different light by researchers working in other regions; Léopold Génicot, for instance, has found that in the Namurois during the twelfth century nobles and knights formed two clearly separated strata, one above the other. I have been fired by his findings to look again at the documentary material I used earlier. I would now like to set out the results of my new research.

Southern Burgundy has few narrative sources for the eleventh century. In particular, we find none of the genealogical writings that in other provinces can provide such enlightening glimpses of the ideas men of those days entertained about the antiquity of their families, that is about their nobility. On the other hand, the collections of charters belonging to the great religious establishments, especially Cluny, provide a documentation that is, for the tenth and eleventh centuries, more abundant and concentrated than in any other locality. As a result the upper ranks of society are more clearly visible here than elsewhere. To make my findings more accurate still, I have chosen to restrict the geographical area of my revision even more narrowly than I did in my earlier study. I have concentrated on a sector where the sources are richest and most continuous—an area of less than two hundred square kilometres in the immediate vicinity of Cluny, where the abbey's acquisitions were early and frequent.

The area covered by my research comprises now about forty rural communes. In the year 1000 it consisted of forty-five parishes, about a hundred peasant hamlets with appendant lands and four castles. One of the castles, Lourdon, belonged to Cluny and the other three, Berzé, Uxelles and la Bussière, were in the hands of lay lords. Of these, each was busily engaged in erecting around his fortress an autonomous domain which had as one of its boundaries Cluny's own *ban*, the protective zone which the institutions of God's peace (*la paix de Dieu*) were attempting to establish around the monastery. The aim of my research is to cut a slice through society at the end of the eleventh century and to list all male owners of lay property who were active between 1080 and 1100 and whose descendants are known to have borne the title of knight in the twelfth century. I have limited myself as far as possible to one generation, thus excluding fathers or uncles still living and sons already grown up at the moment of the survey; I have also excluded certain men holding only small parcels of property in the region and making only occasional appearances there (such were three other masters of castles, those of Bâgé and Montmerle in Bresse, of Bourbon on the Loire, and heads of a few aristocratic families from the Charolais). One hundred and five individuals can be thus singled out, belonging to 34 family groups or 'houses', 7 of which can themselves be divided into two or three related branches, adding up altogether to 41 *fraternitates* or groups of brothers. Starting with this sample, I shall attempt first of all to provide these individuals with a genealogy and then, by following the pedigrees, to trace their most remote ancestors. By sifting through all the charters and entries in records (*notices*), mentioning the social qualifications of these 105 individuals and their forebears, I have endeavoured to discover whether the corresponding lineages were at that time considered either noble or knightly.

In documents dated between 1080 and 1100 family groups are clearly distinguished by a *cognomen*, a surname borne in common by brothers and cousins. In fact, three of these *cognomina* are each borne by two distinct groups. Owning property in the same localities, these groups are related to each other, although only distantly, so that they form separate lineages. It should be noticed, moreover, that of the 31 surnames in use, 7 are nicknames that have become hereditary, another 2, interestingly, belong to two of the three owners of castles, while the remaining 27 are place names, that is of a landed patrimony, an inheritance.

An historian trying to trace ancestors from a starting point so apparently reliable nevertheless comes up against some formidable obstacles, the first of which arises from the fact that the available documentation is very far from uniform. Although plentiful about the year one thousand, it gradually tails off in the course of the eleventh century for two main reasons. On the one hand, the flow of land grants offered to the religious houses gradually lost its momentum while at the same time the gifts which were made were less frequently registered in writing. This means that our principal sources, the collections of charters of the monastery of Cluny and the cathedral of Mâcon, are much less revealing for 1100 than they were a hundred years previously. On the other hand, because lay owners in the area we are concerned with were gradually

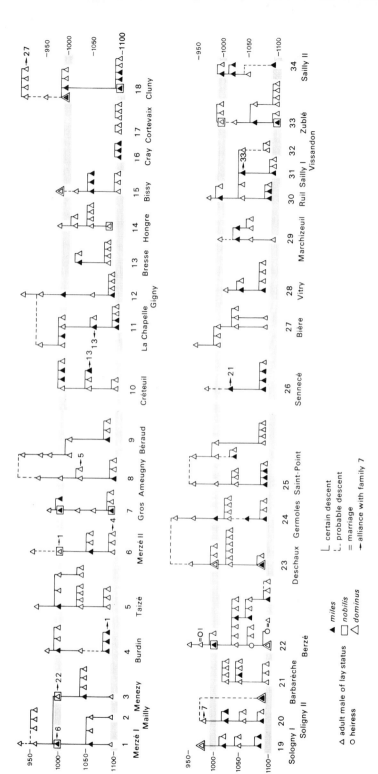

3.1. Genealogy of the 34 family groups under consideration

being pushed out as the landed possessions of the church expanded, they were imperceptibly thrown back onto the lands they owned outside the boundaries of our zone. For this reason, they slowly disappear from our view. If we add to this the fact that the chronology of the deeds, especially the Cluniac charters and entries in records, became much less precise in the second half of the eleventh century, it is obviously not easy to establish the links between the generation of 1100 covered by our initial survey and the generation active a century earlier, around the year 1000.

But to help us reconstruct the link we have at our disposal three kinds of evidence—first, the express mention of a direct line in a document; secondly, 'surnames'; and thirdly, individual or Christian names, themselves inherited up to a point from ancestors according to rules which may not have been compulsory at the time and are not, therefore entirely clear to us nowadays. The first of these clues becomes harder to follow the further back in time we go. Mention of kinship ties in deeds guaranteeing the transfer of rights was in fact most frequent in cases where the ties were strong, and where the individual did not feel himself to be free to dispose his patrimony among men of his own blood at his own discretion. But the framework of kinship—and I shall deal with this at length later in this study—was apparently in the process of being modified during the eleventh century to increase progressively the solidarity of the lineage. The result is that written evidence of direct descent or of kinship is much more frequent in 1100 than in 1000. It is consequently much harder at the earlier date to attach members of the aristocracy to a family group or to connect them with their descendants.

Similarly, the limitations of the second clue are also only too evident. To add a family surname after the name of one of the contracting parties was in 1100 quite a recent practice among editors of charters. Out of our 31 surnames, only 14 appear in deeds before 1070, 11 before 1050, and 5 before 1035, while none at all are mentioned before the year 1000. Can individual, or Christian, names, then, be of any help to us? Their use in the course of the eleventh century is confused by a highly important development which is itself deserving of close study, but which can only be touched on here, that is the gradual reduction in the number of Christian names. The 47 lay males, active in the year 1000 and identified as ancestors of the 105 individuals forming our sample, share 35 names. Already at that time there is some duplication—7 Bernards, for example, and 3 Josserans. But by 1100 their 105 descendants shared only 39 names so that namesakes were much more frequent than they were in 1000: there were 7 Bernards, as before, but no less than 10 Josserans, 15 Hughs, 12 Geoffreys and 5 Humberts. The phenomenon is closely bound up with the fact that family surnames were becoming more usual. It also owes something to a two-way movement affecting the relations of kinsfolk to which I shall have to return later: this was the simultaneous fission of the main family line into separate branches and the fusion of lineages through matrimonial alliances. Nevertheless, if we consider that 17 of the 35 names borne by individuals in the year

1000 had disappeared before many years had passed, and that of 39 names in 1100, 21 had been recently adopted by our selected families, it will be evident that the factor determining a family's choice of name was a combination of two tendencies—one of reduction in the range of names and one of innovation. The actual choice is pregnant with psychological and social significance. It is worth pointing out that, of the 5 most common names in 1100 (borne by 49 individuals, nearly half the total), one, Hugh, was that of the man who had been abbot of Cluny since 1049, and another, Geoffrey, belonged to the lineage of the counts of Mâcon, and that the other three—Josseran, Bernard and Humbert—were the hereditary names of two very powerful families holding the strongest castles. Thus, of names borrowed from ancestors, the preferred ones were those which recalled the memory of the most glorious forebears, or which implied relationship with the most illustrious lineages of the country. The appearance of new names is mainly explained by the fact that aristocratic families were obliged to practise exogamy by marrying their children at an ever greater remove from their immediate kith and kin. But certain innovations can only be understood by a change in mental attitudes, Thus, the appearance of names taken from the New Testament, like those of the four Stephens and two Peters of 1100 probably derives from the slow maturing of religious sentiment, while the fascination exercised by the epic heroes was perhaps another influence; thus Gerald, Roland and Oliver duly take their place among the new names. At all events, changes in the choice of the names for boy babies serve to confuse one of the most reliable and continuous lines of genealogical research. Finally, as bachelors and other childless individuals appear most often in our sources simply because they were more generous to the church than others; as those families whose history is least obscure were the ones which gave most, even to the point of impoverishment, extinction, and total disappearance; and as, conversely those families which were most vigorous, most solidly anchored to their landed estates and least prodigal of alms, hardly ever appear in the charters, it will be obvious that my efforts to establish lines of ancestry could not have been attended with complete success.

The quantity of the documentation and the amount of direct and reliable evidence contained in it are, however, sufficient for the attempt to be well worth while. Moreover, the picture becomes clearer if we use other, less obvious, clues. All these clues taken together firmly support my hypothesis. For instance, it is safe to assume that if two individuals bear the same unusual name and if, at the same time, it appears that their hereditary lands in the same locality are adjacent, then they are blood relations. The presence of certain distinctive features of a patrimony through the generations—a tenure from a religious establishment, a compact estate, a parish church—is another reliable indication of their successive owners being in a direct line of descent. To be sure, in this region of allodial holdings, after a century-long chain of partible inheritances and matrimonial alliances, a landed patrimony could well have been fragmented to a point at which, in most of the localities where the landed wealth to the abbey of Cluny was increasing, neighbouring landowners would make up a whole army of heirs so distantly related that the web of kinship uniting them would be practically impossible to disentangle. Let us take the locality of Sercie (8 kilometres north of Cluny) as an example. About 1090 the cellarer of the abbey, one Hugh of Bissy—first cousin to three of the knights in my sample—undertook to acquire the whole of it, piecemeal, either through *conventiones* or through *comparationes* concluded in the words of the text, 'with his uncles, with other relations and with other men'.[1] Thus, he had to deal on the monastery's behalf with 37 groups of landowners, among whom were 10 peasant holders of allodial land. Twenty of the 105 men included in our study belong to 9 family groups, 3 of them holding their land as fiefs, while 2 more held it from their wives' chiefs. But 5 family groups, including that of the lords of Uxelles, actually appear to share an inheritance in this locality which came to them from a common ancestor. This strengthens the impression, already suggested by our study of individual names, of a narrow group linked by ties of kinship which bind the whole of aristocratic society into one homogeneous bloc. But this very coherence, by inextricably confusing the ties of kinship, makes it much harder for us to build up genealogies, even though it reinforces the presumption of direct lines of descent. In the last analysis, however, the results produced by my enquiry are the best that, in my opinion, we can hope to achieve for any other part of Europe at this particular period. Here, then, are the results of my enquiry.

The first question I asked myself was: exactly how far back can the genealogical trees of these 34 groups of families be pushed? To put it differently, how old were these familes on the eve of the twelfth century? Or, rather, since nobility was before all else a question of remote and well authenticated ancestors, how old was their 'nobility'? Was the aristocracy of this region around the year 1100 formed of heirs to ancient wealth or was it, on the contrary, made up of newcomers who had recently risen by serving a master or by the favour of a benefaction?

(a)   Four groups of brothers in our sample (nos 4, 16, 17, 34) lack all direct evidence of a line of forebears. We do not know who were the fathers of the 12 persons who formed these groups at the end of the eleventh century. But for two groups (nos 4 and 34) there are several clues which make it possible for us to reconstruct with reasonable certainty a genealogy covering four generations. This leaves only 8 persons, therefore, whose origins are totally unknown to us.

(b)   There are 4 other groups (nos 9, 13, 24, 26) consisting of 14 persons about whom we can confidently say we know who their fathers and their uncles were. Moreover, the direct line of one of them (no. 26) can be pushed back with a high degree of probability to four generations and of 2 others (nos 9 and 13) to six generations.

(c)   For the 30 persons who form 9 other groups (nos 6, 10, 15, 18, 20, 21,

[1] C 3034, 3066, 3642.

28, 29, 33), we know with certainty who some of their grandparents were, and for 4 of the groups (nos 6, 15, 18, 33) their genealogies can be carried back to another, or a fourth, generation.

(d)   Then there are 14 groups whose direct line is definitely established for four generations (nos 1, 2, 3, 5, 8, 11, 14, 19, 23, 25, 27, 30, 31 and 32) and for 5 of these (nos 1, 2, 3, 8, 23) we can without hesitation add a fifth generation.

(e)   For 2 more groups (nos 7 and 12) it is quite safe to extend a direct line to five generations.

(f)   For the 34th and last group (no 23) the direct line is definite for six generations.

There are four conclusions to be drawn from this enumeration:

1   Twenty-four of the 34 families which formed the upper rank of lay society at the end of the eleventh century, in other words more than 80 per cent of the total, appear to have been firmly installed on rich allodial holdings before the year 1000; without being overconfident we might raise the proportion to 95 per cent, that is, allowing for the state of our documentation, we might consider that by 1100 the whole of the aristocracy had been established for at least a century. For 12 families, more than a third of the total, the antiquity of their landed possessions could be carried back another fifty years or so.

2   I have already said that 3 of the 34 family groups held castles and the powers to command that were attached to a fortress. These 3 families are indeed among the ones whose direct line can be carried furthest back: the earliest known ancestors of the masters of the castles of Berzé and la Bussière were active around 960 and probably around 940, and of the masters of the castle of Uxelles around 980. Nevertheless, on the evidence available to us in our research we cannot attribute a remoter origin to these families which were more powerful than others in the twelfth century. The most ancient families of all are not to be found among them. The first representative of the dynasty ruling at the castle of Uxelles makes his appearance in our documents definitely later than the ancestor of 8 other lineages and probably later than 11 others. We must not forget, of course, that the documentary sources upon which we base our enumeration are to some extent defective. What caused the members of the lay aristocracy to emerge from the shadows was their contact with the religious houses. Three quarters of the genealogies which can be extended furthest into the past are, in fact, those of families who owned land in the area where the landed wealth of Cluny was expanding earliest, and of course the family of the lords of Uxelles was not one of these. The important thing to note however, is that the lineages of the men who had by the year 1000 begun to erect an independent castellany around the fortress in which they were installed do not seem to have owned allodial property more ancient than many other neighbouring lineages. To put it in another way, we cannot state with certainty that it was a better established local position which had made it possible for these three families, by appropriating the power and the

profits of the *ban*, to begin the rise that had, by the end of the eleventh century, put them so clearly above others in the hierarchy of power and wealth. On the other hand, it is possible to consider that the gradual emergence of these lineages might have resulted from the fact that one of their forebears was already established in an existing castle by an act of delegated authority of which we know nothing.

3   We should note further that the most ancient branches of our family groups (one certainly, and 9 probably) emerge into the light of history only shortly after the point in time when the earldom of Mâcon had become hereditary and definitely before the founder of the most powerful lay principality of the region—the lordship of Beaujeu—reveals himself to have been active. Half, if not two thirds, of them appear to be firmly entrenched before signs of the great political and social upheavals which, about the year 1000, enabled the masters of castles to seize autonomy, the lordships of the *ban* to be established and the movement for the peace of God to be launched. It was also—and it is important to remember this—before the moment when the word *miles*, the title of knight, was introduced into legal vocabulary, and became widely used. If so, the aristocracy in the neighbourhood of Cluny owed nothing to these developments. A spate of early gifts of land about the mid-tenth century throws light on the social scene in the vicinity of the abbey, and everything points to the conclusion that landed wealth had already been firmly based on freeholding. We cannot be present at the birth of the aristocracy: we can only witness the situation after the event as the mists surrounding its infancy begin to dissipate.

4   Finally, if we take account of all the evidence provided by specific references to direct descent and matrimonial alliances, the choice of individual names by family groups of different generations, and the way in which the patrimonies of the aristocracy were intermingled in the localities, we need not feel we are being too audacious in conjecturing that 28 of our 34 groups and 83 per cent of the individuals listed at the end of the eleventh century (that is, 80 per cent of the entire aristocratic circle) were, in fact, descended from no more than 6 founding families. To one of these, whose places of origin stretched into the mountains of Beaujolais and the upper valley of the Grosne, and from which were descended the lords of Beaujeu and several other aristocratic families settled outside the geographical limits of the area we are concerned with, 8 lineages may be traced (nos 1, 2, 3, 24, 22, 23, 27, 5). Two of the latter and 6 others (nos 4, 19, 14, 20, 21, 26) come from another founding family of the Evrards and Alards, whose earliest known representative in the region of Mâcon was a member of the entourage of Charles the Bald and whose ancestral property was situated between Cluny and the valley of the Saône. A third root stock can be located west of Cluny, a fourth on the wooded hills rising to the east of the monastery; from both of these were descended 5 lineages (nos 31, 34, 32, 33, 30, 7, 8, 9, 15, 4), one of whom was also connected to the Evrard root stock. From the fifth and sixth founding families, both located beside the river Grosne, downstream from Cluny, three and four more family groups respectively

appear to have descended, two of which were also connected with the Beaujolais stock.[2]

At all events, we can be certain of one thing: the aristocracy of the year 1100 was a society of heirs. Its members were mostly descended from men who a century earlier, before the possessions of Cluny started to swell, owned huge tracts of land in the region. A further proof of this is that these people still held at the end of the eleventh century (or had held until recently) a number of parish churches: the Béraud family held the church at Chazelle, the Ameugny family held the church at Taizé, the Créteuil family the church at Chassy, the Bière family the church at Berzé-la-Ville, the family of la Chapelle the church at Bragny, from which they took their surname. It all points to the fact that some time in the mid-tenth century at the very latest, six very great patrimonies—whose earlier origins are lost to history—were divided up by partible inheritance to found the landed wealth of the various branches of the local aristocracy. But the process of fragmentation, details of which escape historical observation, appears eventually to have slowed down. By the end of the tenth century we can actually connect 24 individualized branches to our 6 original founding families: afterwards, during the eleventh century, only 4 new family groups make their appearance by a threefold realignment on the part of 2 of the 24 branches. During the same period the 6 families whom we cannot connect with certainty to any of these branches emerge from obscurity and 4 of the family groups visible in our documents about the year 1000 became extinct. Thus, in the eleventh century after a period of dispersion, dissociation and proliferation there followed a phase in which society appeared more or less static. What could have been the reason for this? Could it have been because the relationships between kinsfolk changed? It is this question we now have to consider.

Some twenty years ago I put forward the idea that a change in the family structure of the aristocracy occurred in the course of the eleventh cen-

---

[2] Moreover, we could probably add to this array of cousins stemming from a common ancestry, other relationships engendered by more recent matrimonial alliances, which wove these families even more closely into a web of connections. The use of the name *Wichardus*, for example, while it brought the bearer into the orbit of the sires of Beaujeu, also established a link between six groups descending from the Beaujolais founding family (nos 1, 2, 3, 23, 24, 5), two groups descending from the Evrard family (nos 19, 21) and three more stemming from another founding family (nos 8, 9, 15). A similar choice of the name *Humbertus* at the same time as it connected them with the sires of Beaujeu, apparently linked the Sailly II, Sennecé, Barberèche, Hongre and Berzé families. In addition, we have already seen that the Gros, Bissy, Taizé, Cortevaix and Besornay families had probably inherited land at Sercie from a common ancestor. Finally, in the generation we have taken as our point of departure (the generation at the end of the eleventh century) and in the immediately preceding one, our documents reveal some marriages which tie the threads more closely still; thus, Geoffrey of Merzé II is connected through his wife with the Ménezy family and through his brother-in-law with the Burdin family; Dalmas of Gigny and Letaud of Ameugny had both married sisters of the sires of Uxelles; the Bresse family was joined by marriage to the Créteuils and the la Chapelles, The extent of the endogamy that was practised in spite of the church's disapproval seems to have resulted in making all the 105 individuals into cousins of one kind or another.

tury. Since then some leading experts of the post-Carolingian aristocracy and specialists in genealogical studies (mainly pupils of Gerd Tellenbach) have put forward the hypothesis that the structure of kinship in the Empire gradually crystallized into patrilineal dynasties or lineages.[3] As this idea is so similar to the problem about the nobility under discussion here, a re-examination of the documentary material I made use of earlier is clearly called for, although to be quite frank, I do not think we can yet consider any revisions in this field to be final. The defects of our sources add significantly to our difficulties. The main defect, of course, is that the sources are so few: in the absence of any express formulation of rules or customs, we cannot look for documents defining the practice, but should try rather to penetrate beyond to see what was actually happening, although even then allusions which reflect reality are extremely few and for the most part very hard to interpret. Furthermore, our texts have the more serious defect that during the period in which we are interested they were affected by changes which cast a doubt on all our observations. On the one hand, the wording of the deeds themselves underwent a change; the strict framework in which charters of gift, sale or exchange were drawn up in the tenth century began to break down fast after the year 1000 and eventually to collapse completely. At the same time we find that written deeds drawn up between laymen about property or rights subsequently acquired by the church became scarcer in the archives of ecclesiastical establishments until after a certain date they finally disappeared altogether, either because the archivists had neglected to preserve the titles, or else because the practice of drawing up such deeds was effectively abandoned by lay society. The turning point in the deterioration of documentary material appears to have come about 1035; and the date links the deterioration closely with the disappearance of public jurisdiction, the abandonment of written proof, and the adoption of other means of guaranteeing the ownership of land. In face of these changes in our sources, we have to ask ourselves whether the statistical evidence which supports the hypotheses which I am about to put forward reflects reality and is not merely a result of changes in the outward form of the documents. If we add that the latter reveal only one aspect of kinship relations, the one concerning economic matters and patrimony, we can realize how fragile the basis for our conjectures is.[4]

The outline assumed by family trees leads us to conclude that between the middle of the tenth and the end of the eleventh centuries the biological growth of families without any doubt slowed down. Our primary hypothesis consists in suggesting that there is a connection between the phenomenon and the rearrangement of kinship ties into the framework of a strictly masculine line, and the appearance of a truly

[3] Particularly Karl Schmid, 'Zur Problematik von Familie, Sippe und Geschlecht. Haus und Dynastie beim mittelalterlichen Adel. Vortragen zum Thema: Adel und Herrschaft im Mittelalter', *Zeitschrift für die Geschichte des Oberrheins*, 105 (1957).

[4] In an attempt to reduce the doubtful basis of my conjectures, I have drawn on sources relating not only to the very restricted area selected for observing the most easily visible aristocratic families, but also to the whole of southern Burgundy.

lineal structure. In order to verify my hypothesis I shall have to pose three questions in turn. Do we see during this period an increase in the solidarity of blood relations centred on the inheritance? Can we discern the gradual acceptance of male primacy? Does it seem as if certain privileges were then recognized as belonging to the eldest son?

1   The first of the three aspects of relations between kinsfolk is the most easily seen and lends itself best to statistical treatment. There is no denying that changes led to a greater cohesion of the family group. But the changes themselves are complex and can be divided into four distinct movements—the growth of indivisible ownership by heirs; the increased appearance of kinsfolk among witnesses to deeds; the growing frequency of consent by kinsmen to alienations; and lastly, the multiplication of family usurpations of pious gifts that had been made by ancestors. These four movements will be examined separately. To simplify matters, I shall divide the period into four chronological sections, the two halves of the tenth century, the first half of the eleventh century, and the period between 1050 and 1120. For each of these periods I shall give the percentage of surviving deeds in which the various manifestations of the same development are discernible.

(a)   Unusual before 950, indivisible inheritance subsequently grows at a frequency which stays the same. What does change—and causes the growing consolidation of kinship bonds—is the gradual increase after the middle of the tenth century of indivisible inheritance between brothers, called in the texts *fraternitas*, or *frereschia* (28 per cent, then 33 per cent, and then 50 per cent). Perhaps even more significant is the increasingly clear incidence of indivisible inheritance among more distant blood relations (2 per cent, then 6 per cent, then 14 per cent).

(b)   An examination of the 'life cycle' of our deeds, in the order in which records appear and disappear, will clearly reveal the progressive intrusion of kinsmen among signatories (from 4 to 10 per cent; then to 16 per cent; and then to 20 per cent). Obviously the phenomenon cannot be separated from the simultaneous disappearance of public assemblies. This is emphasized by the fact that in the tenth century the formal indication of family relationship was much less frequently noted in the concluding formalities of documents. But that the scribes did not at that time consider it as useful to record them as they were to do later is by itself a remarkable fact. In any case we note that, among the relations who occur as signatories, fathers and mothers became fewer until they practically disappeared (28 per cent, 7·5 per cent, 4 per cent, 3 per cent). What this proves is that, after the year 1000, sons no longer possessed the independent right to their share of the inheritance in the lifetime of their parents. On the other hand we are reminded of the increasing role of the *proximi*, that is relations further removed than children or brothers (from 3 per cent to 10 per cent, then 14 per cent and 18 per cent). Lastly, it is worth noting that development appears to be continuous without any break in the pace.

(c)   The intervention of relations in order, as the texts put it, to *laudare,*

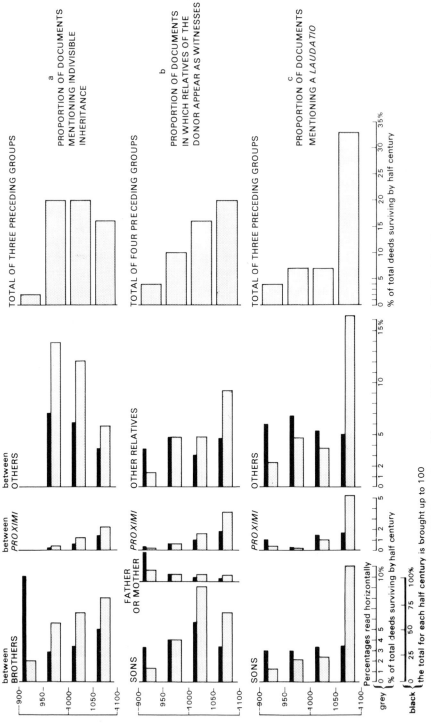

PROPORTION OF DOCUMENTS MENTIONING INDIVISIBLE INHERITANCE

a

TOTAL OF THREE PRECEDING GROUPS

PROPORTION OF DOCUMENTS IN WHICH RELATIVES OF THE DONOR APPEAR AS WITNESSES

b

TOTAL OF FOUR PRECEDING GROUPS

PROPORTION OF DOCUMENTS MENTIONING A *LAUDATIO*

c

TOTAL OF THREE PRECEDING GROUPS

% of total deeds surviving by half century

between BROTHERS

between PROXIMI

between OTHERS

SONS

FATHER OR MOTHER

PROXIMI

OTHER RELATIVES

SONS

PROXIMI

OTHERS

Percentages read horizontally

grey { % of total deeds surviving by half century

black { the total for each half century is brought up to 100

3.2 Increasing solidarity of blood relations with the inheritance *concedere*, to give a *consilium*, on the occasion of an alienation of a hereditary property, itself becomes more and more frequent (4 per cent, 7·7 per cent, then 33 per cent of the deeds). Here, at any rate, there is a break between the first and the second half of the eleventh century. In addition, about 1080 there is the first mention of a cash payment for such an approval. And if the proportion of sons remains the same (about a third) that of 'close' members of the family moves up from 3 per cent between 950 and 1000 to 14 and then to 16 per cent.

(d)   Almost unknown before the year 1000 (I have discovered only three instances), the *querella*, or the *calumpnia* (the claim made by members of lineages to an ancient family property in the possession of a religious establishment), remains rare during the eleventh century. However, with time it becomes somewhat more frequent (from 1·6 per cent to 3 per cent). The important thing is still that the part played in these disputes by 'close' members of the family relatively to the part played by sons or brothers (*consanguinatis objectione vel cupidatis illectione*, as a document of 1030 calls them[5]), gradually increases from 12 to 35 per cent of all disputes.

This statistical analysis of our four aspects provides convergent evidence clearly supporting the gradual strengthening of the solidarity of blood relations in matters concerning inheritance. This continuous movement seems to have been going on from the second half of the tenth century; if the change in the outward appearance of the deeds that I have spoken of is not an illusion, its pace increased in the second half of the eleventh century.

2   Do the rights of sons and brothers grow at the expense of those of their sisters? To put it differently, does our society, at least as far as hereditary property is concerned, become more obviously a masculine one? In dealing with this second question the enquirer feels himself on much less firm ground. Indeed, evidence about the actual practice of succession is both meagre and unreliable. Customs of succession are sometimes alluded to in deeds of gifts and deeds winding up disputes between heirs. But a complete inheritance is never described nor is its partition. We cannot therefore put a definite value on one heir's portion and compare it with the shares of others. Lastly, the references are so few that we cannot even attempt to construct a trend.

It is obvious that women inherited from their fathers. However, references to the transmission of allodial holdings coming from the maternal side from mother to daughter, or sister to sister, are more frequent and more explicit.[6] Again, though some texts lead us to suppose that women's rights to succession might be equal to their brothers', such texts are few and their interpretation is debatable. In fact most such

[5] C 2906.

[6] Alexandra makes a gift in *locum divisionis* to her daughter Landrée; a little later, the latter by an identical deed bequeaths the property to her sister. M 467 [960] and 468 [997–1031]; Elisabeth gives 'a piece of land which came to me from my mother and my ancestors', 'my share of the inheritance'. C 2860 [1031–48].

references seem to imply that male heirs received larger shares.[7] Could this preferential treatment lead at times to the complete exclusion of daughters from the inheritance? The frequency of joint possession of property between brothers only, of partitions in which the number of shares is the same as the number of boys, would alone suggest that we should not reject out of hand the hypothesis that women were excluded from inheritance. It can, moreover, be supported by formal documents. Here, for instance, is a couple with five children, 'four sons and one daughter. . . . One became a monk at Cluny; they have given him his share of the inheritance;' another son, the eldest, gave himself after his father's death to Abbot Odilon who had paid his ransom and, when he in turn died he bequeathed the whole of his property to the monastery 'before his sons and daughters'. 'Then, the third brother . . . became a monk at Cluny and gave his share to Saint Peter. The fourth, the lastborn, alone remained; he had held in fief for life all the shares of the inheritance,' which after his death, passed wholly into the estate of Cluny. There is never the slightest reference to the fifth child, the daughter. In the same way, the married sister of one donor is excluded (one of the 105 individuals in our sample) who offered 'the quarter of the inheritance which came to me by hereditary right after partition with my three brothers'.[8] Of all the theories that we might construct on the basis of these documents, the least unlikely is that of a society where the succession concerned only men and where women had only subsidiary rights, where unmarried sisters remained under the tutelage of their brothers and received at most, as a gift for their funeral alms, a small share in the joint inheritance, usually a part of the property brought into the family by their mother, where the married daughters finally left the household with their small dowry, without being able from then on to claim anything from the family allodial holdings.

If we look at matrimonial law, the general impression is confirmed. There is a perceptible difference between the tenth and the eleventh centuries; the husband strengthened his grip over the wealth of the couple. In fact before the year 1000 the wife seemed to have retained a clear legal independence within the conjugal unit: she managed her own hereditary property, and the husband made her a gift of what was called the *sponsalitium*, which was a third, or sometimes even a half of his entire inheritance 'to do with it what she wishes', 'to have it, to sell it, to give it'. The gift was so complete that there were occasions when a woman transmitted to the children of her second marriage property which was part of the ancestral patrimony of her first husband.[9] But by the eleventh century all that had changed: husbands, supported by their lineages, exercised their power to preserve strict control over the *spon-*

---

[7] A man owned half a manse, the other half belonged to his sisters. C 1899 [991]; a donor held two thirds of an estate from his father, his aunt had the other one third. C 3574 (the partition took place about 1050); gift of two thirds of a church 'which came to me by hereditary right; the other third belongs to my sisters.' C 2860 [1031–48].

[8] C 2118 [c. 1030], 3304 [c. 1080], the brother-in-law appears amongst the signatories of the deed.

[9] M 210 [tenth century]. C 2265 [994]. C 254 [925–6], 370, 798, 953.

salitium. Every precaution was taken to avoid the risk, present in earlier times, of it falling into the hands of any but blood relations. And now, too, it was the husband who took charge of his wife's hereditary property, her dowry, in other words, that small portion of the family wealth given her by her father or brother which had been carved out of the least desirable parts of the patrimony. This would often be a portion of the bequest of a deceased parent which he did not intend to cede to the church, or property received by the mother as her dowry, and as far as possible it was not removed from the heart of the inheritance that had been handed down from the earliest ancestors.[10] A strengthening of marital power is indisputable and seems to reflect a defensive reaction by family groups reformed into a pattern different to what had formerly prevailed. The group is now based on the patrimonial property which appears intended to uphold more distinctly than previously the line of male offspring and which required protection against economic accidents arising from matrimonial alliances which had previously resulted in destruction or fragmentation. A reaction of this kind must have been due to a greater awareness of the lineage such as we see for the first time formulated with great clarity about 1025—the date is crucial—in one of the clauses in a deed of gift: 'if the children, issue of my body by my legitimate wife, should die without legitimate son' my heirs (*heredes* and *proheredes*) shall have no right to my succession. 'And thus, in the course of time, that the legitimate sons, issue of my body, succeeding in turn by right and lawful *ligne* of descent, shall not be able to deliver any part of this property into the ownership or lordship of our other heirs.'[11]

3   One more question remains: was the eldest of this line of 'sons' and males in some way privileged? If so, it is obviously the exact antithesis of the equal rights to the inheritance for all brothers reflected in every text that we can use. Nevertheless, throughout the period in this region we cannot help noticing that the father was himself able to decree how his property should be distributed among his heirs. After direct allusion to some 'charters of partition' come, from 980 onwards, other direct allusions to some 'partitions', which were probably no longer put down in writing. Custom now probably ensured continuity between the written dispositions of the tenth century and the first of the new written wills to have been preserved, drawn up about 1090 in Beaujolais.[12] Unfortunately, the relevant references are no more than allusions. There is no evidence by which we can measure whether eldest sons were at greater or lesser advantage as a result of such partitions, nor as a result of those gifts to children during the lifetime of the parent. Such gifts were frequent up to the beginning of the eleventh century, but disappeared

---

[10] B 12 [1087], M 463 [997–1034]. Dowry given to Saint Vincent of Mâcon 'by the hand of Bernard, her husband'. M 477 [end of the eleventh century]. Dowry constituted by ancient alms: C 3301 [1049–1109]. C 2528 [beginning of eleventh century]: the aunt had given some manses to God; 'my mother, in marrying me, plundered these two *manses*, and gave them to me as a dowry.'

[11] C 2493. The same in 1100 (C 3030) 'if my two sons who I leave in the secular estate, die without heirs, none of my heirs shall claim anything from this allod.'

[12] Printed in the *Cartulaire lyonnais*, edited by M. C. Guigue (2 vols, Lyon, 1893), 10.

thereafter, in the face, perhaps, of increasing family solidarity. It is true we can see the privileges of seniority showing themselves openly on two occasions in our sources. But it has to be admitted that these two examples occurred in the last years of our period as the twelfth century approached, and also in the restricted social circle of castle owners, a position which even though it was 'up for grabs' within the family itself, always kept its public character and was for this reason most likely to be considered indivisible. Here are the cases of two lords of castles. One, on leaving for the Holy Land in 1100, made bequests and instituted one of his four sons as 'heir to the remainder of his honour'. The other, at about the same date, stated that his father was still alive and had made him the 'gift of his honour' having forbidden him 'to give or to sell any of it to anybody, nor his sons nor his daughters'.[13] What conclusions can we draw from this limited evidence of late date? Our knowledge of subsequent successional practices in southern Burgundy would allow us to see in them the first signs of a growing movement. On this point, however, I have my reservations. Even if we admit the persistence of principle that each son should receive an equal share of the inheritance, it is indisputable that the outline of genealogies shows quite clearly, from the beginning of the eleventh century at the latest, the tendency for family lineages to adhere to a single branch, an axis by which, so it appears, the eldest son succeeded. Though favoured by stiffening solidarity between blood relations, by masculine privilege, and probably even more by the new developments of matrimonial custom, this process of crystallization appears, however, to be more the result of a prudent limitation on marriages. Obviously all brothers had the same rights of succession, but they did not share the inheritance on their father's death. Only one of them married and begat legitimate sons. The latter, thanks to the practice of prolonged joint ownership, would later collect without difficulty the rights of their uncles who had remained celibate and hence the entire inheritance, shorn only of what the uncles themselves might have offered to the church as funeral alms.

Evidence abounds that marriage was restricted to one or at most two sons. I can repeat the case quoted above of the family of four boys, of whom two took the habit at Cluny, only the eldest had children, and the fourth died unmarried. Another example is that of the lords of the castle of Uxelles. In 1070 there were five boys, of whom two entered the cloister at Cluny, two others disappeared without trace, and only one carried on the line. It is also noteworthy that, among the gifts made during a lifetime, those made by bachelor uncles to one of their nephews were much the most numerous, and the custom was maintained longest. I can quote indisputable evidence of men who drew up deeds in the names of their brothers, but who acted alone, the other males merely giving their 'advice'. Finally, I can refer again to the results of my genealogical researches. These are obviously not complete: we cannot hope to know about all the adult members of a family group, and those who escape our

[13] C 3737, 3031.

observations are, of course, precisely the members of collateral branches who interest us. We must, however, take account of the following facts: of our 34 lineages 3 only acquired their individuality in the course of the eleventh century through the ramifications of two of the original root-stocks. There are no more than 8 others where in one generation or another, several sons produced children; there remain 23 single lines whose ramifications withered away without offspring. And when the masters of castles are considered from about the year 980 onwards, the time when the independent castellanies first appeared, the superiority of the elder brother over the younger ones is quite evident. Take for example the castle of Berzé where Walter, about 1030, had five brothers; he was a canon and yet he ruled alone—as did his grandson Hugh fifty years later, who had at least three first cousins who we know about. Lastly we should note—and this is one final proof of the privilege conferred by seniority—that the principle of the superiority of direct descendants over collaterals, combined with the effects of restricted marriages, frequently resulted in a daughter who had no brothers inheriting her father's possessions, even though she had uncles and cousins living. Hence, it was her husband who 'held' her possessions. In this way the castle of Berzé fell twice, about 1060 and then again in 1090, into the hands of sons-in-law, men from outside the region who may perhaps even have been upstarts, although the collateral branches of the lineage were well provided with male members. The evidence that I have collected is perhaps inconclusive, but it all points in one direction. My re-examination permits me therefore to maintain the view I first put forward in my book on the society of the Mâcon region. I proposed that there was a narrowing and a tightening of the family around the male line, from which emerged a dynastic spirit that was probably more noticeable amongst the owners of castles, but was nonetheless quite common throughout the aristocracy.

The remaining problem takes us back to our first question: did the self-awareness of the aristocracy relate to the notion of nobility or to that of knighthood? The interest of the argument as so far developed is in fact to relate the study of the social vocabulary and the way it reflects psychological attitudes more closely and reliably to the real world, that is to men themselves, or rather to those family groups which can be individually distinguished in the course of the eleventh century.

So far as the vocabulary is concerned I can repeat what I have said before, but a more detailed statistical treatment of my sources enables me to state it now with greater confidence and precision.

1   The adjective *nobilis* (or its equivalents *clarissimus, illustris*, etc.) was used in the mid-tenth century to show that an individual belonged to the aristocracy. But, on the one hand its use was infrequent and, on the other, in eighty per cent of the cases when it was used it appeared to depend on the requirements of certain traditional records, such as in contracts of leases (*precaria*) and deeds of exchange, when the term was employed to designate the beneficiary of the deed individually, or in

proceedings of judicial assemblies, when it was necessary to describe the juries collectively.

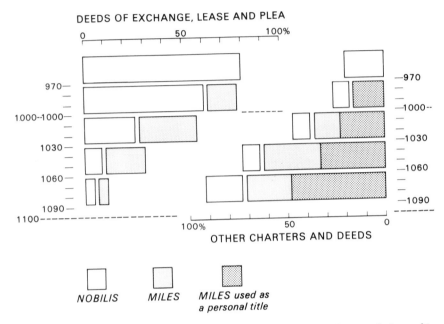

3.3 Distribution of titles showing noble birth in deeds of exchange, lease and plea and in other charters and deeds (as a percentage of documents in which such titles appear)

2   The period after about 970 witnessed a twofold change.

(a) First, the custom of distinguishing those who belonged to the ruling stratum of lay society from other men gradually spread. The diffusion of aristocratic adjectives in the vocabulary of charters and entries in records is evidence that scribes increasingly felt they had to indicate the superiority of certain individuals. This was because the aristocracy was becoming more uniform as well as more important, and because at a certain level the gap in the hierarchy of social standing was getting wider. Thus, in all the deeds where we come across terms indicating that men belonged to the aristocracy, the proportion of ancient formulae in which the employment of these words was traditional gradually decreased—slowly to begin with, then much more rapidly from the middle half of the eleventh century onwards. It shrank from 76 per cent between the years 970 and 1000, to 56 per cent between 1000 and 1030, to 29 per cent between 1030 and 1060 and to no more than 10 per cent in the last period.

(b) Simultaneously among these words appeared a title which soon replaced all the others: this word was *miles*. In a document still preserved it was first used in this way in 971. It penetrated into the old traditional formularies where it was gradually substituted for words like *vassus* or *fidelis*, expressing the subordination of a vassal, and, even more clearly, for the word *nobilis*. Between 970 and 1000 we find it in 20 per cent of deeds of this kind; between 1000 and 1030 in 53 per cent; between 1030 and 1060 in 70 per cent; between 1060 and 1090 the proportion falls back to 50 per cent, but by this time of course, the formulae themselves had almost gone out of use.

In other deeds the triumph of the title of knight is even more obvious: two thirds of the instances of its occurrence were between 970 and 1000, four fifths between 1000 and 1030, and 87 and 85 per cent respectively in the two succeeding chronological periods. Here it should be noted that it was increasingly used as an individual qualification, attached either to the person who was one of the main parties, or to the person who was a witness (16 per cent, 23 per cent, 33 per cent, and finally 48 per cent of the total of all deeds).

3   Here it could well be that it was a genuine substitution, as is proved by these two examples among others, one dating from 1002 and the other from the year 1000. In connection with the court of pleas presided over by the count of Mâcon, mention is made successively of *ceterorum nobilium hominum qui ante eos stabant* and of *ceterorum militum qui ibi aderant*. A formulary of land exchanges brings to our notice one, Bernard (lord of Uxelles) who is described as '*vir clarissimus* according to the custom of the century', but signs himself 'Bernard, knight'. Admittedly the title *miles* does not entirely replace *nobilis*, but from about 1030 it acquires an overwhelming superiority—between 970 and 1000, 31 per cent of the descriptions used to indicate social rank, between 1000 and 1030, 64 per cent, and thereafter 81 and 82 per cent.

But to prove that those who were called noble and those who were called knight were the same people, we have to replace words by real men. Let us go back to our 105 individuals, three of whom, we may recall, ruled over a castle, 96 certainly possessed old fortunes and all of whom were cousins. The adjective *nobilis* (in its superlative form) is applied to only four persons, three of whom are so described in the same deed; but they were not numbered among the most powerful men, nor among those whose most remote ancestors we know about; moreover, two of them were called knights in addition. The fourth was the lord of Uxelles, *nobilissimus* it is true, but the register of deaths at Mâcon which calls him this adds, *nobilissimus miles*.[14] Now let us consider another description also reflecting superior status, the term *dominus*. I have found it used three times, although obviously in a careful attempt to denote social rank, since of the three people who bear the title two are masters of the castles of la Bussière and Berzé.[15] Finally, the word *miles* itself: we find it applied to 34 persons. Its use is clearly more extensive, even though it only relates to 32 per cent of the individuals and 20 out of the 34 lineages. In 4 of the family groups all the brothers who remained laymen bore the title, in 12 other groups it was only applied to the eldest

[14] C 3104 [about 1090]. Register of deaths, M II, p. 28.   [15] C 3671, 3565, 3565.

brother; was it therefore still the privilege of seniority? Among those who were called, or who called themselves, knight, there were, as we have seen, two lords of castles, and the cousin of a third, but in addition there were men whose fathers we do not know, such as the three Cray brothers. Seventy-one individuals are left who had no title, although, it is true, 39 of them were either brothers or nephews of a knight.

Having established these facts, let us go back as far as we can into the past of the lineages to a point about the year 1000. Out of 47 laymen designated as the ancestors of our 105 individuals of the year 1100, 15 bear the title of knight (that is, it should be noted, 34 per cent, a proportion which is a little higher than at the end of the eleventh century, even though the use of the word *miles* had in the interval become, as we have seen, more widespread). Among these 47 persons there were proportionately more *domini* (4) and especially more *nobiles* (6, or 13 per cent, instead of the 4 per cent in 1100). Of these 6 'nobles', 20 owned castles, but 3, including these 2, were also called knight either elsewhere or in the same deed.

Last, if we consider the genealogies as a whole, we can see from the documents at our disposal that in not more than 3 of the 34 lineages had there been no single member in any generation bearing the title of knight. Of these 3, one had suddenly emerged at that moment from the shadows. This is the only lineage for whom we can put forward the rather tenuous hypothesis that it was a family of upstarts who had suddenly broken into the aristocratic circle. The other two were of ancient stock: it was said in the year 1000 of the representative of one of them that he was *prepotens amicus* of the count of Mâcon; one male member of the other family was called 'noble' in 1080. The remainder form 92 per cent of the total. In 7 of the groups the description of knight is not recorded until the generation of 1080–1100; in another 7 it is recorded in the previous generation; in 18 more (53 per cent), two of whom were lords of castles, the title can be traced back to about the year 1000.

On the other hand, the title *nobilis*, or its equivalents, does not seem to have been specially reserved for members of the small elite. The owners of castles were not described as being nobler than others, any more than they could lay claim to the longest pedigrees. It was another word, *dominus*, that marked their particular position.[16] Thus, everywhere, the words 'noble' and 'knight' appear to be interchangeable; everywhere there is continuity in the list of titles. In every family, as in the family of the lords of Uxelles, it seems to have been a matter of indifference whether, in the year 1000 as in 1100 , any male representative was called *vir clarissimus* or *nobilissimus miles*. We may, therefore, conclude without hesitation that aristocratic society was homogeneous. Its members were all brought together into a single coherent group—and this was from the second half of the tenth century, before

---

[16] At Berzé, in the year 1000 the lord was called *miles* and *dominus*, his successor in 1100, *dominus*: conversely, the lord of la Bussière, was called *dominus* in the year 1000 and *miles* and *dominus* in 1100.

the great upheavals connected with the birth of the lordship of the *ban* and the diffusion of the institution of peace. They had common ancestors, formed a group of cousins who still clung to the persistent practice of endogamy, enjoyed an economic superiority that helped to safeguard the reinforced lineages, and lastly, they had a common vocation for power and for the bearing of arms which brought out the masculine features of the whole social circle. It was this common vocation which may explain how it was possible, in circles in which the fief held so little importance as against the allodial holding, to pass so easily from the notion of 'nobility', underpinned as it was by the image of an ancient race and the idea of an inborn authority and power, to the notion of 'knighthood', itself closely linked to the concept of public military service.

Thus, having re-examined my material I am able to reassert with even greater confidence all that I had already stated in my book. In a part of the country so well served by a wealth of documentation, we are able to see a well established landed aristocracy which was in the eleventh century in possession of patrimonies held by lineages had been handed on from one generation to the next and mostly received from even wealthier ancestors. We know nothing about them, however, until the mid-tenth century because for the earlier period there are no written records. Before the year 1000 the cohesion of these fortunes began to be threatened by the customs of inheritance and the relative economic independence of individuals. To prevent the superior position of the social group being compromised the relations of kinfolk were gradually modified within a flexible framework of customs to allow the lineal characteristics to be strengthened. The changes occurred soonest in the families holding 'honours', that is the families with castles and the power to command and punish. The earliest recognizable 'houses' were formed by the families of 'masters' possessing powers which were originally of a public nature. It is at this point that we can see how political conditions influenced the structure of the family. Indeed, these men who had been able about the year 1000 to throw off the effective control of the count and to create little independent principalities around their fortresses belonged to lineages similar, but not richer nor more ancient, than those of some other men. A degree of differentiation began to appear within a homogeneous social group in the course of the eleventh century merely because political events allowed some men to enrich themselves from the profits of 'exactions' raised from peasants and to become leaders of local *militia*. A small dominating layer, the *sires*, emerged by degrees from the upper ranks of the aristocracy. They were wealthier and more powerful than their cousins, it is true, but they were not thought of as being more noble, because from about the year 1000 they had all assumed the same title—that of knight. It seems that this title did not describe any man who was an upstart, who had been suddenly elevated because of faithful service, the bearing of arms, or the holding of a fief. It described in a more definite and explicit way members of an already existing social group. The change reflected by the rapid diffusion of the title did not affect the material structure of society, merely the way men saw themselves. It only remains to point out that a noun emphasizing the military function and service was preferred to adjectives indicating the varying lustre of birth. The date of the change in vocabulary encourages us to connect it with political events, such as the formation of lordships of the *ban* and the spread of the ideology of the peace of God.

4

The history and sociology of the medieval west

I would not think of starting an account of recent French research into the history and sociology of western Europe in the middle ages without mentioning the name of Marc Bloch, or without trying to convey all that he meant to my generation, and especially to me personally. When I was twenty years old *Feudal Society* had just been published, and the *Annales d'histoire économique et sociale* were appearing regularly, filled with his writings in which he demanded that disciplines as yet young and uncertain be opened up and that history be rejuvenated. If for a while the history of medieval society was, in France, in the fore-front of historical research, this I am convinced was due to him.

What then were the directions to which he pointed the way? In the first place Marc Bloch made solid advances in economic history. It is very striking to see in the papers he left behind how much space he devoted to the foundations of social development—to monetary history, to demography, to technology. The founding fathers of medieval economic history had, of course, concentrated until then upon cities and trade, but medieval society was, after all, agrarian and Marc Bloch had a particular interest in everything to do with the land. Thus it is to him that we must, perhaps, attribute this vital switch to the history of the countryside. The decisive change in the direction of research was to a great extent made possible by the existing links between social history and human geography. By 1940 this bond had come to seem not only essential but perfectly natural. In addition, through his studies Marc Bloch opened up two further lines of approach. One was towards com-parative history by which he attempted to arrive at a typology of medieval societies. His other approach was towards a definition of the 'intellectual tools'. Since his time the need for this definition has been at least tacitly admitted. These, then, were the points of departure for those of us who have followed after him.

If we now ask ourselves what were the materials with which we conducted our research, one thing is clear. During the last twenty years all researchers into social history have made use, as did Marc Bloch himself, of documents in archives, supported by cadasters, maps and aerial photographs, that is to say, the tools of the geographer. For the period between the tenth and the thirteenth centuries (studies of earlier periods are still rather limited in France) our basic material is to be found in charters and entries in cartularies. To take some examples from recent research, this is the kind of evidence used by Robert Fossier for his excellent thesis on rural Picardy, as also by Pierre Toubert and Pierre Bonnassies in their studies of Latium and Catalonia respectively. In the studies of the succeeding period (where most scholars are concentrating at the present moment) the most fruitful sources are fiscal and legal documents and notaries' registers. From this point of view, southern France is particularly well endowed, and a sort of compensating activity has been taking place. Previously, because research was conducted mainly in Paris, the southern parts of the country remained almost unknown. Now, however, it is to this area that most of the work is being devoted. Of course towns have attracted most of the attention, and here I must mention books by Philippe Wolff on Toulouse and Jacques Heers on Genoa, as well as studies on the Provençal towns pursued by my own pupils.

As to the methods used, the following is a very brief account. Every researcher tries at the outset to locate a source of documentation which is both compact and coherent, which does not have too many gaps and provides a continuous series—as do, for example, the eleventh-century cartularies of the abbey of Cluny, or the notarial registers of Toulouse in the fourteenth and fifteenth centuries. What the researcher hopes to find is a body of evidence giving sufficient continuity to reveal the broad development of a social group over several decades. The second distinctive feature of recent research is that it is usually confined to a limited area; in this it follows the example of the excellent regional and urban monographs completed by French geographers in the 1930s and 1940s. A third feature is the attention given to the counting of everything capable of being counted in a continuous documentation. This is an attempt at a statistical treatment of increasing refinement. Here I should mention as an example the experimental use of ordinators in an effort to utilize the numerical material contained in the exceptionally detailed Florentine cadaster of 1427. These attempts at quantification have had their influence on the questions asked, on the area investigated and, consequently, on the direction in which the greatest progress is being made.

Here demography in its widest implications is in the forefront. It may be a question either of quantitative changes in total population based on the evidence of censuses made for tax purposes, the first of which appeared at the end of the thirteenth century (a notable example is Edouard Baratier's demographic study of Provence), or of more detailed researches into the composition of households; it may involve the history of individual families, or research into the variation in the density of settlement; then there are enquiries into the distribution of wealth.

The most important consequence of these uses of statistical methods has been to put the emphasis on the purely economic aspects of the social structure. This is why legal history has had to surrender the position it occupied in the history of society before 1945. But perhaps the fascination with numbers and quantification has led to our overestimating the economic influences. More specifically, and perhaps more dangerously, we may have built up a picture of the economy of the middle ages (especially between the tenth and the thirteenth centuries) which does not correspond with the ideas entertained by contemporaries about their own wealth.

But, and this point needs stressing, it is clear that for some years historians of medieval society have been aware of other problems to an extent that amounts to a wholly new departure. This widening of the scope of the problems goes hand in hand with an extension of the documentary material used.

In considering the sociology of western Europe in the middle ages, then, we can observe trails leading in two directions. The first leads towards an outline of the archaeology of material civilization. This is a completely novel idea in France where, up to now, medieval archaeology has been restricted to works of art serving the aim of a history of artistic creation. Following in the steps of foreigners, particularly from eastern Europe, French scholars have now turned to the study of more prosaic remains. The leading teams in this field are working at the Institute of Medieval Archaeology in the University of Caen, at the VIth Section of the École Pratique des Hautes Études in Paris, and at the Laboratory of Medieval Archaeology in the University of Aix-en-Provence. At present work is concentrated on sites of villages. The choice reflects the dominating position occupied by problems relating to the economy and to population in social history. Indeed most medieval archaeologists are working on the problems of the villages which were deserted in the latter part of the middle ages, during the course of the fourteenth century when there was a downturn in economic and demographic growth. These excavations are proving most useful in revealing the material basis of the social structure. As an example of what can be done, Gabrielle Demians d'Archimbaud's excavations on the site of a Provençal village illuminate how wealth was distributed and output organized among a group of shepherds and arable farmers living in the shadow of a fortress. But recourse to the archaeology of everyday life also enables us to enlarge the field somewhat and to free social history from its dependence upon economic history. Something of this can already be seen from the results of the research, under Michel de Boüard's direction at Caen, into the castle, the seat of political power during the feudal era. Fundamental social problems such as the distribution of different ranks of the aristocracy, the gradual dissolution of military 'households', and the appearance of dynasties of knights, can be directly tackled by examining the remains of the mottes, by analysing the way the living quarters of the castle were laid out and by comparing what we read in documents with what we find in excavations. But we can also hope that through archaeology we shall gradually enlarge our knowledge of the outward signs of social differentiation, such as emblems, costumes, or anything reflecting personal luxury, at all levels of wealth, even down to the most lowly.

However, by referring to signs and symbols I come to the second perspective, the one that attracts me personally and continues to hold my attention. What in my opinion could most effectively stimulate research in social history, open it up and enrich it, without in any way neglecting its quantitative aspects, is a return to the study of its social basis. Here the disciplines from which historians could expect most encouragement and vitality to come are linguistics, social psychology and anthropology. Indeed the structure of a society cannot depend solely on the system of production or the way in which wealth is divided among the different groups, ranks and classes. It is influenced quite directly by other things which may depend on ritual, and which may stem from powers that are not solely of economic origin; by the self-awareness of that society; by the system of reference which it respects, and by the very words that it uses; by all the different phenomena of culture and ideology, whose movements are, it is true, closely linked to economic factors, but are not necessarily synchronized with them in every particular. The important thing is to associate the concrete image of an economic sociology with the abstract image of a psychosociology that was deeply felt by contemporaries and by which their behaviour was to a large extent governed. To be able to interpret this abstract image, we have to rehabilitate a certain kind of document, used patiently and in great detail in the nineteenth and early twentieth centuries when history was all about politics and events, but which has been neglected since attention became focused exclusively on economic facts. The documents I have in mind, of course, were the chronicle narratives. Chronicles contain words, or rather associations and constellations of words, which place individuals or groups of individuals in relationship to each other. It is the task of the historian of society to define which of these expressions are the most significant, to reveal their meaning, to follow their semantic trail, as far as possible, to trace any discordances between the categories and relationships which these terms are intended to designate and those which establish the effective connections of power. Other forms of liturgy, ceremony, or ordering of precedence, intended to command the social body periodically and to make it conform to the ideals of collective awareness, as revealed by these texts, must also be similarly interpreted. In fact these forms and all the other cultural models, which determine social relations just as imperiously as the unequal distribution of wealth does, have to be dissected and laid out to view.

As a straightforward example let us take the problems presented by the formation and consolidation of the social group called 'knighthood' (*la chevalerie*) in France during the eleventh and twelfth centuries. The example is a conclusive one, for Marc Bloch was one of the first to blaze the trail and to establish a master plan for others to follow. By going through the documents and making a preliminary statistical analysis of the material much can already be learned. From these texts we can isolate an entire social vocabulary which is introduced into them belatedly only to be crystallized in the language of professional scribes. By counting and classifying words it is possible to distinguish the group of persons to whom they apply, to see it take shape and attach to itself a title that was first borne by individuals in the last thirty years of the tenth century and came to be used collectively after 1030. Charters also permit the economic base of this rank of society to be explored, to be placed in relationship to inheritances, prerogatives and the economic power established by its members in one zone of the scale of wealth. The main thing the use of the words shows is that in the neighbourhood of Cluny everyone who bore the title of knight at about the year one thousand was a free landowner; as landowners knights were also holders of fiefs, but these were absurdly small in comparison with the totality of their holdings, and most individuals appeared to be descendants of the great lords of the Carolingian period. The words also reveal to what extent the social group shared such mobility as was taking place elsewhere in the population at that time, as well as indicating the remarkable stability of its membership during the eleventh and twelfth centuries. Moreover, if we use the results of archaeological exploration in conjunction with investigations into narrative sources, the mists surrounding other large areas of obscurity begin to dissipate.

Thus, a study of fortified places reveals two facts. The first is that the knighthood in the eleventh century did not comprise the entire aristocracy; the latter was actually dominated by a much smaller social group made up of a few individuals who were in command of a fortress to whom knights were attached and were in fact subordinate. The second fact is that castles of more modest dimensions, later called 'fortified houses', began to multiply in the course of the twelfth century. This phenomenon shows, among other things, a desire on the part of the knights to emulate the way of life of the owners of real castles, to appropriate their prerogatives and to raise themselves up to their level. It reveals a deep-seated movement which resulted in aristocratic behaviour being gradually vulgarized. The effect of the movement was to blur the lines between the hierarchy within the seigneurial class and to make it more uniform.

But to appreciate the scope of the movement and to elucidate the changes which determined it, we have to undertake a parallel investigation into the narrative sources and into the things they express. It appears that ideas and cultural models played a leading part in the development. In the upper levels of the aristocracy, among the 'princes' and the 'magnates', to use the language of the documents of the period, an ancient concept of nobility was still current. The essence of this concept was the hereditary aptitude—I might even go so far, since it was transmitted through blood and was not affected by education, as to call it the biological aptitude—to command, an inborn charisma of power. It was this notion which had created the gulf between 'nobles' and plain knights. But the gulf soon began to disappear; in the neighbourhood of Cluny this happened quite early, by the end of the tenth century. An idea began to spread that knights were also noble and possessed similar virtues because of their birth. But the idea does not seem to have been the result of a material fusion, for there was no intermarriage between the two groups and the economic gap remained clear cut. Changes in manorial profits, far from reducing the differences, only made them more obvious. It seems more likely, then, that what was responsible was the influence of an ideology known as the peace of God (*la paix de Dieu*), which originated in the south of France during the last years of the tenth century. The movement was the outcome of a political event, the collapse of the royal powers, which was itself a direct consequence of economic factors. It was a response to conditions in an enclosed, agrarian society, no longer nourished by the profits of war which had formerly been put into circulation by the sovereign. The spread of the peace of God transformed the view which aristocratic society had of itself. Collective attitudes and idea were affected in four different ways:

1   Those who bore arms were segregated from other men, and an exclusive, homogeneous group was thereby created which, because it was set apart, came to form a strictly limited social class. This helps to explain the diffusion after the end of the tenth century of a common description, a special title, the word knight, which by emphasizing the military specialization was intended to circumscribe the group's membership.

2   The diffusion of the ideology of peace also hastened the acceptance of an ethic pertaining to all warriors, which was made possible because military activity had acquired its own value. In this way the intellectuals of the church were able to find spiritual justification for the violence implicit in the knight's calling. They held up the exemplar of the *miles Christi* for the approval of the entire lay aristocracy, including 'magnates' and 'nobles' as well as other members of the upper stratum, and by so doing they prepared the way for the crusading ideal. From the last forty years of the eleventh century onwards it was a point of honour for the great nobles to behave like knights and even to take the title of knight. The two groups of the aristocracy thus found that they had much in common. What finally completed the process of fusion was that the values attaching to noble birth, particularly the notion of hereditary 'virtue' transmitted by blood and race, fitted in quite naturally with the common ethic.

3   The popularization of the idea of noble birth brought with it one more change of immense importance, although up to the present it has hardly been studied. There was a shift in the attitude towards kinship in aristocratic society as a whole, and a strengthening of family solidarity within the framework of lineage. The idea of ancestry, as patrilineal, solid, strict, at first prevailed inside the ranks of the greatest nobles, but in the end it seems indeed to have become vulgarized and to have been diffused throughout the lower levels of the knightly class. One thing certain is that knights, many of whom had in the eleventh century still lived in the households of masters of castles as members of their households, began to settle on small estates and that most of them took the

name of the estate as their own. The name was hereditary, as was the land, which encouraged the sentiment of belonging to a lineage. The knighthood thus became a society of heirs, all the more solid and shut in because, in order to maintain their position of wealth, families attempted to limit births mainly by strictly controlling marriage. This behaviour accounts for the stability of members of this social group as revealed by an analysis of the cartularies.

4   This last attitude, moreover, explains the significance of bachelors within the knightly class. These were the young men, known at the time as 'youths', who had not had the means to acquire a separate establishment. Their presence in the world of chivalry was responsible for that wanderlust, turbulence, aggression and the other characteristics described and exalted in the literature of pleasure written largely for the benefit of a public formed by the 'youths' themselves.

This example that I have quoted encourages us to re-examine our methods of research. It is essential when using narrative writings, as when using archival sources, to start with an accepted knowledge of economic conditions as the groundwork of social relationships. It is not so much a matter of confining oneself to what the modes of expression of a minority reveal about a culture, as of discovering the 'lay', or material basis of attitudes of mind. However, it is no less necessary to seek out the repercussions of any ideologies prevailing at any moment of time. These attitudes can in fact achieve a certain degree of independence from the very political and economic realities that presided over their inception. They may outlive them and we can see many a discordance between the outward form of a social group and the picture its members see of themselves. Consequently, it is very important to pursue the study of economic conditions concurrently with the study of ideas in order to be in a position to mark out the areas of harmony and discordance.

5

The origins of a system of social classification

Historians of society must examine closely any system of classification that has come to impose itself on the collective mind. Social behaviour is directly governed by ideas of this kind because it is through them that people are made aware of their position in the world and their relationship to one another. The simple and rigid forms assumed by such mental systems make it possible for them to be generally accepted over a period of time and also to survive without obvious modification by economic or political developments. The latter, however, gradually remove them from the realm of reality until a mutation, usually of an abrupt nature, replaces them with another system of ideas. Thus, for many centuries, human relationships over a large part of western Europe were dominated by a system of ideas which divided men into a threefold hierarchy. The first category contained all men of religion and the second all men whose business was war. The third, by far the largest, class of men was lumped together indiscriminately. In it were all those workers who were compelled to maintain by the fruit of their labour the members of the other two, superior and privileged, groups. It must be admitted that the history of this classification, familiar though it be, remains somewhat vague. This is primarily because we do not know over what precise area this view of society was imposed in the course of time, neither do we know how far within this area it was more or less mixed up with other views. Nor, even inside the area where it was accepted without question, can we discern the original meanings which it may have reflected in different places. Up to the present time there have been no studies to help us trace the development of this system of ideas or to observe in what manner it was unconsciously deflected to conform, more or less closely, to transformations taking place in the way power was exercised or wealth distributed. We need, therefore, to see more clearly when, how and why the system itself took shape and replaced other types of classification. Problems concerned with origins are never straightforward, so in this instance it is proposed to restrict the consideration to some questions of method.

It is generally acknowledged that the earliest clear-cut formulation of this tripartite system in France is to be found in two writings. One is a poem composed about 1028–30[1] by Bishop Adalbéron of Laon, dedicated to King Robert. The other is the *Gesta episocoporum cameracensium*, written by order of Bishop Gerald of Cambrai about 1025 but relating to matters of interest in the year 1023. True enough, historians frequently use these two sources, but have they made sufficiently sure that other, less obvious but perhaps earlier, traces of a similar picture of the social hierarchy do not exist? At any rate a preliminary enquiry seems essential, and this entails re-reading certain by no means numerous texts,[2] both contemporary or slightly earlier, and subjecting the assembled evidence, no matter how tenuous it may seem, to a rigorous scholarly analysis. The evidence is, of course, mainly confined to Adalbéron's and Gerald's writings which are less well known than is generally believed. In what linguistic forms was the character as well as the functional vocation of each of the three social divisions expressed before that time? Without having first provided some kind of an answer to this preliminary investigation we cannot know how to continue our enquiries into the antecedents of our system of ideas nor into its genesis.

There is an obvious relationship between the model of social organization set out in the writings of Adalbéron of Laon and Gerald of Cambrai and, from quite another direction, the tripartite functional division which, as Georges Dumezil has shown, imprinted such a profound mark on the structural forms of Indo-European culture. The latter model was also a threefold one based on the distinction between the religious, warlike and productive functions. It is therefore permissible to regard its appearance in the kingdom of France soon after the year one thousand as a revival of the system of ideas which Georges Dumezil showed to have been part of the culture of ancient Rome. But the mere fact of demonstrating the revival does not by itself solve anything. What we have to explain is why the idea came into use again and what caused it to be found necessary and useful at that particular time and place. Of course a difficulty arises directly from the fact that societies in the eleventh century and in Roman antiquity were so very different. There is, to begin with, one fundamental difference: the former system was one of social classification. The latter was a composite picture formed from the different fields in which human activity takes place under the aegis of gods, heroes and princes. Moreover, our two cases are separated by an enormous lapse of time extending over more than a thousand years. During that interval the ideas it represented had been totally lost, or at least so confused that they did not enter into intellectual activity, the only medium available for their transmission.

It is true to say that the discontinuity is considerably reduced if we

---

[1] The last scholar to discuss this dating was J. F. Lemarignier in *Le Pouvoir royal au temps des premiers capétiens* (Paris, 1969), note 53, p. 79.

[2] J. Batany has recently dealt with the *Apologeticus* of Abbon of Fleury. 'Abbon de Fleury et les théories des structures sociales en l'an mille', in *Etudes ligériennes d'histoire et d'archéologie mediévale* (Auxerre, 1975).

take into account the fact that the Anglo-Saxon period provided an intermediate stage. The division of the social body into three groups possessing respectively the functions of worship, combat and labour appears unequivocally at the end of the ninth century in an interpolation Alfred the Great introduced into his translation of Boethius and, again, one hundred years later (a very short time before the writings of the poem to Robert the Pious and the chronicle of the bishops of Cambrai) in a description given by Aelfric of the society of his own times. There were intimate links at that time between educated ecclesiastical circles on both sides of the Channel; the transmission of ideas can thus be easily explained. But a hypothesis like this about the spread of ideas merely removes the problem to another plane, and raises one more fundamental question. When, why and how was the three-functional division introduced into England at the level of written culture to reflect changes in the exercise of power, and what role is to be attributed to possible borrowings from the culture of Brittany? To answer these questions it is absolutely essential to widen our enquiry into French texts of the eleventh century to include Celtic and Anglo-Saxon literature. But having done this, we still have to ask ourselves why it was that a system of classification of this kind came to be adopted slightly later on the continent. We can see that reference to structural forms does not by itself provide an explanation which satisfies the historian: it merely stimulates his curiosity and turns it to new directions.

If we take as our starting point the two explicit pieces of evidence provided by Adalbéron and Gerald and if we take it as established that firstly, a threefold system was adopted in France by a particular cultural circle, that of the bishops most intimately connected with the royal authority, and that secondly, the adoption took place at the beginning of the third decade of the eleventh century, it then becomes possible to reject the likelihood of a possible imitation of an Anglo-Saxon model or a probable revival of forms described by Georges Dumezil. We can then allow ourselves to interpret the adoption of a threefold system simply as a recourse to one formal framework selected from among several others and thus to recognize the direction our researches should follow. Is not the appearance in the thinking of prelates of a threefold division a final combining of several systems of classification which had been formerly in use but which had, on the eve of the eleventh century, clearly become ill suited to represent the reality of social relations?

The thought and practice of the Carolingian period had left behind four such systems. The first, probably the most generally accepted in educated, or ecclesiastical, circles was itself also threefold in nature. It related three conditions of men—monks, clergy and laity—to each other and distinguished them as representing the three steps towards perfection (based incidentally on sexual morality)—*virgines*, *continentes* and *conjugati*. The other three systems were all twofold, and were based on political organization. One, ancient but now in the process of a slow dissolution, still distinguished between free and unfree men. Another, in which two functions, priestly and warlike, were mingled, we can associate with the concept of royalty. It placed those who contributed to the victory of the sovereign by prayer, the *oratores*, in apposition to those who helped him by force of arms, the *bellatores*. The fourth system which, after the beginning of the ninth century, tended to replace the first, condemned by a gradual shift in juridical concepts, reflected the distribution of private power, since it put men into two simple categories: the 'powerful' and the 'poor'.

Changes in ecclesiastical society and the powers of government, running parallel and conjointly, gradually affected these four systems. Unquestionably, the most directly influential was the development connected with the church, for it must never be forgotten that any picture we have of society at that period was the creation of churchmen. The tendency was towards modifying the tripartite model. Two movements, which both achieved their full effect after the year 1000, united in blurring and finally effacing the distinction between monks and clergy. The first, following on from the triumph of monasticism and the efforts of the Cluniacs to disengage themselves from episcopal control by means of privileges of exemption, seems to represent an attempt on the part of the bishops (for whom Adalbéron was only the mouthpiece) to reaffirm their authority over the monasteries. To merge all the men of prayer in one category, to assemble monks and clergy in a single order, and thus to reunite them under episcopal jurisdiction, was to be the means of achieving this end. In fact, the movement was closely connected with a second, much broader one, which was also animated by the expansion of monasticism and aimed at a general reform of the church. The church was to intervene in two ways. First, through the endeavour, of which it was the spearhead, to widen the distance between the spiritual and the temporal powers, it tended to strengthen the cohesiveness of the whole body of ecclesiastics as against the laity. Secondly, it set in motion after the year 1000 a generally purifying process aimed at segregating all churchmen from the threefold contamination of the carnal world—the sexual act, the handling of money and the bearing of arms. Prohibitions of this kind, until that time placed only upon monks, were now imposed on all churchmen. Thus the reforming spirit and the tension between episcopacy and monasticism on the eve of the eleventh century resulted in the reduction to a dual system of the tripartite system formerly accepted by the church. But by the same token the second part of the system also began to undergo a fission. Reformers proposed for a group of laymen a major precept of perfection, that 'powerful men' had a duty to defend and help the 'poor'. For this purpose one of the three bipartite systems of classification most suited to the development of a political framework was adapted.

The second, political, development itself had repercussions at three levels:

1 In the long term, the growth of the great estate, the fortunes of serfdom and the transformation of military techniques resulted in an erosion of the notion of liberty and the gradual disappearance of the ancient distinction between slaves and others. The essential line of

cleavage was thus shifted to establish a group of 'powerful men' which had absorbed the 'warrior' group of another bipartite system and another group, the general mass of the 'poor', deprived of the use of arms, symbol of full independence, and placed under the special protection of the sovereign.

2   At the same time, changes occurring in France in the 1030s to the institution of kingship, particularly revealed by the weakening of royal authority, led to the separation of the two functions exercised by the king, liturgical and military, one going to the *oratores*, the bishops, and the other to the *bellatores*, the lay princes, leaders of armed bands. These changes called into being the movement for God's peace, which can be seen spreading across northern France at the precise moment when Adalbéron wrote his poem and Gerald gave utterance to the ideas we have noted above. In fact the movement confided the protection of the 'poor' (formerly undertaken by the king) to the church and gave rise to a major distinction between the king and other laymen, men of blood, violence and war—those whom the canons of the councils of peace called the *milites*.

3   Finally, as public authority disintegrated the process institutionalized the private powers of the 'powerful' within the framework of the lordship of the *ban*. It led to the establishment of a fiscal system which, sparing those who specialized in battle, weighed exclusively on other laymen who did not carry arms and had to be defended. Thus, beyond an even higher barrier, the exploited workers (who might or might not have been 'free') were set apart from the defenders of the social order, and the soldiers. The latter were privileged through being entrusted with a mission either because they were themselves 'powerful men' invested with the powers of the *ban*, or else because they were simple *milites,* armed auxiliaries, without whose aid the local leaders would not have been able to fulfil their protective function.

An analysis of the combined changes in the framework of church and state makes it easier for us to understand the emergence in episcopal circles of a threefold system of functions. At a time of tension about dogma when heretical movements in northern France, within the ranks of clergy as well as laity, called the prevailing ideology into question, it behoved the bishops to defend the orthodox view of a universal order. In fact Adalbéron's political and social ideas are inseparable from his theology. For this reason, and because they set out to explain and justify certain aspects of the visible world, the bishops had to fall back on the tripartite system of classification traditionally used by the church. But because they intended both to exalt their own ministry and to swim with the mainstream of moral renovation, they had also to modify it. Thus two bipartite systems best suited to a new reality were combined. One, by separating the spiritual and the temporal worlds, isolated those who served the Lord from everyone else, and the other, supported by the process of feudalization, made a fundamental distinction between those men who were both exploited and protected and those who were not. In the threefold system, stemming naturally from such a selective combination, the accent was placed on function. In reality, and with reference to the new ethic and its precepts, and the relationships henceforth laid down between institutions and the exercise of power, what justified the differentiation of each of the three categories was their function. The system of classification proved most durable because its demarcation lines correspond to two major divisions in the social framework which had not been very obvious up to that time. At the deeper level, lords and peasants were bound together because of agricultural production on the manor. At another level, there were changes in the institutions of kingship, court and palace, the struggle for power and a fundamental and increasingly obvious cultural split between the great churchmen and the secular lords. Thus the framework of our system truly reflected innovations at the heart of social structure that were becoming more obvious every day.

But to formulate hypotheses of this kind and to try to draw conclusions about the different manifestations of society, the changes that affected them, and the means by which they were related to real developments in the exercise of power, entails a confrontation: on the one hand, we have a tentative scholarly analysis reached by sifting through all statements, whether verbal or otherwise, about the new system of classification and, on the other, our knowledge about political institutions, religious attitudes, economic relations and, in fact, every individual feature of the social system. In addition, it must be done with a precision sufficient for us to see how far the different time scales coincide. For we cannot arrive at valid explanations without placing the correlations in their exact place in time. There is no other way of approaching the wider problem of how to unite, in their respective time scales, the various images of the structure of society with the real shape assumed by society as a whole.

6

The nobility in medieval France

Some years ago Marc Bloch invited medievalists to enquire into the development of the nobility in the various countries of the west, and particularly in France.[1] There was a notable response to his appeal, but the most worthwhile contribution, and perhaps also the most pertinent, came quite recently from Professor Léopold Génicot, of the University of Louvain, who has devoted the second volume of his economic history of the Namurois in the early middle ages to a study of the nobles in that small country.[2]

Throughout the 370-odd villages and hamlets which make up the county of Namur, he finds, at the beginning of the twelfth century, no more than about twenty families of which the chief member was called, in the Latin of the charters, *nobiles*. The group was thus very small, but it was formed of very rich men, who enjoyed large and widely dispersed fortunes spread across the lands of the neighbouring provinces, and who had, according to the most likely hypothesis, been established several generations earlier by princely endowment. Set up on the borders of the principality, the leading branches of these lineages appear, in the uncertain light of a far from abundant documentation, to have possessed parish churches, often castles and certainly the power to command and to punish. Indeed, it seems as if, in the vocabulary of the editors of the acts, 'noble' and 'free' were interchangeable appellations. It is certain that all nobles were called free. But Génoicot is inclined to think also —although I feel that he is less than certain about this point—that there were not at that time outside the nobility any genuinely free men, or men who were free in the sense of not being in any way subject to the customs of the *ban*, of being judgeable by the few public tribunals there were and of being able to dispose of themselves entirely as they wished.

[1] 'Sur le passé de la noblesse française; quelques jalons de recherches', *Annales d'histoire économique et sociale* (1936), preceded by 'Projet d'une enquête sur la noblesse française', set up by the count of Neufbourg.

[2] *L'Economie namuroise au bas moyen age II, Les hommes, la noblesse* (Louvain, 1960). Recueil de travaux d'histoire et de philologie de l'Université de Louvain, 4th series, fasc. 20.

Lastly, this 'privileged nobility' was a hereditary one and its qualities and titles descended by blood.

In distinct contrast to the 'nobles' there were the men whom the texts say belonged to a *familia*, that is to a company of servitors in households grouped around a master. Who, then, were these masters? The count himself was surely one, as were probably the great religious establishments. Perhaps also some nobles, though we should like to know more definitely whether, in this country, the castles were the sole foci of such households. Those who belonged to the *familia* were not all of servile origin, but even so they did not enjoy complete liberty. They did not possess a seal, they lived in hereditary dependence, and they did not escape payment of dues. Nevertheless, about 1150, we begin to notice some of them being distinguished by a special epithet—they were decorated by the title of *chevalier* or 'knight'. Apparently mounted military service was an honour. The prince had need of them; at all events they appear to be in comfortable circumstances. These *milites* form an aristocracy which increased in strength even though still remaining very much inferior to the elite of the 'noble' families who, as a result of natural increase, were themselves becoming slightly more numerous and at the same time less rich.

Génicot's study is based on a fuller documentation after the year 1200, and it becomes better explored and more reliable. It shows how the families of the nobility were gradually weakened by the break up of inheritances, the competition of the princes who opposed their power of the *ban*, the liberation of rural communities, and the fall in seigneurial incomes which could, however, be compensated by strokes of luck and especially by the success of some of the colonizing enterprises on waste lands. Only a few family lineages succeeded in keeping their patrimony safe: in the mid-thirteenth century they formed a small group of 'peers'. But the greater number of the 'nobles' had not been able to maintain themselves in the aristocracy, and this at the very moment when the position of the knights was rising. Much more numerous, and by now holding the reins of authority, adding turrets to their residences and sitting in judgment on the peasants, the *milites* had in the course of the century seen their title assert its prestige. People had begun to call them sir (*messire*), and soon they alone had the right to this epithet. In lists of witnesses, the distinction between nobles and knights disappeared about 1280; knights were placed apart from all others and—a fact of importance in a world so conscious of precedence—a nobleman who had nòt been knighted had to yield to knights who were not noble. Finally, at the same time, knights gained their personal liberty, the prince having exempted them from the customs of the *ban*. Their franchise was a hereditary one, since children of a knight could enjoy it even if they did not carry arms. By the second half of the thirteenth century the knightly class was thus transformed into a genuine nobility. However, for several more generations, the 'nobles' of ancient race still kept themselves jealously apart. It was only in the last years of the fourteenth century that both groups merged through matrimonial alliances, and the extension of the title 'nobleman' to all knights was finally accepted. By 1420 there was no more than a single upper class of 'gentlemen' among the inhabitants of Namurois.

For at least a century the class had been wide open. To be included, it was sufficient for men who had become wealthy through administration, business or even patient peasant saving, merely to submit themselves to the ceremony of dubbing. Nor does the ceremony of dubbing seem to have been very strictly controlled. It should, moreover, be noted that the descendants of these self-made men soon ceased to arm their sons. Knights among the ranks of gentlemen were very few, especially after 1350. We do not lack reasons why there should have been so little interest in knighthood. It entailed great expense on arms and horses, it imposed tiresome obligations, and it exposed the holder to physical danger, while the condition of the simple esquire was increasingly well thought of. The main reason, however, was that it was sufficient to count a knight among one's ancestors to the seventh degree in order to profit from fiscal, legal and military privileges, and to be 'free' and place oneself alongside the 'men of law and lineage'. In Namurois it was this legally defined class which, during the later middle ages, took the place of the old 'nobility' whose memory had passed away. Its majority was formed by rich men, owners of fortified houses, with motte, tower, *bloquehut* and chapel, but the new class also included many persons of modest estate, as well as craftsmen and even menservants. For, as with the *nobilitas* of olden times, the privileges of the class were based solely upon birth and the quality of one's ancestors.

I have thought it right to give a thorough summary of this excellent book if only in order to be able to appropriate its methods. A detailed examination of all the written sources relating to a small region imparts rigour to the study and, more particularly, provides the sole medium for following closely the changes in patrimonies and tracking down the fortunes of individuals. So far as these aims go, the narrative abounds with concrete details and is entertainingly lifelike.[3] It should be particularly remarked that the research relies on the one hand on a systematic inventory, a chronological classification and a grammatical examination of all the terms used to describe men of those days; and on the other hand, that it is largely based on the patient reconstruction of a great number of genealogical tables which form, as they should, the most illuminating part of the study.

The wide scope of the family trees actually reveals the main weakness of the study, which is that before the beginning of the thirteenth century its supporting documentation is extremely limited: indeed for the eleventh century it is practically nonexistent. The deficiencies of the older sources noticeably reduce the range of Génicot's observations, of the kind that P. Bonenfant and G. Despy were able to make about the nobility of Brabant.[4] For instance, the poverty of sources at times pre-

---

[3] It is to be regretted that there are no sketch maps to bring reality to the countryside.
[4] P. Bonenfant and G. Despy, 'La Noblesse en Brabant aux XIIe et XIIIe siècles: quelques sondages', *Le Moyen Age* (1958).

vents him from concluding with certainty whether the owners of castles, holders of the right of the *ban*, were the only persons in the twelfth century to be described as *nobiles*. This poverty also raises an obstacle to genealogical study of the antecedent past. In particular, it is impossible to discover whether there were not some *milites* in the second half of the twelfth century who belonged to the lateral branches of the great lineages of the higher aristocracy. In Saxony[5] and southwest Germany,[6] as in the Mâconnais, it has, in fact, been possible to establish the existence of a vigorous lesser nobility springing entirely from the governing families; in the Germanic countries, this 'old' lesser nobility eventually came to share the title of knight with the 'new' lesser nobility formed by officials (*ministériaux*). Finally, we must ask ourselves whether a less exiguous body of evidence would not have enabled us to see more clearly the relationship between *libertas* and nobility. The statement that in the twelfth century there was a complete identity between nobles and free men is, in fact, rather surprising, for in many regions of France, Germany and even Lotharingia, there are documents proving that there were at that time many free men who never claimed to belong to the nobility. Even if we consider that all knights who were members of a *familia* were officials, we must take cognizance of the opinion of those German medievalists who consider, as does H. Dannenbauer,[7] that many free men of modest estate entered the service of magnates as mounted men. For example, a Brabantine act of 1180 mentions three *milites ingenui* in a count's *familia*.[8]

At any rate Génicot's researches throw into relief the fact that in feudal times the features of aristocratic society in this part of the Empire differed from those in most French provinces. The differences were the continued vigour of households described by the word *familia*; a more complex, differentiated, and hierarchical notion of liberty; a greater influence of maternal ancestry, perhaps, as revealed in legal statutes about heredity. But we ought not be surprised if the criteria determining nobility in the region of Namur turned out to be unusual, or if they proved to be not at all like those we believe we can observe in Burgundy or in the Forez. We know how different the development of the social structure in France and Germania was during the Carolingian period. These differences have once more been underlined by A. Borst in a very intelligent essay on this precise subject of the dignity of knighthood, its ramifications, content and literary expression.[9] But even within the boundaries of these great territorial areas there were quite distinct regional customs and a whole range of forms intermediate as between the French and Germanic types in the lands of the Meuse,

[5] A. Hagemann, 'Die Stände der Sachsen', *Zeitschrift der Savigny-Stiftung, Germ. Abt.* (1959).

[6] K. Bosl, 'Der Wettinische Ständestaat im Rahmen der mittelalterlichen Verfassungsgeschichte', *Historische Zeitschrift* (1960), p. 191.

[7] H. Dannenbauer, 'Königsfreie und Ministerialen', *Grundlagen der mittelalterlichen Welt* (Stuttgart, 1958).   [8] Bonenfant and Despy, 'la Noblesse en Brabant', p. 40.

[9] A. Borst, 'Das Rittertum im Hochmittelalter. Idee und Wirklichkeit', *Speculum* (1959).

Saône, Jura and the Alps. Génicot's conclusions do not weaken those of other scholars who have tried to ascertain conditions elsewhere; on the contrary, they have the merit of giving a solid base to the debate, bringing it to life again and refreshing the discussion of the older hypotheses on the subject. His studies actually encourage us to pursue the quest into French lands, in three main directions in particular.

In the first place it will be necessary to examine closely the manner by which the quality of nobility was transmitted. Génicot's researches indeed place on record one fact which will henceforth be taken as incontrovertible, that the medieval nobility was independent of the knighthood and preceded it. Nowhere is this proposition more vigorously stated than in a recent book by another Belgian historian, L. Verriest—a book of passionate feeling, which is, alas, badly organized, occasionally disfigured by sophistry and always marred by an immoderate desire to annihilate all views not wholly in agreement with his own most original ideas; a book which, nevertheless, makes some very pertinent points,[10] and in particular offers a critique of Marc Bloch's theses. The latter thought, and I myself was for long in agreement, that in feudal times, when the noble families of the earlier middle ages became extinct, a totally new nobility emerged from among the common people, who attained a certain level of wealth and adopted a distinctive mode of life, more especially an aptitude for the exercise of arms. In fact, we may now consider it to be established as axiomatic that the Carolingian nobility was transmitted by blood to large numbers of feudal descendants and that, in a more general way, every noble claimed first of all to be *de nobilibus ortus*, or 'gentleman': in other words, that he did not rely in the first instance on his authority, or his wealth, but on his forebears. All prestige originated from them alone and none from his own person. We need do no more than consider the present-day notion of nobility[11] to realize that it must always have been founded upon the honour of ancestry and that it must naturally have become stronger as it went back into the past through the ramifications of the family tree. This is so to such an extent that it seems pointless to question the 'origin' of nobility since no one is noble who has not risen with the reputation of a forebear, even if the latter should be mythical. We have seen that Génicot's study was based on genealogies, so that an enquiry into nobility merges directly into the wider, but nonetheless arduous, enquiry whose object is the medieval family.

In this enquiry one question presents itself immediately. The importance of ancestry is, of course, obvious; but which side is the more important? The father's or the mother's? Or both equally? For want of

---

[10] *Questions d'histoire des institutions médiévale. Noblesse, chevalerie, lignage. Condition des gens et des personnes. Seigneurie, ministérialité, bourgeoisie, échevinage* (Brussels, 1959).

[11] The short book by P. du Puy de Clinchamps, *La noblesse*, in the series *Que sais-je?* (Paris, 1959), contains nothing new on medieval nobility, but has useful material on the nobility of the *ancien régime* and its survivors of today. The legal and sociological aspects of the modern institutions of nobility can provide the medievalist with food for thought.

any clear indication until the modern era, Génicot's answer is very circumspect. It presupposes that nobility, implying liberty, was transmitted, like liberty itself, only through women, but that after 1200 the growing prestige of knighthood, as a purely male attribute, caused the role of the father in the transmission of a superior legal status to widen. L. Verriest presents his answer in a brutally simple way. According to him—everywhere and always—the blood of the maternal line alone ennobles. Admittedly his interpretation relies on texts which are both late and very local in application and to this extent cannot command unreserved acceptance.[12] To arrive at a valid conclusion we need detailed studies of family structure in the various regions of feudal France.[13]

For this purpose—since no documents drawn up with the direct object of proving nobility have survived for the period before the fourteenth century—it might be useful to examine the genealogical literature that flourished in certain provinces between the tenth and the beginning of the thirteenth century, much of which has survived. Documents of this kind can teach us a great deal about the attitudes of mind of the men who drew them up, about men's recollections of their forebears and about the efforts they made to celebrate them. They also give a much more accurate picture of the views of the family actually held at the time than do the genealogies reconstructed by modern scholars according to their own ideas. Therefore, to begin with, it would be sensible to survey these sources systematically, because quite a number of genealogical sketches are incorporated in literary works and even in charters.[14] This could be followed up by a study of their contents which would allot their respective places in the ancestry on both male and female sides and take note of the terms used to describe and to compare the lustre of the ancestors.

I shall use as an example the interesting tree of his own family drawn up by Canon Lambert, the author of *Annales Cameracenses*, who was born in 1108.[15] We shall note that his memory does not go back beyond his grandparents, although it takes in many blood relations of the preceding generation, even quite distant ones, and is most explicit about the more illustrious branches. Indeed the accent is most definitely

---

[12] In particular I do not think much can be deduced from the genealogies drawn up for their defence by the *sainteurs* accused in the courts of being serfs and who, in those regions where the taint of servility was inherited strictly through the female heredity, insisted on the superior birth of their grandmothers alone without mentioning their father's condition since it would.have been of no use to them.

[13] A study of this kind has been going on for several years in my seminar for research into ideas and social structures at the Faculty of Letters of Aix-en-Provence; publication of some of the provisional results is in preparation.

[14] A short while ago Professor Vercauteren of the University of Liège drew the attention of the participants at my seminar to the family trees which Gislebert of Mons, chancellor of the count of Hainault, used to introduce into the deeds that he drew up at the end of the twelfth century in the name of his master.

[15] MGH SS XVI, pp. 511–12. This belongs to Professor Vercauteren, who has been kind enough to bring this document to my attention, and to comment on it in the detail it deserves in the presence of my pupils.

placed upon the glory of his predecessors, their warlike activities and the memories of them kept alive in the *jongleur*'s verses. Lambert's paternal grandfather as well as his maternal uncles and his cousins on both sides bear the title *miles*. Nevertheless the word *nobilis* and its derivatives are not used except in connection with his maternal grandmother and her relations. But if women are referred to as 'noble' in this text, as well as in many others, this might well be because the word 'knight' has no feminine form and because (as I believe I can detect in the charters of Mâcon) *nobilis* appeared to be the more suitable way of describing a woman holding the equivalent social position.

However, if we restrict ourselves to literary works which are genealogical in the narrow sense and which were composed in honour of the few lords of the highest rank, we shall have to admit that the direct descent of the male line occupies practically the entire attention of the authors. Apparently, in the eyes of the magnates who caused the works to be drawn up for the celebration of their noble status the male line alone mattered. An example is the genealogy of the counts of Angoulême, included in the *Historia pontificum et comitum Engolismensium*, excellently edited by J. Boussard, which was compiled about the year 1160 by one of the canons of Angoulême.[16] It goes back through eight generations, down to the middle of the eleventh century, to one William Taillefer, a legendary hero. The genealogy is not totally indifferent to the female ancestry, since it mentions the wives of the counts who gave birth to heirs, but it is arranged strictly by descent from fathers to sons and is never diverted to the female line. Preliminary soundings in literature of this type[17] show that similar linear arrangements emphasizing male primogeniture, by which family glory and the memory of the forebears was transmitted through men, were widely adopted throughout the top ranks of the aristocracy in the twelfth century. But a closer look reveals that genealogies composed at an earlier date probably gave a much larger place to female lineages. Eleventh-century family trees, such as those of the counts of Anjou for instance, are also so constructed as to establish first of all the descent of the title of count from father to son, and then expand in a supplementary manner to include matrimonial alliances and the bonds of kinship formed through the intermediary of women. Even more clearly, the most ancient genealogical writing of all, the one describing the ancestry of Count Arnould of Flanders, drawn up between 951 and 959, places the greatest emphasis on women and their illustrious lineage. The only dates mentioned in it are those of marriages, and the whole point of the genealogy is to establish the nobility of Count Arnould by connecting him, through his grandmother, with the family of Charlemagne. A shift

[16] *Historia pontificum et comitum Engolismensium*, edited by J. Boussard (Paris, 1957).

[17] Cf. A. Hönger, 'Die Entwicklung der litterarischen Darstellungsform der Genealogie im deutschen Mittelalter von der Karolingerzeit bis zu Otto von Freising', *Mitteilungen der Zentralstelle fur deutsche Personen und Familiengeschichte* (1914); K. Hauck, 'Haus und Sippengebundene Literatur mittelalterlicher Adelsgeschlechter', *Mitteilungen des Instituts für österreichisches Geschichtsforschung* (1954), p. 62.

in the perspective of this kind could well be one of the indications of a change which, near the year 1000, affected the structure of the aristocratic family in the west from the shape it bore in the collective consciousness.

The point could indeed be reinforced by some of the results of a general enquiry into the nobility of the Rhineland made a few years ago in Freiburg-in-Breisgau under the direction of G. Tellenbach.[18] From the published results I shall pick out K. Schmid's for special notice, because he attempts to tackle the study of prominent lineages in the post-Carolingian and feudal period from a new angle.[19] The point of departure for his research is a consideration of the method formulated by Tellenbach.[20] For the period prior to the eighth to tenth centuries it is very difficult to pursue the trail of aristocratic families; the difficulty obviously springs from the fact that the persons in the documents no longer have family surnames and that, as they bear one name only, they are consequently easily confused with other individuals bearing the same name. But it is not merely a question of sources; the real difficulty is the mental attitude of the nobility who did not at that period accord agnatic ancestry (that is ancestry from father to son) the superior status it enjoyed in later periods, but considered cognate relationship and agnate ancestry on the same footing. By making a close examination of the nobility of Alemania, Schmid has been able to discover a clear difference between the two periods. By the twelfth century the concept of the family was a resolutely dynamic one; men traced their ancestry back through males, and when the use of armorial bearings began to spread at the end of the century, the symbolism of heraldry was so arranged as to preserve the memory of the common agnatic origin through all the lateral branches from the moment these had formed themselves into independent lineages. This idea was mainly attached to a common residence, the cradle of the family, handed down from father to son, which gave its name to the lineage. Thus, the 'race' came to be thought of as the 'house'. But before the year 1000 the bonds of kinship wore a very different aspect in written sources. Family names did not exist; there were only individual names. Instead of the *Geschlecht* (meaning the lineage uniting all the men who claimed a paternal ancestry from a common forebear) there was the *Sippe* (a nebulous grouping of men allied to each other). For the first half of the tenth century, a period for which documentation is particularly poor, Schmid uses the *libri memoriales* in which were entered the names of the benefactors of the great religious establishments for whom the community had to say prayers. The way in which the names in these books were arranged in relationship to each other reflects the reality of the

[18] G. Tellenbach, *Studien und Vorarbeiten zur Geschichte des groszfränkische Adels* (Freiburg, 1957).

[19] K. Schmid, 'Zur Problematik von Familie, Sippe und Geschlecht, Haus und Dynastie beim mittelalterlichen Adel. Vortragen zum Thema "Adel und Herrschaft in Mittelalter" ', *Zeitschrift für die Geschichte des Oberrheins* (1957) p. 105.

[20] G. Tellenbach, 'Zur Bedeutung der Personenforschung fur die Erkenntnis des früheren Mittelalters', *Freiburger Universitätsreden* (1957).

bonds of kinship as actually acknowledged in aristocratic circles. It then appears that the role played by kinsfolk of the wife and the mother in the life and consciousness of the family was on an equal footing with the paternal ancestry. There are other indications confirming and explaining this attitude. Names taken from the mother's side of the family were freely given to children. Of the two lots of blood relations the one whose nobility was the most splendid, whose reputation was the greatest, whose ancestors were the most glorious, was placed first; as daughters had the right to inherit land, marriages united in the same community possessions allied to and descending from both lines. Finally, magnates were not settled in permanent residences. For families such as these with their widely dispersed possessions and with a mobility depending on inheritance and alliance, there was no 'house', merely many places of shelter. And it followed, therefore, that there was no 'race'.

The important questions are: how did one system of kinship turn into the other and how can we date the transformation and compare it with changes in the social structure as a whole? Unfortunately it happened during the most obscure period of the middle ages, but it is nevertheless one of the fields that historians of the French nobility should address themselves. For Alemania, Schmid sketches out an explanation, whose great merit in my view is its links with the history of political institutions, since the very notion of nobility and its content is closely associated with the attributes of authority. In the Frankish period there existed at least one 'house'—the king's—and it is remarkable that the royal family was the first to show the signs of being a race, by limiting the names of its sons to the *agnatio* and by assigning a subordinate position to alliances made through women. Moreover, at that time a noble could only make his fortune by joining the house of the king, by going to live there as an adolescent with the other men maintained (*nourris*) by the king and by receiving benefactions and honours from him later on. This was a household nobility (*Hausadel*), therefore, whose members, because of their position, could not live in a 'house' of their own. But, when they apportioned court responsibilities, the Carolingian kings made their choice, within the allied group of original office holders, from amongst descendants, or blood relations, or those related by marriage, without restricting themselves to any agnatic line and even less to any first-born man.[21] Thus it was not until noble families broke away from the royal household, acquired autonomous authority and private lordships, that they organized themselves in dynasties. 'The house of a noble turns into a noble house when it becomes the central point around which an independent and lasting race crystallizes and to which it owes its power.' In this way the change from *Sippe* to *Geschlecht*, the gradual strengthening of the male line reserving to itself the hereditary transmission of authority, landed

---

[21] Cf. R. Louis, *De l'histoire à la légende, Girart, comte de Vienne (819—877) et ses fondations monastiques* (Auxerre, 1946) I, p. 5.

wealth, ancestral glory and, as a result, nobility, comes to represent one of the aspects of the advent of 'feudality'.

The feudal system arrived by successive stages not always contemporaneous in every province—in some places it came earlier, in others later. Autonomy was achieved first of all by the houses of the counts (the heads of which were distinguished in the Latin texts by the title *dominus*), then by the masters of castles with the authority of the *ban* (whose families in the Mâconnais were organized into lineages by the year one thousand), and lastly, a good deal later, by knights in their own homes which had, by the end of the twelfth or early thirteenth century become 'fortified houses'. Appropriation of the power to command and to punish, exercised only by a male or transmitted to his son, together with those purely masculine heritages of honour, fief, title, family surname and coat of arms, and the gradual exclusion of married daughters from the paternal inheritance, had all without doubt helped to confer dynastic features on noble families, especially the more illustrious ones, while at the same time pushing the maternal line into the background and restricting its role in the transmission of the quality of 'nobility'.

We must now ask whether such happenings did not coincide fairly closely with the exaltation of the vocation of war, the sword and the *militia*. In any event, in order to test these hypotheses, we must look further into the literature of genealogy, the history of successional customs, the matrimonial policies of the great families, and (heraldry being one of the most valuable of related sciences for this kind of study) the evolution of armorial bearings. We might expect an enquiry of this kind to bring out strong regional diversities in the different parts of France, and to reveal more precisely the areas where the custom of transmitting the quality of nobility through the female line was kept up. These areas were the Empire and its fringes, such as Champagne, Bar-le-duc, Franche-Comté or Namur; elsewhere it seems that the ability of the male line to transmit 'nobility' (as well as 'servility'[22]) had, from the end of the eleventh century onwards, been accepted.

The study of the relationship between nobility and knighthood is the other avenue along which we might hope to see research proceed. Génicot's conclusions on this point have been joined by recent contributions from German scholars which have clearly distinguished nobility combined with authority, lordship and, hence, race, from the knighthood, connected with service of a domestic nature, consequently conferring an entirely individual title.[23] This was the contrast between *Herrschaft* and *Dienst* which had long been maintained in Germanic countries, since the German aristocracy of the thirteenth century still embodied the antithesis between the *herren von geburte fri* and the

---

[22] The rules of mortmain in the region of Paris bear witness to the early importance of the agnatic line for the servile population; cf. *Cartulaire de Notre-Dame de Paris*, edited by B. Guérard (Paris, 1850) I, p. 375 [1109].

[23] In the last instance see, K. Bosl, 'Über sociale Mobilität in der mittelalterlichen "Gesellschaft"', *Vierteljahrschrift für Sozial- und Wirtschaftsgeschichte* (1960).

dienestman, ritter und kneht.[24] But the opposition between the two was gradually reduced by the successful rise of an exemplary social type, the *miles christianus*, the man who fought for God, and was exalted by the church. His success was relatively late: A. Borst places it in the second half of the twelfth century and relates it to the expansion of the military religious orders in the Germanic lands. The same was true in Lotharingia. Thus about 1175 we can see the nobles of Brabant arming themselves as knights and bearing the title of *milites* at the precise moment when the Hospitallers and Templars were establishing themselves in the duchy.[25]

However, we know that the social structure in the territories of the Empire is characterized, at this period, by the archaic and complex 'estates' separated by a clear distinction of status and by a formidable obstacle to matrimonial alliance between different groups. It is possible that in France these developments did not continue in the same way. Once more it appears necessary to investigate the social structure closely, allowing as usual for regional differences. Judging by appearances, France also saw a higher aristocracy gravitating around the royal household, a *nobilitas*, becoming stronger and more involved in Carolingian times. K. F. Werner's recent study on Neustria contributes evidence on this point that is of paramount importance.[26] In search of the origins of great princely families and the groups of vassals by whom they were surrounded, this enquiry manages to surmount the obstacle presented by the increasing scarcity of documents in the mid-tenth century and even more the problem presented by the changing relations of individuals to others of their kin. Research proves that the apparent emergence of new men as 'nobles' in this obscure period is an illusion created solely by the laconic nature of our sources. The reality is that in Touraine, a region which was ravaged more than others by the Northmen and which needed help from other imperial provinces, the leading families were already firmly established in 845 and formed, around Robert the Strong, a stable network of faithful vassals. Werner is able to destroy Marc Bloch's hypotheses by establishing the continuity of the aristocracy in the Paris basin between Carolingian times and the mid-tenth century, the point of departure for reliable feudal genealogies. But he also reveals that there were different strata politically defined within the social body. At the summit there was the *Reichsaristokratie*, as defined by Tellenbach, made up of a few groups of kinsfolk dispersed over the entire Empire and charged with the very highest honours; in this area it was well represented by Robert the Strong who arrived in the region of Tours from eastern France, but who found there relations and friends. The members of this small elite group were highly mobile and the command they exercised here and there was somewhat ephemeral. On the other hand, from about the mid-ninth

[24] Borst, *'Das Rittertum'*, p. 233.
[25] Bonenfant and Despy, 'la Noblesse en Brabant', p. 39.
[26] K. F. Werner, 'Untersuchungen zur Frühzeit des französischen Fürstentums (9–10 Jahrhundert)', *Die Welt als Geschichte* (1958–60).

century we can see below them a regional aristocracy which was more securely fixed[27] and which was itself divided into two echelons—the counts and viscounts on one side and the *vassi dominici* and the *vicarii* on the other. By the second quarter of the tenth century the latter group, that of the *vassi* and *vicarii*, had ceased to be directly connected with the royal authority and had passed entirely under subordination of the former group which had enabled them to participate, through the system of *precaria* (tenure), in the landed wealth of the great religious establishments. The two echelons remained quite distinct. When they entered the church, the sons of the *vassi dominici* became canons, while the sons of counts became bishops; we do not notice any matrimonial alliances between the two groups. The second group was partly recruited from lateral branches of the lineages of counts, but these, in cases when the main branch happened to be disinherited, did not acquire the great honours that were previously conferred on other members of the upper class. Nevertheless the two groups formed together a body of 'nobles' who were separated by a wide chasm from humbler free men. The latter, vassals of the *vassi dominici*, do not appear on the lists of witnesses who in the ninth and tenth centuries put their names to the acts of the Robertians. There was thus, from the early middle ages onwards, a 'nobility' which shared the public authority, was bound to the royal house, but was becoming detached from it little by little, and yet was aware of its honourable status and the honour of its ancestry, and was consequently closed to self-made men.[28] From this nobility sprang the upper aristocracy of feudal times—the *vassi dominici* of the ninth century are the ancestors of the castellans of the eleventh, and the 'barons' of the twelfth. It kept its distance from the families of the middle aristocracy, who later became the knights, but who from then on (although this does not agree with Génicot's conclusions) enjoyed full legal liberty.

Somewhere about the year 1000 the word *miles* became a title common in French lands to describe certain persons. Should we conclude that all these knights were *ministeriales*, armed servants of the great families, hardly to be distinguished from other menservants? Some of them it is true, occupied modest situations. P. Petot recently drew attention to the existence in Flanders and in Champagne, but also in Berry and the region of Paris, of serf knights, occupying a status rather like that of the German *Ritter*; this causes him to impute Beaumanoir with the simplistic notion of a clear opposition between knighthood and servitude.[29] The remark invites a closer examination of the status of the men whom eleventh- and twelfth-century texts called *milites castri*, and who have specially attracted the attention of J. Richard in his studies on

---

[27] 'Die Herren an der Loire mögen wechseln, ihre Vassalen bleiben' (Werner, 'Untersuchungen', p. 188).

[28] 'Wo es Schichten gibt, die auf ihren Rang achten, ist kein Platz fur Emporkömmlinge' (Werner, 'Untersuchungen', p. 186).

[29] P. Petot, 'Observations sur les *ministeriales* en France', *Revue historique de droit français et étranger* (1960).

Burgundy.[30] What was their relationship to the master of the fortress to which they were attached and which they had to protect in an emergency? Did they form part of his household? Did they owe to him alone all the lands we see them occupying in neighbouring villages which assured them of an independent economic position well above that of other peasants? It seems indeed (at least in central France) that eleventh-century knights held very small fiefs and that their wealth was essentially formed of free holdings. E. Perroy's comments about the two knightly families attached to the castle of Donzy[31] in the Forez complements my own observations in the region of Mâcon which has such a wealth of documentation. Knights in the Forez, indubitably regarded as free men, belonged to families in comfortable circumstances and mostly claimed the same ancestor as their lords, the castellans. To their sons the duties of knighthood seemed to have been a strictly hereditary function. But this picture is not true for the whole of France; we can state without hesitation that the conditions did not apply in northwestern France in the regions bordering the North Sea and the English Channel. In these areas, right up to the twelfth century, many knights lived in the castle of their lord on a stipend as members of his household. Among these an early emergence of primogeniture often forced younger bachelor sons to seek their own fortunes, by turning to a life of adventure and joining military companies of vassals formed in the 'houses' of the magnates.[32]

It seems, moreover, that the rise in general esteem of the knight's estate occurred much earlier in French lands than it did in Germania. The development in ecclesiastical ideology of the notion of the *miles Christi*, auxiliaries of the church who won salvation by performing the duties of their estate in the service of Christian morality, must have originated in the Carolingian period,[33] and the idea of an 'order' of soldiers composed of men of God, charged with a general mission of protection, and hence worthy of some legal privileges, rapidly became current in the tenth century. It was already accepted when God's peace was established and made its position secure. The rules of God's peace established a special status for those who were *milites*, far more favourable than the status of the peasants. A new distribution of the power to command was taking place at this time, which generally accepted the 'customs' wielded by the holders of the right of the *ban* and from which knights were themselves exempt. They were thus, from the eleventh

[30] J. Richard, *Les Ducs de Bourgogne et la formation du duché du XIe au XIVe siècle* (Paris, 1954) pp. 99–102, 260–2; 'Châteaux, châtelains et vassaux en Bourgogne aux XIe et XIIe siècles', *Cahiers de civilisation médiévale* (1960).

[31] E. Perroy, 'Deux lignages chevaleresques en Forez au XIe siècle', *Bulletin de la Diana* XXXIV (1957).

[32] My own seminar has begun an enquiry into these *juvenes*; its point of departure is the *Historia ecclesiastica* of Ordericus Vitalis, and the *Historia comitum Ghisnensium* of Lambert of Ardres. See also below, chapter 7.

[33] E. Delaruelle, 'Jonas d'Orléans', *Bulletin de littérature ecclésiastique* (1954); The doctoral thesis of J. Chelini, assistant at the Faculty of Letters at Aix-en-Provence, on the attitudes of laymen towards religion in Carolingian Europe helps to clarify the chronology of the evolution of these ideas.

century onwards, clearly established as a separate group, well before the founding of the military religious orders;[34] the latter were bands privileged in worldly as well as spiritual ways, to whom the church recommended the practice of special virtues and an exemplary religious life adapted to their professional calling. Ordericus Vitalis describes how a priest in the entourage of Hugh of Avranches, marquess of Chester, preached the *emendatio vitae* to knights and chose for his sermons themes from the lives of the soldier-saints—Demetrius, George, Sebastian, Theodore, Maurice, and Eustace, as well as the count-monk, William of Aquitaine.[35] The corresponding 'germanic' concept, still voiced in the twelfth century by Honorius Augustodunensis, showed the human race after the deluge divided into three hierarchical orders—the 'freemen' who were descendants of Shem, knights who were descendants of Japhet, and serfs who were descendants of Ham. This can be contrasted with another system, older by a hundred years, a system well known to Adalbéron of Laon, by which laymen were divided into two categories only and in which knights, 'protectors of churches and defenders of the people', who were not subject to any constraint, were placed above serfs.[36] It is true that the idea of a nobility of blood whose reputation preceded and exceeded the honour of knighthood was kept alive in France. Adalbéron expressed it when he said that 'the titles of nobles come to them from the blood of kings from whom they are descended.'[37] It was also forcefully proclaimed at the end of the twelfth century in works of fiction: Perceval was noble without being aware of it, but his mother wished to bring him up in ignorance of chivalry. However, the power of his noble blood triumphed over his timid education and attracted him to the knightly virtues: 'gardez que chevalerie soit si bien emploiée en vos que l'amors de vostre lignage i soit sauve' (take care that chivalry is so well exercised that the love of your lineage is preserved by it) is the advice that Galaad, in the *Queste du Graal* gives the king's son whom he has just knighted.[38] But it is clear that from the eleventh century onwards French customs distinguished two groups in law—knights, free from the exploitation of the *ban*, among whom were the nobles; and all others. Lay witnesses to legal documents were divided in this way, and nobles already bore the title of knight. The viscounts of Marseilles, recalling their grandfather and paternal great-uncle, described him in 1040 as *nobilissimus miles*; their father William who thirty-six years earlier had come to die in the Benedictine community of Saint Victor, had already announced that he had abandoned the *militia saecularis* for

[34] It seems as if the nobility and the knighthood in the Latin kingdom of Jerusalem were intermixed from the legal point of view in the period immediately after the first Crusade; the documents used by J. Prawer for his article, 'La Noblesse et le régime féodal du royaume latin de Jérusalem', *Le Moyen Age* (1959), should be carefully studied in this connection.

[35] H. Wolter, *Ordericus Vitalis. Ein Beitrag zur Kluniazensischen Geschichtsschreibung* (Wiesbaden, 1958), p. 100.

[36] Honorius Augustodunensis, 'De Imagine mundi', PL 172, col. 166; Adalbéron de Laon, *Poèmes au roi Robert* translated by Pognon, *L'an mil*, p. 226.

[37] *Poèmes*, p. 219.

[38] J. Frappier, 'Le Graal et la chevalerie', *Romania* (1954).

the service of God.[39] At this point it becomes plain that we have to look more closely at the ceremony of dubbing and the development of its rites, because hardly anything is so far known about the subject.

However, in central France as well as in Brabant and Namurois from the first years of the thirteenth century, we can see how the different levels of the aristocracy were brought nearer together by the knighthood. Here and there, some contemporary phenomena are identical: the description *dominus* or *messire*, until that time reserved for the holders of the authority of the *ban*, is henceforth assumed by all knights and by them alone. At the same time, knights' sons, becoming more and more numerous, are no longer invariably dubbed knight on reaching manhood and are distinguished by a new title, 'esquire' or 'page' (*damoiseau*). However, to explain these changes we should not be content merely to invoke the prestige of the rank of knighthood (far older, as we have just seen, in France) or the economic difficulties of the nobility. (It is by no means certain that many nobles had yet actually experienced any embarrassment, nor was it the most modest families who were the first to give up dubbing their sons.) A much more significant part in the change was played by the increased authority of the princes. A levelling of the ranks of the aristocracy had, indeed, occurred under the reconstituted authority of the territorial princes when they subdued the independent castellans by reducing their power at the same time as, at the parish level, the lower *ban* was being abandoned to the village knights. It was then that the latter took possession of seals and transformed their residences into fortified houses. Raising simple knights to the level of the ancient *nobilitas* of castellans coincided with a redistribution of seigneurial rights, such as tallage and the lower justice, and with the popularization of the power of the *ban*.

Besides, at that moment the rearrangement of social estates opened up in a different way a new phase in the history of the nobility. To be noble was, in fact, to escape taxation. The prince had therefore to exert control over the composition of this group and we can see that there were rules as to who was to be exempt. The main criteria were twofold—the blood, and the ceremony of dubbing—and here we can at last see nobility and knighthood mingling. To be free from the liability of taxation a man had to claim a knight as his ancestor and the necessary degrees of ancestry were laid down. For the 'men of law' in the Namurois it was the seventh degree. The statutes of Fréjus governing 'knights' liberties', enacted in the thirteenth century by the count of Provence, exempted knights from the count's *quiste*, and also their sons and grandsons, although they lost their franchise if they had not been knighted by the age of thirty. Here it should be mentioned that in order to preserve their status, Provençal nobles were henceforth forbidden to set their hand to peasant tasks.[40] Control of a man's condition thus introduced at an early

[39] The municipal archives of Arles, edited by L. Blancard, 'Arlulf, origine de la famille vicomtale de Marseille', *Mémoires de l'Académie de Marseille* (1887).

[40] In 1205 a sentence delivered at Arles established that 'quisquis possidebat terram si miles est dat decimam, si alius agricultor tascam et decimam'; knights thus normally

stage the notion of social demotion, and we cannot follow L. Verriest when he denies that there was any connection between an individual's economic condition and his legal status. At any event, from this time onwards, the nobility had to show proof of its claims and produce to the authorities the original deeds by means of which their ancestors supported their particular qualifications. It is not irrelevant at this point to observe that, during the seventeenth century, titles were not the same in every French province: 'esquire' and 'knight' were in use everywhere, but the title of 'noble' was general in Flanders, Artois and Hainault, Franche Comté, the region around Lyons, Dauphiné, Provence, Languedoc and Roussillon, while in Béarn, Guienne and Normandy the title was that of 'nobleman'. The very diversity of the titles to nobility is one more reason why we should not treat the whole of France as a single homogeneous unit in our researches into the connections between nobility and knighthood.

One last problem remains: to what degree was the medieval nobility an open society? How far was the social group refreshed and renewed by the entry of self-made men? Génicot demonstrates plainly how the few noble families of Namurois at first proliferated and divided into lateral branches, then after the thirteenth century were gradually reduced by the extinction of one lineage after another. I wish other historians would follow his example and study the demography of aristocratic families in the various French provinces, since these families might not necessarily show the same characteristics as families of other social levels. It is especially striking to see how quickly some noble families in the feudal era petered out. As an example I take from the *Historia comitum Ghisnensium* of Lambert of Ardres[41] the story of Henry, castellan of Bourbourg, who died after 1151; he had twelve children, of whom seven were sons; two of these sons entered the church; two others died accidentally, one *adulescentulus* and the other as a knight; a fifth was blinded in a tournament which, so it seems, prevented him from trying to keep the succession by marrying; the eldest son, Baldwin, who succeeded his father in the castle, was married twice but neither of his wives was able to provide him with an heir; the seventh son then became castellan and although he married, his only male child died in infancy in 1194, and thus the whole of Henry of Bourbourg's magnificent inheritance reverted to Beatrice, his only granddaughter on the paternal side. She proved a tempting prize for young nobles in search of establishments of their own and was at last conquered, after a bitter struggle, by Arnould, son of the count of Guines. This story demonstrates how the biological fate of the nobility was threatened, first by the inherent perils of military calling, a brutal enough life sometimes subject to real danger, and

enjoyed franchises (*miles* is here a legal qualification) and some of them were engaged in working their land (Archives of the Department of Bouches-du-Rhône, 60 H, 24, no. 4).

[41] C 122, 'Genealogia Broburgensium', MGH SS XXIV, p. 620–21. The whole of this text, which is of such importance for the history of the feudal family, is the subject of detailed study by my seminar.

secondly by the customs restricting births. To avoid dissipating the inheritance, and to assure an intact lordship for the eldest son, heir to titles and honour, as many as possible of his younger brothers were put into the church and the others prevented from marrying. The continuance of the line was therefore at the mercy of an accident of war or of a barren marriage. A brief investigation into the genealogies of the higher nobility of the Paris basin has shown me how frequent were these two separate, but related, situations within this social group in the thirteenth century—the bachelor adventurer, forced to seek his fortune outside his father's house and often dying in armed combat, and the solitary heiress, target for matrimonial intrigues.

In his study of the personal circumstances of 60 nobles in the Forez, who, belonging to 43 families, banded together in 1314–15 to resist royal taxation, E. Perroy provides the most important recent contribution to our knowledge of the real structure of the aristocracy.[42] Among the 60 members of the league were 4 widows of knights and 29 knights, but there were in addition 27 men who had not been dubbed knight and thus only bore the title of *donzeau*; 11 of these died in this condition and of the 16 others, only 6 were armed as knights before they reached the age of forty, 5 before the age of fifty, 4 before sixty, and the rest at an even greater age. We cannot say, therefore, that the desire to solicit the honour of knighthood was very urgent. Eleven members of the league disappeared without leaving a male descendant and the family line of 26 others was extinguished within a century of the alliance of 1315. Figures like these allow us to measure the pace of renewal of the nobility, for new men who had recently joined the ranks of gentlemen fought alongside powerful barons of ancient race in defence of their common privileges. Such a man was William Fillet, agent of the count, a commoner by birth, who had been knighted seven years earlier; such, also, was Peter du Verney, still a burgess of Montbrison in 1304, son of one of the count's bankers; and Pons de Curnieu, a *donzeau* of peasant origin. I may add that 14 of the 56 nobles had married heiresses to whom they owed the greater part of their wealth. It can also be assumed that it was lucky marriages of this kind that made it possible for Peter du Verney and his nephew William to acquire the knightly rank and, although they came from a trading milieu, to take their place among other nobles. All these cases fit in perfectly with the results produced by Génicot's researches about the aristocracy of Namurois in the last centuries of the middle ages, and reveal that, in spite of efforts by the princes to restrict tax exemptions and to maintain control over entry to the nobility, the aristocracy was still wide open in the fourteenth century. As older families became extinct they were constantly replaced by new families, raised up through marriage, occupation or wealth.

However, I find it difficult to renounce the impression which emerges from the enormous quantity of documentary evidence relating to the Mâcon region of an astonishing continuity among knightly families

[42] E. Perroy, 'La Noblesse forézienne et les lignes nobiliaires de 1314–1315', *Bulletin de la Diana* XXXVI (1959). E. Perroy has made a genealogical study of all these lineages.

between the early eleventh and the end of the twelfth centuries. These sources demonstrate that, in fact, descendants of those very same men who, soon after the year 1000, had been raised to the knightly rank in the households of castellans are still to be found living on the same estates and in the same economic condition as their ancestors did. At this level there are no self-made men, only cousins stemming from the same lineages. Within this throng of families those who became extinct without leaving any posterity seem to have been very few, and the gaps they left were not filled by the intrusion of commoners but by branches of older families who found room to expand. The genealogical studies of Perroy into the lists of the Forez families in 1315 will show whether the unstable condition of the nobility and its rapid renewal on the eve of the fourteenth century, of which there is evidence in the southeast of the kingdom of France, was also there earlier in the thirteenth century.

We must ask ourselves, therefore, whether the aristocracy, united in a single group throughout most of France with legal privileges gained from 'knighthood', did not as a whole remain relatively stable until about 1180, even though the 'nobles', forming a smaller elite of descendants of ancient families related to the Frankish kings and of men who inherited the exercise of the rights of the *ban*, remained apart from the mass of simple knights, their cousins of collateral branches, and the descendants of the wealthy freemen of the early middle ages. Might it not rather have been that, only after 1180, an increase in the circulation of money, the attractions of urban residence and consequent changes in life style, the strengthening of the princely authority and the widespread restoration of the power to command which produced a hierarchy of legal status, all combined to accelerate those changes in the structure of feudal society damaging to the position of the nobility? It seems appropriate to close my investigation of the field of enquiry by suggesting these questions which other researchers may like to pursue.

7

Youth in aristocratic society

Northwestern France in the twelfth century

In the narrative writings composed during the twelfth century in the
northwestern part of the kingdom of France[1] certain well-born men are
mentioned: they are described either individually by the adjective
juvenis (young) or collectively by the substantive *juventus* (youth). All
our evidence suggests that these terms have a precise meaning and that
they were used to indicate membership of a particular social group. The
word could sometimes be used in connection with churchmen, particularly to denote one section of the monastic community,[2] but more frequently the description applied to warriors and was used to assign them
to a clearly determined stage in their careers. It is essential at the outset
to recognize the limits of this stage. The person described is quite clearly
a 'youth' and no longer a child, having passed through the educational
process and the exercises preparatory to a military career. Indeed the
authors of these writings always used other terms when they referred to
the sons of the nobility who were still learning the usage and techniques
appropriate to their station. These terms (*puer, adulescentulus, adoles-
cens emberbis*) described boys who were obviously beyond what we
should call childhood; they might be fifteen, seventeen or even nineteen
years of age, but they had not completed their apprenticeship. The
'youth' on the other hand was already an adult person. He had been
received into the company of warriers; he had taken up arms and had
been dubbed. He was, in effect, a knight.[3] We notice, moreover, that a
knight was usually called a 'youth' until his marriage and perhaps even
afterwards. In the ecclesiastical history of Ordericus Vitalis married
knights who have not yet had children are described as being 'youths'
while others who are younger but are already fathers, are never called

[1] I use these in my general enquiry into noble families in feudal times, some preliminary
points of which are dealt with here.
[2] Thus, by Ordericus Vitalis, HE 3 (II, pp. 47, 94). For the use of books 3 to 7 of HE, my
comments rely on the unpublished study by J. Paul, *La Famille et les problèmes familiaux
en Normandie au XIe siècle d'après 'l'Historia ecclesiastica' d'Orderic Vital* (Aix, 1960).
[3] HE, 8: Robert de Rhuoddan, described as *puer* until he became *miles*. D'Arbois de
Jubainville, *Histoire des ducs et des comtes de Champagne* (Paris, 1859–66) VII, I, 70;
Baldwin VI, son of the count of Hainault, *juvenis etiam miles*.

juvenis, always *vir*.[4] Thus in the world of chivalry, the warrior ceased to be regarded as a 'youth' when he had established himself and put down roots, become the head of a house and founded a family. The stages of 'youth' can therefore be defined as the period in a man's life between his being dubbed knight and his becoming a father.[5]

Our sources also reveal that this phase in a knight's life could last a long time, although it is admittedly hard to define its duration for most individuals since our documents provide few biographical indications capable of being exactly dated. Two examples, however, can be quoted. In 1155 William Marshal, left the paternal roof at the age of eleven or twelve to be a *puer* with his uncle William of Tancarville. In 1164 he took up a knight's arms; in 1166 and 1167 he took part in tournaments and led a life of 'adventure' and 'feats of valour'.[6] In 1189 he married, by which time he was about forty-five years old; thus his 'youth' had lasted a quarter of a century. This may well have been an exceptional case, although Arnould of Ardres, son of Count Baldwin of Guines, dubbed knight in 1181 and married in 1194, remained a 'youth' for thirty years. Therefore what we are to understand as 'youths', that is to say persons belonging to a certain age group and occupying a particular position in military society and family life, accounted for a large component in the world of chivalry, and contained a considerable number of individuals. Accordingly the group had important connotations at this period in history for the aristocracy as a whole.

Moreover the importance of the group was not due entirely to its size, but also to the peculiar behaviour of the men who composed it. Indeed, in our epics and tales, 'youth' appears to have been a time of impatience, turbulence and instability. In the earlier and later periods in his life, the individual's position was a fixed one, either as a 'child' in the house of his father or the patron responsible for his education, or else as a married man and a father in his own house. In the interval between he roamed abroad. The roving life and the refusal to 'stay put' are revealed as a fundamental characteristic in all the descriptions we have of the condition of 'youth'. The youth is always on the point of departure or on the way to another place; he roams continually through provinces and countries; he 'wanders over all the earth'.[7] For him the 'good life' was 'to be on the move in many lands in quest of prize and adventure', 'to

---

[4] HE, 4 (II, p. 219); Richard, son of Hugh of Chester, *juvenis adhuc liberisque carens*; HE, 3 (II, p. 25); Ernauld of Montreuil, who when he died leaving a son, was called *vir*.

[5] In order to explain this idea, 'bachelor' certainly seems in the romance language, to be the exact equivalent of *juvenis*. GM, v. 1477; *Charroi de Nîmes*, v. 23–5; *Chanson de Roland*, v. 3018–1020.

[6] GM, v. 1895; 1901.

[7] 'To wander', GM, v. 2399, 2444, GM, v. 1890:

> Que nus qui velt en pris monter
> N'amera ja trop long sejor . . .
> . . . Ains s'esmovit en mainte terre
> Por pris e aventure quere
> Mais souvent s'en revenait riche . . .

Lambert of Ardres, H Gh, 91: 'torniamenta frequentando, multas provincias et multas regiones . . . circuivit.'

conquer for reward and honour'.[8] It was thus the quest for glory and 'prize' which was to be achieved in war and even more often in tournaments.[9]

This life of vagabondage was originally considered to be a necessary part of a young man's development, a period of 'study', *studia militiae*, such as, for example, the young Arnould of Pamele pursued, but eventually gave up, on his journey to enter a monastery where he died bishop of Soissons and a saint.[10] A youth's journey was not usually a solitary one. He was, at least in the first phase of his wandering, accompanied by a mentor chosen by his father: this was another knight, also a 'youth', but with greater experience, who was charged with advising him, restraining him, perfecting his education and also directing his itinerary towards the most profitable tournaments. This was the role Ogier fulfilled for Roland in the *Chanson d'Aspremont* and William Marshal for 'young' Henry, son of Henry II of England. When Arnould of Ardres was dubbed knight, his father and his father's lord, the count of Flanders, designated as his counsellor *in torniamentis et in rebus suis disponandis*, an older man who, as he was not himself free to travel all the time, appointed as his tutor-in-arms one of the own nephews, companion until then of 'young' Henry of England.[11] However, in a more general way, the 'youth' found himself caught up in a band of 'friends' who 'loved each other like brothers'.[12] This 'company', or 'household' (*maisnie*)—to use the words of the documents written in the common tongue—was sometimes formed, immediately after the ceremony of dubbing, by the young warriors who had received together the 'sacrament of knighthood' on the same day, and who remained together thereafter.[13] More frequently the company collected around a leader who 'retained' the young men, that is who gave them arms and money and guided them towards adventure and its rewards.[14] The leader was sometimes an established man, but he was more frequently another 'youth'. In such cases the group often centred around the newly dubbed son of their fathers' lord, and were thus the 'youths' of vassal families. Thus Ordericus Vitalis tells us that Robert Courte-Heuse brought with him

[8]   Puis mena si très belle vie
         Que plosors en orent envie
         En torneiemenz e en guerres
         E erra par totes les terres.
                              (GM, v. 754; 2997–8)

[9] It should be noted that young men of good family who were not dubbed but had taken vows to study also went adventuring in a very similar way, in which scholarly disputations, occasions for prowess and reward, were substitutes for the tournament. The behaviour of the young Abelard, even the language he uses, in the first pages of the *Historia calamitarum*, are very relevant to this point.

[10] *Acta sanctorum*, August III, p. 232 A.

[11] *Aspremont*, v. 7517–16. GM, v. 2427–32. Henry II placed his son in the care of William Marshal, who simultaneously taught him and took him to places where there were tournaments: GM, 1959–67; H Gh, 92.

[12] In the case of the sons of William Marshal and the earl of Salisbury, GM, 15884.

[13] H Gh, 91.

[14] Young Henry of England knew how to 'retain' young men: at his instigation older men distributed arms and money to the young men. GM 2673–5, 2679–85.

the sons of his father's vassals who were of his own age, and had been up to then 'maintained' and 'armed' by him.[15] In this way, a gang of 'children' reached maturity and left the great seigneurial roof together, led by the heir who had just acceded to the knightly estate and who escaped into the wandering world of the 'youth'. The group sentiment which arose from their fathers' condition as vassals was reproduced among the 'youths'; within the band it was prolonged into a new generation. Nevertheless, the company was usually formed in a more complex way. In the *familia* maintained by Hugh of Chester, *pueri* undergoing their apprenticeship, clergy and courtiers mixing with knights were all called *juvenes*.[16] Who were the 'youths' led to adventure by Arnould of Ardres? They were two bosom friends, his inseparable companions, knights from distant parts, like Henry le Champenois, who were not part of his father's household. All three took part in tournaments in the father's principality.[17]

Within these bands of companions pleasure was pursued. The leader squandered his money for he loved luxury, play, miming, horses and dogs;[18] morals were far from strict.[19] The main business, however, was fighting 'in tourneys and in war'. Three days before Lent a troop of French knights turned aside to visit Clairvaux, so Saint Bernard exhorted them to refrain from taking up arms, but 'as they were youths and great knights, they refused' and, after drinking, left bent on military exploits.[20] Companies of youths like these formed the spearhead of feudal aggression. Always on the lookout for adventure from which 'honour' and 'reward' could be gained and aiming, if possible, 'to come back rich',[21] they were mobile and ready for action with their emotions at a pitch of warlike frenzy. In an unstable milieu they stirred up turbulence and provided manpower for any distant expedition.[22] It was a 'youth' who directed the military activity of the Erlembaud clan at the time of the Flemish troubles; it was 'youths', 'poor bachelors', who were harangued by William of Orange when he organized the expedition against Nîmes 'to replenish his household'. And how many 'youths' must there have been among the bands of armed pilgrims and crusaders?[23] Dedicated to violence, 'youth' was the instrument of aggression and tumult in knightly society, but in consequence it was always in danger: it was aggressive and brutal in habit and it was to have its ranks decimated. On this point our information is abundant. Indeed, the most frequent references to 'youths' in the documents consulted here, are

[15] HE, 5 (II, p. 381), 7 (III, p. 190).   [16] HE, 6 (III, p. 4).   [17] H Gh, 92.

[18] Cf. the *familia* of Hugh of Chester, HE 6 (III, p. 4) in which the leader, *in militia promptus, in dando prodigus,* kept jugglers and prostitutes.

[19] When Roger and his companions left the household of Hugh of Chester to be converted, Ordericus Vitalis describes them coming back *Quasi de flammis Sodomiae.* HE, 6 (III, p. 16). On the subject of the depraved habits of the *juvenes.* see, among others, Guibert of Nogent, *De vita sua* (edited by Bourgin, Paris, 1907) I, 15, p. 57, III, 19, p. 220.

[20] *Fragmenta Gaufredi,* Analecta Bollandiana, 50 (1932), p. 110.

[21] GM, v. 1897.

[22] HE, 3 (II, p. 54); the duke of Salerno received as reinforcement *de electis juvenibus Normanniae aliquos.*

[23] *Charroi de Nîmes,* v. 641–6.

connected with their violent deaths, either accidentally when out hunting, or in the exercise of arms or, more frequently in military confrontation.[24] Death continually claimed many victims and sometimes the entire offspring of a family could be cut down. Two sons of the castellan Henry of Bourbourg died as 'youths', while a third was blinded in a tournament.[25] When Lambert, author of the *Annales Cameracenses*, describes his kinsmen in a very curious passage in the tale, he recalls ten of his ancestor Raoul's brothers killed on the same day in a fight, whose memory was kept green in the ballads (*cantilenas*) of the *jongleurs*; and, of the fifteen male blood relations that he mentions elsewhere, three were killed in combat and a fourth in a fall from his horse.[26]

The aristocratic vocation for war, together with biological pressures and the circumstances of their age group, all combined to condition the behaviour of these men. But I think we may reach a better understanding of the deeper influences at work by considering the family background of these 'youths', since this accounted for much of their cupidity and also forced them into adventurous and turbulent behaviour. Statistical computations based on a large number of genealogies lead us to conclude that, in aristocratic society of this region and period, the average span of the generations was about thirty years. Moreover, at the end of the twelfth century the eldest son normally came of age and took up arms between the ages of sixteen and twenty-two, that is to say when his father, in his fifties, still held the patrimony firmly in his hands and felt himself more than capable of managing it alone. It certainly seems as if it was the accepted custom for the wealthier father, who tended also to be more solicitous for the glory of his house, to provide his eldest son, after the ceremony of dubbing, with the means to lead a group of 'youths' on an expedition lasting one or two years.[27] The excursion over, the 'youth', once more under the paternal roof, became bored. He felt frustrated for he had tasted economic independence while away and had had the freedom of spending money. To be deprived of this freedom was intolerable and he cast envious eyes on an income he considered his due. If his mother was dead evil counsellors encouraged him to demand what she had left. This, at least, is what Arnould of Ardres did.[28] Long arguments followed and in the resulting confrontation, the father sometimes had to give way. But even so the returning youth's 'sojourn' in the family household weighed heavily and tension against paternal rule mounted. The stories of great families abound with such quarrels in which the son, by now full of aggressive feelings,

[24] Richard, son of William the Conqueror, killed hunting, HE, 5 (II, 391); Hugh, son of Giroie, *juventus florens*, died of spear wounds in an exercise, HE, 3 (II, 29); Ernauld of Montreuil who was not a youth, killed fighting a *juvenis*, HE, 3 (II, p. 25); William of Guines, 'strenuissimum quidam militem, sed in flore juventutis apud Colvinam mortuum', H Gh, 72; Simon of Ardres, *jam adultum et juvenem mortuum*, H Gh, 134; of the fifteen men who made up the band led into Apulia by William Giroie, only two returned to their native land.

[25] H Gh, 122.   [26] MGH SS XVI, pp. 511–12.

[27] Henry the youth *bien erra an e demi*, GM 2444; H Gh, 91. Arnould of Guines 'multas regiones fere per biennium non omnino sine patri auxilio et patrocinio circuivit.'

[28] H Gh, 92.

was often provoked to depart once more. The eldest son who as a 'youth' was surrounded by 'young' companions, in a similar condition, began to struggle openly against the old lord.[29] In any event, 'a long stay at home disgraces a young man' and, even if family peace was not rudely broken, the youthful heir, not satisfied with his limited domestic role, once again took to the road.[30] His father would give him leave to depart with some relief,[31] and he would not recall his son until his own powers waned.[32] It seemed quite normal to both parties that a son who was an unmarried knight without an establishment of his own should take the field and go far away.

The rules of managing the aristocratic patrimony thus encouraged the eldest son to set forth in quest of adventure, but he had of course brothers, sometimes many brothers. From Ordericus Vitalis we learn that, in the houses of the nobility, five, six or even seven sons usually reached manhood. They too, even more urgently than the first-born, felt driven to leave. From the beginning of the eleventh century, the eldest son's privilege to succeed to the seigneurial powers of his father and house was firmly established in the families of the greatest lords, such as kings, counts and castellans. In families of lesser degree, the prerogatives of primogeniture made headway more slowly. However, by the end of the twelfth century they were accepted throughout knightly society in this region where land was becoming scarce and where feudal law presented an obstacle to the break up of fiefs. The care taken by writers to specify the eldest son, and even the eldest daughter, in genealogies is proof of this.[33] What, then had the younger members of the families to hope for? Two or three of them could expect lucrative positions within the church. The others sometimes received a small part of the inheritance, usually from some recent acquisition or from possessions coming

[29] Robert Courte-Heuse, HE 5 (II, p. 381); William Marshal's eldest son accompanied by another 'youth' supported the king of France's party who fought against his father, GM, 15884. In the eleventh century, the son of Robert the Pious with a troop of *socii* of his own age, ravaged his father's lands, Raoul Glaber, *Histoires*, III, 9.

[30] H Gh, 93. Arnould of Ardres preferred to go to other countries *propter torniamentorum studium et gloriam*, rather than to stay in a country where there was no war; GM, 2391 (the young Henry):

> En Angleterre sejornèrent
> Près d'un an qu'ils ne s'atornèrent
> A nule riens fors a pleidier
> Ou a bois ou a tornoier
> Mais al giemble rei pas ne ploust
> Tel sejor, anceis li desplout
> A ses compaignons ensement
> Ennuia molt très durement
> Car esrer plus lor pleüst
> Qu'a sejornez, s'estre pleüst
> Quer bien saciez, ce est la somme
> Que lonc senor honist giemble homme

[31] GM, 2404; Henry II gave his son leave to depart; William Marshal, 'youth', asked leave of his father, GM 1391–4.

[32] HE, 5 (II, p. 457). Ansould of Maule, an eldest son, was recalled from the Crusade by his aged father; he returned, married and succeeded his father. The other sons were far away from the home. See also HE 5 (II, p. 463).

[33] H Gh, 63; *Annales Cameracenses*, MGH SS XVI, pp. 511–12.

from their mother's side.[34] But possession in such cases was precarious, and fragments such as these bred discord between brothers, encouraged cupidity and sharpened the temptation of other brothers or nephews to seize whatever they could by force.[35] When deprived of any hope of certain inheritance, younger brothers had often no other prospect but adventure.

The pressures which forced twelfth-century knights after they were dubbed into a life of errancy must therefore be attributed to customs regulating the distribution of inheritances and of family wealth. But in order to cast more light on the position of 'youth' we must examine matrimonial habits more closely, since, as we have seen, the condition of 'youth' continued until marriage and usually ended then. There is no need to underline the fact that all marriages were at that period a matter of negotiation, conducted and concluded by the father and the elders of the family.[36] This practice, it is true, dealt primarily with the marriage of the eldest son. But as this union could put the future of the whole family at stake, much care was taken over it, and those responsible were prepared to wait for a really suitable opportunity. This, of course, even further prolonged the period of 'youth'. Where the younger sons were concerned, the attitude of the family to marriage was yet more circumspect, but for quite different reasons. It was in fact essential not to permit too many younger sons to take wives for fear of the lateral branches of the family multiplying to such an extent that they would overwhelm the main branch. Furthermore, and this was the really important point, when a son got married something had always to be cut out of the patrimony in order to establish the new husband and provide the jointure, or marriage settlement, for the wife.[37] In the case of the eldest son this was inevitable, but there was great reluctance to repeat the process in the case of younger sons. Younger sons were therefore condemned to a prolonged 'youth'. Another obstacle was that within the neighbourhood of the family, marriageable daughters were scarce. Indeed previous alliances would already have united the entire knighthood of a country into single cousinhood. Ideas about incest current at that period, and the interdicts on consanguinity imposed by the church erected a formal obstacle. These problems were compounded by the lottery that marriage turned out to be in practice. Genealogies reveal that, for the most part, heads of families were often widowers several times over. In order to form advantageous alliances, they often married either older widows or else a weakly member of families of feeble physique. There were also, of course, the hazards of childbirth. At any

[34] In the southwest of the country the old lord used to proceed during his lifetime to *dispositio* his succession. See *Historia pontificum et comitum Engolismensium*, edited by J. Boussard (Paris, 1957), pp. 26, 31, 36.

[35] *Historia pontificum et comitum Engolismensium*, p. 30.

[36] H Gh, 149. The marriage of Arnould of Ardres was decided by the father of the husband and the uncles of the bride.

[37] The dower (H Gh, 149); Manassé, third son of Count Baldwin of Guines (the second son had died *in juventute*) was established on his marriage on a manor formed by his father out of recently acquired lands.

rate, as widowers, well established and provided for, these men sought new wives within their circle, and their position, prestige, and worldly wisdom favoured remarriage. Thus, they had first call on the most eligible brides and thereby further dimmed the prospects of 'bachelors'. Everything, therefore, conspired to prolong 'youth' and to force 'youths' into adventure in far-off places.

In fact, these adventures were also revealed as quests for wives perhaps first and foremost. Throughout their wanderings the bands of 'youths' were animated by hopes of marriage. They knew that their leader, once settled himself, would consider it his first duty to help to marry off his companions.[38] All *juvenes* were on the lookout for an heiress. If they came across one, they tried to reserve her before she was nubile. Sometimes they took the child with them on their journey, and were prepared to restore her to her father if they should find a more desirable match on the way or if another 'youth' should come to claim her too insistently. Here I shall borrow another example from the *Historia comitum Ghisnensium*. A certain adventurer who had been promised the castellan of Bourbourg's daughter had taken her to England with him. But Baldwin of Ardres, having gained the friendship of the castellan by his warlike exploits, received permission to dispute her. The heiress had to be brought back; and he finally married her.[39] Thus, the desire to be married seems to have dominated the behaviour of a 'youth', encouraging him to shine in combat and to parade at sporting events. In this way Arnould of Guines attempted by feats of valour to seduce the countess of Boulogne. Later, he bound himself to the daughter of the count of Saint Pol. Finally, as soon as he realized that she was worth the taking, he broke all his previous attachments and set himself to win the heiress of the castellan of Bourbourg.[40]

The search for a rich girl with a fine establishment was thus not always doomed to disappointment. But certain obvious hazards and obstacles of the hunt were inherent in the uncertain supply of suitable quarry, that is by the frequent eclipse of noble families which resulted in the entire inheritance devolving upon an heiress. Indeed, the whole phenomenon is intimately bound up with the existence of the class of 'youths', with their peculiar circumstances, their adventurous life, and the dangers they ran which so reduced their ranks. This leads us back to consider the demography of these families. Scrutiny of the family trees of great lords is in this conection very instructive and rewarding. Here are two by no means exceptional cases. The first concerns the descendants of a Norman lord, Hugh of Grentemesnil. Ten of his children grew up, including five sons. Two died as 'youths' in our special sense of the word; two others went to seek their fortune abroad, one settling in Apulia and the other nearer home, in England. The latter had himself two sons who were both drowned in the wreck of the White Ship while on

---

[38] *Aspremont*, 5572–3: war leaders gave wives to soldiers as a reward. H Gh, 64: when Arnould of Ghent established himself in the county of Guines, he summoned all his companions, and 'retained' several of them in his house, *illos in terra maritabat.*
[39] H Gh, 39/60.   [40] H Gh, 93, 149.

their 'youthful' wanderings. Only one of Hugh's sons, Robert, the elder, had stayed behind on the family estate, perhaps because he had been married off earlier and was thus preserved from the dangers of 'youth'. He had only one child, a daughter, and consequently the entire fortune passed, through her, to another family.[41] Another such case was that of the castellan, Henry of Bourbourg. He had been established for twenty-four years during which time his wife presented him with twelve surviving children (such facts demonstrate that the infant mortality of this social class should not be exaggerated). Seven sons were found places in ecclesiastical prebends; the eldest held the castle on the death of his father and was married twice without issue; three others, as I have previously mentioned, died or became invalids while still young; the last born succeeded his brother as castellan and was married, but his son died in childhood; the whole inheritance therefore came to his daughter, the girl who was won by Arnould of Ardres.[42]

It is obvious that it was the bands of 'youths', excluded by so many social prohibitions from the main body of settled men, fathers of families and heads of houses, with their prolonged spells of turbulent behaviour making them an unstable fringe of society, who created and sustained the crusades. They were also responsible for the craze for tourneys, the propensity for luxury and concubinage, and their life style exercised a decisive influence on the birthrate of the nobility and the fortunes of partrimonies in the region. While most of the young men were kept in a state of celibacy and danger the risk of fragmenting inheritance was certainly less. But at the same time the chances of a family line surviving were also reduced and the extinction of many families was thereby hastened. The continuity of the nobility was in these cases dependent on the chance matrimonial successes of men of lesser birth. It is therefore incumbent on the scholar wishing to enquire into the behaviour and destiny of the knighthood to investigate this social group closely.

I would also like to point out that the presence of such a group at the very heart of aristocratic society helped to sustain certain ideas, myths and forms of collective psychology. These can be found at once personified and reflected in the literature—and the typical personages depicted therein—of the twelfth century written for the aristocracy. That literature tends to sustain, prolong and stylize the spontaneous reactions, emotional and intellectual, of contemporaries. To begin with it should be noted that the group of 'youths' themselves provided the main audience for this so-called literature of chivalry which was obviously composed mainly for their amusement. I have already mentioned the mummers whom Hugh of Chester maintained in his household, and the ballads (*cantilenas*) which reminded the author of the *Annales Cameracenses* of his ten great-uncles killed in combat. During the wasted days when the 'youth', Arnould of Ardres, was kept at home kicking his heels he encouraged the telling of tales. His kinsman, Walter of Sluys, not only entertained the band with the legends of

---

[41] HE, 2 (IV, p. 167, note 2).   [42] H Gh, 122.

Gormont and Isembart, and Tristan and Iseult, but also, told of the exploits of the former lords of the castle.[43] We should not therefore be surprised if we find that typical events in the life of the 'youth'—quest for adventure and feats of arms—provided both the background and theme for epics and romances, not to speak of the sermons composed for domestic consumption. Gerald of Avranches, priest to Hugh of Chester's *familia*, found it useful to take as the theme of his sermon, *emendatio vitae*, the lives of the soldier-saints, Demetrius and George, Maurice and the martyrs of the Theban legion, Eustace and Sebastian.[44] We should certainly not find it unrewarding to consider the themes of the literature of chivalry anew in the light of the tastes, prejudices, frustrations and daily behaviour of the 'youths', but here I must restrict myself to no more than two points.

First, there was the transfer to twelfth-century genealogical writings in northwest France of the major theme, that of the hopes and dreams of the *juvenes*, of the young adventurer who gains the love of a rich heiress by his valour, and thus succeeds in establishing a great lordship far from his own people and founding a powerful dynasty. K. F. Werner has shown that, in the milieu of the magnates of this region, family trees were preserved in the collective memory which when pushed back to the ninth and tenth centuries, came up against the awkward fact that before then there were no ancestors. They had to be invented, and writers specialized in thinking up original ancestors for great princely families: they had to be strangers, young and brave, *miles peregrini*, famed for their warlike qualities, who had won their lordships, sometimes through marriage.[45] Such was the case in the families of Anjou, Blois and Bellême. When Lambert of Ardres, priest in the service of the young Arnould, imbued with the literature enjoyed by the 'youth', traced the line of the counts of Guines back to the first quarter of the tenth century, he discovered the person of Siegfried the Dane. This forebear was a 'youth' who had sought adventure. His quest had brought him to the household of the count of Flanders, where he had served the count's sister with love. He could not marry her, but he made her pregnant and her bastard son was the first count of Guines.[46]

The second point I want to make about the literary transformations of the attitudes of mind entertained by the youthful knights concerns precisely this growth of courtly love. Here we must leave the northwest of the kindom of France and move southwards to the scene of the troubadours of the generations around 1150. Cercamon, Marcabru, Allegret, all praised the idea of *jovens*; but it appears that by this word they meant not so much an abstract virtue as an ideal animating the group of 'youths'. 'Youth', for whom the troubadours were themselves the spokesmen, appears in their songs to have been vanquished by the social system: 'youths' could never find a woman to welcome them for all

[43] HG, 96.   [44] HE, 3, 3–18.
[45] 'Untersuchungen zu Frühzeit der französischen Fürstentums', *Die Welt als Geschichte* (1960), pp. 116–18.
[46] H Gh, 9–11.

women were married. And when these women enjoyed adulterous love, their partners were not 'youths' but married men. What, therefore, the love songs of the second half of the twelfth century suggest is a new kind of erotic relationship, better suited to the position of the *juvenes*—that husbands should no longer pay court to ladies, and that they should no longer prevent their wives from receiving 'youths' and accepting their services of love. For the triangle 'husband–wife–married lover', the poets of the 'youthful band' wanted to substitute another triangle 'husband–lady–young courtly servant'. They wanted to break into the erotic circle to the advantage of 'youth'.[47] We know how well this ideal theme succeeded. The game came to pass indeed but in so doing, of course, it changed its form somewhat. In conclusion I return once more to Lambert of Ardres and his patron and hero, Arnould, the 'youth'. His quest for valour had brought him to the notice of the Countess Ida of Boulogne who, as mistress of the lordship, appeared to him a magnificent prize carrying the promise of a marvellous establishment. He exchanged secret messages of love with her; he loved her—or at least appeared to love her. Indeed, 'ad terram tamen et Boloniensis comitatus dignitatem, veri vel simulati amoris objectu, recuperata ejusdem comitisse gratia, aspiravit.'[48]

Such was the aristocratic youth of France in the twelfth century, a mob of young men let loose, in search of glory, profit and female prey, by the great noble houses in order to relieve the pressure on their expanding power.

[47] R. Nelli, *L'érotique des troubadours* (Toulouse, 1963), pp. 108ff.
[48] H Gh, 93.

8

Laity and the peace of God

'In the year one thousand of the passion of our Lord', writes Raoul Glaber in the fourth book of his *Histoires*, bishops and abbots began 'at first in the country of Aquitaine, to collect all the people together in synods. The bodies of many saints and countless shrines containing relics were assembled. Afterwards, through the provinces of Arles, of Lyons and Burgundy and thence to the uttermost corners of France, they carried tidings announcing that councils would be held in every diocese in certain places, bringing prelates and princes from all countries together for the purpose of reforming the peace and the institution of the holy faith.'

This quotation gives an accurate picture of the movement known as the peace of God. Indeed, every document preserved confirms that vast assemblies took place, often in fields outside the cities in order to accommodate the crowds, and there is no doubt that the display of relics was an essential part of the proceedings. Moreover, the initiative seems to have come from bishops and heads of monasteries, particularly Abbot Odilon of Cluny; the prelates succeeded in winning over members of the higher aristocracy of regions to their case, and at the very least gained their cooperation by persuading them to join in presiding over the councils of peace. Effectively the movement was born in southern Gaul, in Aquitaine and the region of Narbonne; it travelled northwards along the valleys of the Rhône and the Saône, and by 1033 it had reached the northern frontiers of the French kingdom. Nevertheless, in actual fact it spread more slowly than Glaber's text would have us suppose. In the present state of our knowledge we could place the date of its departure from Charroux and Narbonne at about 989–90; and we can also observe how it had by the year 1000 extended throughout the whole of Aquitaine; it penetrated Burgundy about 1023–5, and soon spread thence into northern France; there followed a second active phase which, according to Raoul Glaber's description, began about the year 1033, but which extended widely through the whole of Gaul between 1027 and 1041, and with special intensity in the south.[1] For half a

---

[1] B. Töpfer's chronology in *Volk und Kirche zur Zeit der beginnenden Gottesfriedens-*

century the phenomenon was thus mostly limited to Gaul and particularly to Aquitaine and Provence; it also seems quite clear that it was
inspired by the church under the direction of the bishops. To what extent
was the position of laymen modified by the order it created and the ideas
to which it gave birth?

It seems to me that, in order to answer this question, we must not lose
sight of the fact that, as with other aspects of religious history, the
movement of the peace of God had two facets, or if you prefer, two levels,
which can be placed in direct contrast to each other without running
counter to intellectual and ecclesiastical thought current during the
period. These two aspects were, of course, the spiritual and the temporal. On the one hand, the institutions of peace were conceived and
established in accordance with certain aspirations of perfection and
salvation: they were presented as a means of achieving the kingdom of
God and became in this way the vehicle for moral values. Consequently
at this level they tended to modify the position of the laity within the
church.[2] But on the other hand, the movement resulted from the
church's penetration into the very heart of the world's problems and
developments; certain particular changes in the social structure pushed
it onwards; indeed, this forward impetus generated it, with the further
result that it reflected, fixed and, to some extent, consecrated the new
forms assumed by power and wealth, politics and society in the material
world of this period.[3] To express it in another way, if we consider the
peace of God as an agent of the renewal of ideas about laity, and also as
one of its first manifestations, we can observe it participating in the
great forward thrust which convulsed western Christianity at the end of
the eleventh century and culminated in what is now called the Gregorian reform and the Crusades. At the same time it played its part in
the advent of what we know as the feudal society, and contributed a
great deal to the formation of its special features. In my opinion we have
to consider the movement of peace from these two points of view jointly.
This is the way I propose to examine the three separate stages by which
it developed and widened in the course of the eleventh century.

When he described the movement of peace in his *Histoires*, Raoul
Glaber made it a part of the general efforts of dignitaries of the church to
disengage the latter from the pressures of the material world and to give
it the dominant position which would enable it to perform the erstwhile
royal mission of leading the people of God towards their salvation. He
was indeed right to do this. In the first years of its growth the movement
did find itself moving in this direction and recent changes in political
forces provided the impetus. The period during which the first councils

bewegung in Frankreich (Berlin, 1957), should be corrected by R. Bonnaud-Delamare's in
Les Institutions de paix en Aquitaine au XIe siècle, La Paix I, Société Jean Bodin, XIV
(Brussels, 1962).

[2] These aspects are well explored in R. Bonnaud-Delamare's study published in
Mélanges Halphen (Paris, 1951).

[3] The relationship of the ideology of the peace to the social structure is fully discussed by
Töpfer in *Volk und Kirche*.

of peace met, the last decade of the tenth century, seems to have corresponded to the period when the public institutions of the Carolingian monarchy in the southern parts of Gaul had finally decayed.

In this part of western Europe and by the year 990 the king had lost all power to restrain the local strong men. Henceforth the latter exercised for their own private profit the *regalia*, the prerogatives of command which were formerly delegated by the sovereign and were now held by hereditary right. To judge and to punish became occasions for levying lucrative taxes, the *consuetudines*, on the population. Every lay lord who had inherited this right sought to extend it, and they laid special claim to the lands and men of the church; although these were protected by privileges of immunity, the defection of the royal authority had rendered useless the documents conferring the immunity. Moreover, among the *regalia* that passed into the private patrimony of the counts in southern Gaul was the right to nominate candidates to the highest ecclesiastical dignities, to dispose of the episcopal throne and the office of abbot. Thus temporal authority menaced the church's liberty in two ways. On the one hand the wealth which belonged to God and the saints, and on the other hand pastoral offices had both by 990 passed under the control of, and been exploited by, a private power, not sacred as the king's authority had been, but wholly regulated by bodies of custom. Spiritual leaders found themselves in thrall to worldly leaders, and naturally sought to free themselves. This at least was the oath taken by those members of the higher clergy who were not too much contaminated by the practice of simony. These men were mostly in the monasteries which had been affected by the Cluniac movement that was so very active at the time and in the same provinces in which the ideas about peace were circulating.

The dispositions of the first councils were thus simple. They were plainly aimed at protecting the 'sacred things', that is the sanctuaries and the servants of God and, in addition, the poor from the violence and intrusions of the new emergent lay powers which confronted them so aggressively. The texts are unambiguous. I shall quote from two, one at either end of what I shall call the first phase of the movement of peace. In 989 at Charroux three types of violence were to be curbed and their agents punished with anathema—those who violated a church or who took something from it by force; those who struck an unarmed member of the clergy; and those who despoiled a 'peasant or other poor man'.[4] In 1031 at Limoges Bishop Jordan denounced the 'secular powers' in his diocese 'who violated sanctuaries, oppressed the poor who had been entrusted to them, and the ministers of the church'.[5]

Historians have been aware for some time that, on these points, the decisions of the councils of peace repeated the terms of earlier legisla-

---

[4] In spite of some imperfections, the collection of texts contained in L. Huberti, *Studien zur Rechtsgeschichte der Gottesfrieden und Landesfrieden* (Ansbach, 1892), is the most useful, and my references throughout this essay are to this work: in this instance, see Huberti, *Studien*, p. 35.
[5] Huberti, *Studien*, p. 212.

tion, notably the Carolingian capitularies and edicts,[6] but with one fundamental difference. The peace invoked in the ninth-century texts was the peace neither of God nor bishops; it was the king's peace. The king alone was charged with defending 'the poor, orphans, widows and the churches of God'. Whoever violated this protection became liable to a royal fine of sixty sous. In 857, for example, Charles the Bald had enjoined his *missi* to respect the immunities of the holy church, not to oppress in any way enclosed nuns, widows, orphans and the poor, and to see that their possessions were not pillaged. Consequently, what could the first stipulations of the peace of God have signified if not the intention in the years before and after the year 1000 of carrying out a slow take-over of this royal authority because the king's power was gradually weakening? In a region where, more than elsewhere, the king's writ was ceasing to run, the bishops undertook to assume the proper functions of an absentee and ineffective sovereign. They wished themselves to protect the holy things for which they were responsible against a rising lay power that was certainly less brutal and less rapacious than the decisions of the councils proclaimed, but was nonetheless unlawful in the eyes of the clergy because it was not hallowed. The bishops would themselves make the peace of God prevail by imposing spiritual sanctions. They would work, as was said at the first council of Poitiers in 1011–14, 'for the restoration of peace and justice'[7]—an eminently royal task.

The movement of peace thus appears as an attempt to alleviate the decline of the royal authority which had hitherto combined spiritual and worldly elements. The result was to bring the spiritual power of bishops face to face with the temporal power of dukes and counts. The confrontation led to a stricter separation of laymen from clergy and monks both socially and in the eyes of the law. This tendency was of great significance in that the *restauratio pacis* conveniently dovetailed into wider aspirations. It took its place in the reaction against the Carolingian order in which church and Christianity had been intimately merged in the person of the king. The movement of reaction was a vehicle for Gregorian ideas. We should be grateful to Roger Bonnaud-Delamare for formulating the theory that the prescriptions of the first council of Charroux were part and parcel of the reproof pronounced at the same time by the abbot of Fleury against clergy who were too fond of money or who wielded arms like laymen.[8] It should also be noticed that the first council of Poitiers did not legislate solely against the violence threatening sacred things, but against simony and the concubinage of priests as well.[9] All these things were connected. The

---

[6] Töpfer, *Volk und Kirche*, p. 35, note 26, p. 88; Bonnaud-Delamare, *Paix*, p. 422.

[7] Huberti, *Studien*, p. 136. But was this indeed the prelates' role? When the movement spread to the boundaries of the Empire in 1023, into regions where the royal power appeared perfectly capable of fulfilling its functions, some claimed the contrary. Bishop Gerald of Cambrai objected that 'it was for the king to suppress sedition, put an end to wars and encourage peaceful relations; as for the bishops, they had only to exhort kings to fight for the salvation of the country and to pray for their victory.' Huberti, *Studien*, p. 162.

[8] Bonnaud-Delamare, *Paix*, pp. 425–6.   [9] *Ibid*. p. 447.

church in the narrow sense of the word was to form henceforth a group which wished to set itself apart. We can discern that there was a right to special protection guaranteed by spiritual rather than pecuniary sanctions. But at the same time and by the same token it was considered that secular clergy also should respect the rules of conduct that had until then only applied to monks. In this way clergy and monks, the two principal *ordines* of the Carolingian social system, began to merge into a single body that was more completely separated from the laity. Thus the legislation of the peace of God resulted mainly in greater segregation of the lay and ecclesiastical groups. Nevertheless, it introduced a new distinction into the very heart of lay society. In their efforts to protect more effectively the things that were God's and, in particular, to prevent, as the canons of the council said, the church's lands from being 'dishonoured by some bad custom',[10] the bishops, as judges and defenders of clergy and monks, were in effect led to include under their protection the part of the lay population whom the kings had previously been called upon to safeguard. From that time on, so far as spiritual power was concerned, laymen were divided into two categories—those who had to be defended and those whose aggressive impulses had to be curbed. The first category was the poor. By the poor, the first council of Charroux meant chiefly the peasantry. The men for whom the church felt responsible, those who they mobilized at Bourges in 1038 in the defence of peace, were *agricultores*,[11] *villani*[12]; and in the text of the vows of peace in 1023–5 merchants, pilgrims and noblewomen were added to country dwellers.[13] What all these people had in common was that they were unarmed—and it was indeed people without arms, *multitudo inermis vulgi*, whom the bishop of Bourges set in 1038 against agitators to their greater disadvantage. The texts sometimes crudely juxtaposed 'nobles' with *pauperes*,[14] but it was obviously the *milites*, or knights whom bishop Jordan of Limoges excommunicated, cursing their weapons and horses, that were the instruments of their turbulence and the insignia of their social position.[15]

It was a plain fact that all violence, covetousness, exactions and other activities prejudicial to churches, God's servants and the poor, came from the class of professional warriors, men who in the new structure of society had the privilege of military activity; in effect, segregation within the laity was a function of the bearing of arms. *Milites et rustici*, horsemen and peasants, this was indeed the fundamental juxtaposition among laymen created by the decisions of the councils of peace. But a coincidence in chronology of paramount importance must be noted here. At the very moment when the vocabulary of the conciliar decisions began to distinguish between horsemen and peasants, the vocabulary of the charters drawn up in southern Gaul also set the same social categories in juxtaposition. It was about the year 980 that the word *miles* began to take on legal and social significance. Thus it can be said that the de facto division of lay society into two classes became

---

[10] Huberti, *Studien*, p. 24.   [11] *Ibid.*, p. 35.   [12] *Ibid.*, pp. 123, 166.
[13] *Ibid.*, pp. 123, 124.   [14] *Ibid.*, p. 183.   [15] *Ibid.*, p. 214.

institutionalized by the installation during the fifty years on either side of the year 1000 of the lordship of the *ban*, whose agency by exempting the *milites* from, and subjecting the *rustici* to, the lords' customary dues and repressive justice, turned the former into a privileged group and the latter into an exploited group. The prescriptions of the peace of God thus came to add to the division introduced into the heart of lay society by the new separation and in some way legitimized it. In the last resort, the legislation of the councils of peace, and the wider movement on which it was based, came to initiate in the last years of the tenth century a rearrangement of the *ordines* into which the Creator had divided the *societas christiana*. There were still three orders, but henceforth only one was ecclesiastical while the other two were lay. It is true that this system was already in existence in some sections of religious thought during the first councils of peace. But we should do well to remember that Adalbéron's poem to King Robert was exactly contemporaneous with the councils. When Bishop Gerald of Cambrai, who opposed the propagandists of the peace of God because in his country the king was himself able to keep the peace, argued that 'the human race had been divided since its origin into three groups, the men of prayer, the warriors and the tillers of the soil,'[16] he was in fact assuming the same model of society as that laid down in the canons of the council.

The first councils of peace did not deny the *milites* their right to fight. That was, after all, their vocation: the arms they bore had been bestowed upon them by the divine will, which also gave them certain other powers, notably the power to judge and to punish. From the very beginning the legislation of the peace of God foresaw that the only 'poor' to be sheltered from the secular threat of being despoiled of their property were those who had not committed any offence.[17] 'Let no man take the goods of a peasant,' proclaimed the Council of Narbonne in 1054, 'except his person for a crime committed by himself, and let no man subject him to force except by law.'[18] It was unjust pillage that was condemned. By contrast court fines and regularly levied exactions were considered just; the authority of the *ban* and the submission of the *rustici* to the territorial lord, to the *dominus loci*, or to the master of his body if they were *homines proprii*, were made lawful by the legislation of the peace. On the other hand, knights, men who were dangerous as well as threatening, had a perfect right to confront and attack their enemies when these were men-at-arms like themselves, even if they should be clergy; the peace of God, it must be remembered, protected only unarmed clergy. Fighting, and particularly what the texts called *werra*,[19] or private war, was not condemned. The first councils of peace merely attempted, by a system of sanctions and collective agreements, to contain lawful activities within limits; they protected certain approved places and social categories against aggression and pillage; they defined clearly marked zones of safety within which the turbulence of knights was

---

[16] *Ibid.*, p. 206.   [17] *Ibid.*, p. 35.   [18] *Ibid*, p. 320.   [19] *Ibid.*, p. 166.

forbidden. From now on warlike behaviour, the privilege of the social group, was not to cross these borders. The peace of God, at the very beginning, merely aimed at restricting military violence to one sector of Christianity, composed of men who carried swords and shields and rode on horseback.

However, the reforming spirit continued to ripen and develop and soon certain prelates came to consider that the building of the kingdom of God needed more radical measures. From the moment when the church took over the king's mission of guiding men into the straight and narrow path, it became necessary to work towards the goal of extirpating the sins of the world. It was here, in southern France about 1020, when the foundations of feudal society were laid, that the period of instability came to a halt. The church no longer, as in the early days of the movement of peace, wanted merely to adapt itself to the innovations brought about by the peace movement or to protect itself, or even to promote its ends in a direction more favourable to the immunities of the spiritual world. It could go further. The first decisions were now taken which set the idea of peace on a new tack.

From its birth, as I have said, the demands of peace were part of a more general desire for purification. In the eyes of those clergy who were in forefront of the reforming movement, fighting, bearing arms and wielding them began at the end of the tenth century to seem evil in the same way as the love of money and the sexual act. To enter the cloister had always meant renouncing the sword as well as gold and women. Within the body of God's servants where, in contrast to the laity, the state of the clergy and the condition of monks tended to merge and where, as a result, priests were invited to share in the renunciations and purifications of monasticism, the pacific aim became bound up with the dual ideals of chastity and poverty as championed by the Gregorians. There was no lack of helmeted prelates or canons engaged in warlike exercises for whom *militare* did not merely mean to serve God, and none of them were protected by the sanctions proclaimed by the first councils of peace. But the abbot of Fleury had already expressed the opinion that these armed clergy were not acting in conformity with the mission of their order. The concept moved forward under pressure from the institutions of the peace of God: the poor were by definition without arms; and it became more and more evident that, in order to be pure and truly worthy of their estate, priests ought also to be poor, and to lead the communal life as monks did. It was only a short step from there to the notion that, like monks, they ought to lay down their arms and place themselves among the *inermes*, the unarmed. The development of the formulae of the peace bears obvious witness to the success of this notion during the eleventh century. The documents dating from the end of the century forbid any attack on the clergy; they do not give any detail except to say that unarmed clergy are alone guaranteed; and at this period clergy did not normally carry arms.[20]

[20] *Ibid.*, pp. 406, 417 (1095, Council of Clermont; oath of peace taken by Fulk of Anjou and the magnates of Touraine).

But the same idea was soon proposed to laymen as a salutary act of penitence. Indeed, it appears that after 1020 councils of peace display a much more marked penitential character. By gathering crowds around reliquaries charged with powers of propitiation and imposing on the assembled company a collective profession of renunciation, their aim was to appease the wrath of God, to combat disaster and fend off famine and pestilence. We might even consider that the deliberate intention to invoke penitence was a part of the propaganda for universal purification, aroused as the millennium of the passion approached by the belief, in certain circles of monks as well as in the collective conscience, that the end of the world was at hand. In any event Raoul Glaber unmistakably introduces the movement of peace into his discourse; he links it to the great religious conversions then occurring at all social levels which led to the proliferation of pilgrimages. And it is quite evident that when Adhemar of Chabannes compiled his chronicle in 1028 he recognized that there was a close connection between the epidemic then raging and the curative properties of the relics, as well as the preaching of the *reformatio pacis*.[21]

In this way the peace of God changed its character. It was no longer merely a social pact, held together by the threat of spiritual sanctions. It became a pact direct with God himself, a matter of appeasing him by promises of voluntary abstinence, of being purified from sin in face of his wrath and of following for that purpose the monastic example. Before that time the ceremonies of public penitence had demanded that the sinner should put off his weapons at the same time as he renounced his worldly goods, made the vow of chastity, and then took to the road on his pilgrimage of redemption. In the years around 1033, the church proposed further that those laymen, nobles, *milites*, whose calling it was to bear weapons, should also associate themselves with the universal task of renunciation: they should no longer be content merely to respect the laws in operation before the peace by not attacking churches, God's ministers or the poor during their military operations or in the exercise of their seigneurial authority, but they should also accept that what was allowed by law could be considered a danger to the soul, in other words they should deprive themselves of the pleasures of fighting and pillaging. Knights were urged to abstain from war during certain periods much as everyone else was urged at certain periods (sometimes the same periods) to abstain from eating foods that gave too much pleasure, and to do so in a spirit of poverty. Indeed, the new dispositions of the laws of peace—and contemporary chroniclers reveal this fact clearly —appear inseparable from a strengthening of the penitential system and especially of the fast.[22]

---

[21] Bonnaud-Delamare, *Paix*, p. 432.

[22] Huberti, *Studien*, p. 241; the canons of the Council of Elne in 1027 punished incest and repudiation of a wife as well as violent acts; *ibid.*, pp. 203, 205. Raoul Glaber and contemporary chroniclers seem to indicate that the councils about the year 1033 laid down abstention from wine on Thursdays and from meat on Fridays at the same time as they reformed the peace.

The pledges of the peace were, therefore, transformed. To the obligation to respect *pax*, peace, ancient royal peace, that guarded the vulnerable areas of the community at large, was added a *tregua*, or truce, a general and temporary suspension of military activity. War was supposed to be a source of sin. It was a pleasure that had to be denied, and at certain times the warlike class, by an act of conversion with monastic overtones, had to renounce its pursuit. The first dispositions laying down the new attitudes can be seen in the vows of peace, drawn up in 1023–5 first by the Burgundians and then by the French. The version proposed by Bishop Garin of Beauvais[23] extended the safeguards which the jurisdiction of the peace of God promised the poor, to the knight who voluntarily put aside his military weapons during Lent; nobody was to attack him. The measure was quite natural: as a penitent the knight had given up his arms and rejoined the poor and in this spirit of poverty he became part of the group of *inermes* and had therefore a right to claim the same security. But the stipulation was an innovation to the extent that it revealed what was perhaps a new inclination among men of war to consider that to abstain from fighting was to earn salvation and that this abstention could be practised during the redeeming period of Lent. Four years later the Council of Elne imposed a truce on Sundays.[24] This was also quite natural, since on this holy day all servile labour was considered to be unlawful and the Carolingian edicts had already even included private war into a Sunday interdict.[25] These early dispositions, and the underlying feelings of disapproving military activity which was now represented to public conscience as a pleasure to be condemned, served as the foundation for an entire legislation with all its articles united in one corpus at the Council of Arles in 1037–41. Peace was to reign from Wednesday evening until Monday morning 'between all Christian men, whether friend or foe, neighbour or stranger', and this was to be done in memory of Christ, his birth, passion, entombment and resurrection.

Thus, the idea of a truce followed the idea of a peace. The peace was widened and deepened in a special way. It offered the class of knights, henceforth well established in the new society, a kind of asceticism appropriate to the function of their *ordo*. The same ethic which demanded from the *pauperes* that they should submit with a good grace to their lord's domination, extolled the ideal of the penitent knight. The latter's honour demanded not merely that he should refrain from attacking and despoiling unarmed Christians, but that, for the love of Christ, he should not draw his sword on holy days. This time the laws of the truce were part of attempts by the feudal church to christianize the warrior's ethic. Consequently, it was connected with the church's growing influence over the ceremony of dubbing, an area of knowledge which has, as yet, hardly been explored.

[23] Huberti, *Studien*, p. 167.
[24] *Ibid.*, p. 240, 'No man shall attack his enemy between the ninth hour on Saturday and the first hour of Monday.'
[25] Capitulary of 813 cited by Huberti, p. 246.

But from the moment when the aggression of the knights came to be kept in check by the peace and, still more, by the truce, there were other matters that needed to be tackled. In fact the idea of the Crusade germinated in the dispositions of the councils of peace, since the latter had gradually extended the fields in which war was forbidden to God's people—to begin with, to certain places and for certain social groups, then in certain periods dedicated to penitence or to glorifying the Lord, until finally it came to be rejected altogether between Christians. Its condemnation was pronounced in the first chapters of the canons of the Council of Narbonne in 1054 devoted to the truce.[26] 'Let no Christian kill another Christian, for there is no doubt that he who kills a Christian spills the blood of Christ.' For if God had given the knight his mission of fighting, he was now no longer permitted to fulfil this mission within the Christian community and the body of Christ; he could only fight against the enemies of the faith. To this battle for the faith, the only fight that was henceforth truly lawful, he had, according to the ethic of the assemblies of peace, wholly to consecrate his weapons, blessed by priests in the ceremonies of dubbing. He had become, as the new literature for his perusal repeated over and over again, the 'soldier of Christ'. It is for this reason—and here we reach the third stage in the maturing of ideas—that the Council of Clermont in 1095 was above all else a council of peace. First, because the injunctions to became a penitent were repeated;[27] second, because it gave a universal value to the stipulations about the truce of God, until then only local in application,[28] and last, because the intervention of the pope secured for all who undertook the penitent's voyage to the Holy Land privileges until then reserved only for the poor and unarmed.[29] The Crusade unquestionably carried the demands of the peace of God to its ultimate goal, since it was the direct cause of the departure of a mass of *pauperes* to Jerusalem, to the divine kingdom. It thus released a flood of confident, pacific and unarmed people that was to carry all before it, as had earlier the march of the *multitudo inermis vulgi* mobilized by the bishop of Bourges in 1038. The new exodus had to include the penitent knights, to protect them and if necessary to ensure their progress by doing battle with miscreants. All the rules for the Crusade were taken from canons of earlier councils in southern Gaul, even to the symbolism of the cross, that rampart against violence, the insignia of protection and shelter.[30] The ideal of the *reformatio pacis* was, in fact, realized by the journey to Jerusalem.

The *reformatio pacis* had been made necessary by the decay of royal institutions and by the growth of a society in which warlike behaviour had become the privilege of a well defined class. In fact all the deliberations of the reforming councils were aimed at this new class and the

[26] Huberti, *Studien*, p. 317.
[27] *Ibid*, p. 406 (and particularly the imposition of the fast).   [28] *Ibid*., p.406.
[29] *Ibid*., p. 411. It should be noted that the Council of Arles of 1037–41 had specified a pilgrimage to Jerusalem as penance for a homicide committed during the truce of God. *Ibid*., p. 273.
[30] *Ibid*., p. 408.

aggression with which it was charged. First a defence had to be found against it, then it had to be disciplined, and finally it had to be diverted into a holy purpose. Only one part of the laity, the group of *milites*, or knights, fell directly under the influence of the institutions of peace, but that influence was very profound. The edicts drawn up by the councils fixed the boundaries of the social group, gave it consistency, and turned it into an *ordo*. Then it forged a particular ethic for it. By the eve of the twelfth century the *nova militia*, bearing arms that had been blessed, saw itself devoted to a dual task—the 'gentleman's' tasks which above all others Saint Louis himself tried to perform—first, to defend the church and the poor, and second, to fight the enemies of Christ. In this way it was hoped to inaugurate the reign of the peace of God.

9

The structure of kinship and nobility

Northern France in the eleventh and twelfth centuries

For many years I have been studying one strand in the history of ideas which needs to be woven into the main fabric of social history to provide perspective as well as illumination. This strand is the story of family ties in feudal France, and in particular those of the aristocracy since this sector of society is the only one to be sufficiently well served by documents. By the nature of things these studies follow two parallel directions, of which the main one is towards a better understanding of kinship as it actually operated. This understanding can be obtained by observing the demographic movements of the family, its wealth, its location (place of residence and burial), its power, its marriages, its wider or more restricted range and all those signs, such as patronymic surnames or heraldic emblems, which are an outward manifestation of the cohesion of its members. But the study has another aim of equal significance and that is to discover in what way men of that period and that position in society themselves viewed their relationships and situation within the group. My researches aim at uncovering what was the mental picture of family relationships in order that the ideal form may be compared with the actuality of experience.

One of the basic instruments for such a study is obviously genealogy, but in actual fact there are of course two kinds of genealogies. On the one hand there are those reconstructed after the event by historians patiently uncovering evidence of consanguinity and intermarriage such as is found in cartularies, titles of ownership and documents of an obituary nature. This kind of genealogy, necessarily incomplete, and often uncertain, gives us a true, one might almost say a biological, picture of the family group throughout its existence and is obviously indispensable for the understanding of the material conditions in the family history. On the other hand there are genealogies differently constructed, but invaluable nonetheless, that are able to provide evidence of family psychology, and the reactions which at that period the ties of kinship produced. These genealogies are of course the family trees drawn up by contemporaries. These trees reveal an awareness of family cohesion; furthermore (and this feature is most significant), they were able to create this consciousness, and to impose it on the members of the group in a lasting fashion, thus to some extent influencing the conduct of subsequent generations. It would be of paramount interest to compare the ideas about the family in these genealogies with the real structure of relationships, and it is most unfortunate that genealogies of this sort are so rare.

I have started my systematic study of eleventh- and twelfth-century genealogical literature in the kingdom of France. I shall begin by pointing out that this literature was particularly flourishing after 1150 and that it was almost exclusively developed in France's western provinces between Gascony and Flanders. This literature is itself worthy of consideration and interpretation in the light of cultural traditions, literary modes, educational systems, and has political and social realities. The two late twelfth-century documents that I propose to comment on here come from the northernmost part of the kingdom bordering on the Empire. My aim is to try to find in them some answer to the following questions: what sort of a picture would a man of the aristocracy have had of his kinship? What was the extent of his picture and how precise were the outlines? What memory would he have had of his ancestors? To how many individuals, living or dead, would he have felt himself bound by ties of blood or marriage? What respective place did the paternal and maternal blood relationship occupy? Finally, how was this mental picture of aristocratic society connected to the two facets, ideal and real, of consciousness of noble status on the one hand and seigneurial power on the other?

I owe my knowledge of the first text to Fernand Vercauteren, who has himself written an important article[1] on the subject. The author of the document is one Lambert who in 1152 began writing a chronicle which he continued until 1170. While composing this chronicle, known as the *Annales Cameracenses*, Lambert interpolated at the year of his birth, 1108, what he called the 'genealogy of his ancestors', *genealogia antecessorum parentum meorum*.[2] This is a valuable, not to say unique, piece of evidence because the table of kinship was not drawn up to order nor was it intended to glorify a patron or to illustrate a great lineage. It was composed by the author quite spontaneously for himself alone. True enough, he was an 'intellectual', educated in a monastery, careful to use fine words, and a member of the church. By profession he was a regular canon of Saint Aubert of Cambrai, and was consequently someone—and this undoubtedly distorts his vision of kith and kin—who lived apart from the family, adhering to another group. Above all he was a man who, because of his calling, had put himself in a position in which he could not participate in the ancestral patrimony and heritage. But even

---

[1] 'Une Parenté dans la France du nord aux XIe et XIIe siècles', *Le Moyen Age* LXIX (1963), pp. 223–45.
[2] MGH SS XVI, pp. 511–12.

though he was a priest he remained preoccupied with his rank and birth. The genealogy itself is what one might call naive: it is not the fruit of documentary research, but is a record of a purely personal memory of a man of about forty years old, based only, as he tells us himself, on oral evidence. Finally—and this is what confers such an exceptional value on the document—the family tree is not that of a great lord but of a member of the lesser aristocracy. Lambert came from a line of small Flemish knights. His paternal grandfather had been, at the end of the eleventh century, one of the bishop of Cambrai's household knights (*miles et casatus*). To analyse effectively this first piece of evidence, it is necessary to begin by summarizing the table of kinship, respecting scrupulously the order which Lambert himself followed in drawing it up.

Lambert begins by telling of his birth and his birthplace. He names his father and mother. He then quotes his ancestry and describes the paternal side first. To do so he goes back immediately, through his father and grandfather, to the latter's uncle, the only representative of this older generation known to the author who, in any case, was in his own opinion his original 'ancestor'. Having arrived at this point Lambert then descends by degrees; he names this man's sons and also mentions the eldest son's marriages. Then he passes to his own father's brothers and their spouses, but does not name their descendants with the exception of one, who was nearest to the common ancestor. He finally comes to his own brothers and sisters. Then he returns to the maternal branch, which is arranged in the same manner—the grandfather and his brothers, then his sisters; the grandmother, her brothers and their issue; then Lambert's uncles and aunts and their descendants. The table is arranged in this simple way. It should be immediately noticeable that, in the picture Lambert forms of his family, men always took precedence over women, elder over younger, and that kinship by marriage was as important as blood relationship. The coverage of the family tree reveals that the range of family association is a relatively limited one.

Although Lambert alludes on his mother's side alone to some distant branches of the family—'celebrated knights', 'men eminent because of their birth', 'some others who are very noble'—he gives specific mention to only 73 individuals. Only 35 are designated by name, 18 on his father's side and 17 on his mother's side. Of those named, men and women, 17 belong to his parent's generation, while in the earlier generation, the third, his recollection becomes vaguer and he remembers only 7 names. Further back into the past, in the fourth generation, only the oldest member of the paternal line and his wife escape oblivion. This is a man who appears in documents about the year 1050 and was thus active about sixty years before Lambert's birth and barely a century before the time when he was writing. We cannot fail to note how short was the memory of forebears.

Lambert speaks very little about relations of his own generation. This can partly be explained by the fact that he lived in a community of regular canons withdrawn from the world; moreover, as he clearly states, his intention was to talk of his 'ancestors'. On his father's side, he names but two men of his own generation—the eldest of his five brothers who was already dead, killed in a fight, and one other person, bearing the title 'knight' reinforced by the adjective *potens*. This man bore the name of the most distant ancestor (the knight was, in fact, the first descendant in the order of male primogeniture of the paternal grandfather, and we may infer that he held by inheritance the fief which had formerly been granted to the grandfather: in any case he was the actual head of the lineage). Thus no more than two men are named. F. Vercauteren was surprised by this limitation and put forward an hypothesis to account for it. If Lambert put so little emphasis on his contemporaries on his father's side, he says, it is because, at the time when he was writing, the family was in the process of rapid economic decline. It is indeed almost certain that Lambert's nine brothers and sisters, whose father and mother were themselves the last members of their families, were far from comfortably off. At any rate his choice of names on this side of his family is significant: he mentions only men, and men of war at that; he places the accent firmly on primogeniture. It was his understanding that the father's family was ordered as a 'house', a line of warriors, in which being the eldest counted for much.

On his mother's side, Lambert mentions by name seven individuals of his own generation, all of them more distantly related. The table on this side thus covers a wider field. These men were, it is true, almost all members of the church and this may have a deeper significance. There were three first cousins, one a monk of Mont-Saint-Eloi like Lambert himself, and the other two were, like himself, regular canons. In addition there are more distant cousins—connections of the maternal grandmother—also ecclesiastics but of higher degree, two abbots and an abbess. However, the last individual to be named was a layman, belonging to the military hierarchy; he was standard bearer to the count of Flanders and was also killed in battle. Here was another hero. Thus, in the description that Lambert gives of his own generation, his maternal relations were important because they were socially more prominent.

Among the former generations of his forebears, however, the paternal side was of greater significance with sixteen named individuals of whom twelve were men.

To begin with, there are his father, the father's three brothers and his grandfather. Lambert says nothing about the latter's brothers. Did he have any? Our difficulty is that, in spite of the detailed researches of F. Vercauteren, we do not possess a real and complete genealogical table that we can superimpose upon the tree drawn up from memory, which would reveal exactly the areas where his memory failed. The least we can do is to justify the exclusive presence of these five men by basing ourselves on what Lambert tells us of the family life. His grandfather lived at Néchin, on an estate which he acquired from his wife. In establishing himself there by a fortunate marriage he left his birthplace and thus broke the community of life he shared with his father and brothers, if he had ever had any. For Lambert, himself born at Néchin, the memory of his great-uncles and his grandfather was in this way effaced. His own memories were of the hearth, the house and the men who actually lived together.

In the second place, however, he also recollected from the previous generation, the most distant that he could remember, one of his grandfather's uncles. He calls him by his name and also by his *cognomen*, which was the name of a place and of another house, Wattrelos. For him, this surname had become a symbol of his very race and of its unity. This race and this man, probably by right of seniority, represented the main branch; this is why Lambert, mute about his own great-grandfather, mentions all the sons of this ancestor, with the exception of one whose name, so he says, for the moment escaped his memory.

In the third place, he enumerates four other men on the father's side of the tree. They belonged to three houses allied to the lineage of Wattrelos through women. They were the brothers, elder brothers and therefore heads of houses, of three wives—wives of two of Lambert's uncles whose line was not extinct (the eldest uncle died before his father and his children were no longer living, which is doubtless the reason why he is not mentioned in the lineage of his wife) and the wife of the eldest son of the earliest representative of the line. The fourth man was the son of the former. He represented, in fact, the most brilliant match which united Lambert's race with one in a higher plane of aristocratic society, the family of a castellan, the sires of Avesnes.

Lastly, on his father's side, Lambert mentions four women—his grandmother who brought with her into the patrimony of the line the landed property where Lambert was born, the wives of two of his uncles, and finally the wife of the most distant head of the house of Wattrelos. The only woman he mentions without giving her name is an aunt who died unmarried. On this side the women whose memory was preserved where those who shared in the increase in the family patrimony or who, though coming from other families, shared the household life or united it to other lineages.

On the mother's side remembrance is wider but less precise. There are only ten names in the ancestry, a higher proportion, up to one half, of whom are women. The grandfather and grandmother are named. The social standing of their respective brothers are described without the individuals being named. The memory here is of the splendour and the glory, a recollection of honour but not at all of domestic familiarity. Above all, the relationship on this side is not attached to an inheritance or a community of landownership. All the maternal uncles and aunts are named although he does not designate the aunts' husbands by name. He does not seek to find out the houses in which they entered. He gives the name of the married uncle's wife, but not of her brother, nor of the family she belonged to. The family memories of lineages of matrimonial alliances on that side do not seem to be retained as they are on the paternal side.

What are we to make of this analysis and detailed enumeration? In the first place, one fact is evident. In the family memory men occupy a clearly preponderant place; among the seventy-three individuals mentioned only nineteen are women. The proportion (thirty per cent) is slightly higher among the individuals mentioned by actual name (although it must be pointed out that all the women named were close relations with the exception of one who was abbess of a great monastery). In addition, it must be repeated, that in the order of enumeration men always appear before women and, in its general construction, the genealogical table places the *agnatio* in the front rank. Masculine preeminence is partly explained by Lambert's personal situation: he was himself a man and moreover a churchman. But it obviously reflects quite directly the influence of rules of succession which reserved the inheritance of real estate to men. These rules of succession, particularly those which applied to the fief (Lambert lived in a region and belonged to a social group where most lands were subject to feudal tenure), also explain the close attention he devotes to the order of births. He takes great care always to indicate and to place special emphasis on primogeniture, whether it is a matter of sons or daughters. It should, however, be pointed out that the preponderance of men is more clearly acknowledged to be on the father's side, where three quarters of the named individuals are male, whereas on the mother's side his memory gives equal place to men and women.

In the second place, on the father's side the remembrance is clearly arranged to fit the consciousness of a race and family feeling whose expression was the bearing of a patronymic surname, a *cognomen*. The name is that of a place, a piece of land; it was borne by both Lambert's grandfathers and it bound both of them to the ancestor most distant in time who, in the author's mind, was the recognized founder of his line. Had the two grandfathers, surnamed 'de Wattrelos', in fact kept ownership in this territory? It is probable that the maternal grandfather, whose eldest son, a knight, was afterwards mayor of Wattrelos, did so. But it is very unlikely that the paternal grandfather, a feudatory of the bishops of Cambrai, who set himself up on the hereditary estate of his wife where his son lived and his grandson was born, should have done likewise. But, even in this case, even though these men lived on a personal fief, installed on the landed property of their wife or of their mother, they henceforth (after the end of the eleventh century at latest) laid claim to the name of the ancestral land, in which, by the way, they no longer had any direct share. This name, already for them an abstract name, indicated that they belonged to a 'house', a 'line', a 'race', organized in a strictly agnatic way and governed by rules of primogeniture. The name of the founding house of the line was the cement binding the line together as well as the mainstay of the family remembrance. And if we ask ourselves why Lambert's recollections do not go back further than to an ancestor of the fourth generation, to a man who lived about 1050, would it be wrong to say that it was because, in this region, the mid-eleventh century was precisely the moment when, in the milieu of the *milites*, at that lower level of the aristocracy from which Lambert came, family groups formed themselves into lines? They did so by attaching themselves to the land, either on freeholdings or on indivisible fiefs which had become, in keeping with recent developments in feudal custom, definitely hereditary through primogeniture. It was in this way that they now organized themselves in 'houses' and simultaneously adopted the *cognomen*. Previously, before this chronological threshold, family relationships of the knighthood were probably arranged in a different way. There were no houses, therefore no family *cognomena*, and no 'races', but only groups of kinsfolk who congregated around the residence of a lord, an employer. Of such family networks, much less coherent, much more diffuse and changing as marriages took place, remembrance was quickly lost. The memory of ancestors only became definite at the time when the structure of relationship was modified and took on a clear-cut agnatic form centred on a landed 'household', an inheritance, a bundle of rights clearly defined and attached to a patrimony. On the evidence of Lambert de Wattrelos, therefore, we may place this fundamental transformation in this particular region and for this particular social class around the middle of the eleventh century. What we know about the history of the aristocracy and structure of the feudal system seems at first sight to contradict the hypothesis.

Moreover, it appears clear that on his mother's side Lambert's family tree is also arranged as a lineage: among the grandfather's sons, only one, the eldest, is married and it is he who owns the hereditary possessions of the line. Two of his brothers remained 'youths', by which we mean knights errant, bachelors without an establishment of their own, while the third entered the church. But in any event, in Lambert's view his mother's line occupied a somewhat different position, and this brings us to the consideration of a further point—the role of women and matrimonial alliances.

As I have already said, women on both sides of the ancestry did not carry the same weight nor had they the same significance, and not without reason. It is true that when she married, a wife entered the house of her husband and became incorporated in it. On his father's side Lambert considered his uncles' wives to have been annexed in this way. He calls them by name, but he also names either their father, or at any rate their elder brother, or the latter's son, whichever individual happened to be the head of the lineage at the time when the *Annales Cameracenses* was drawn up. This was because by their intervention a bond between the men of Lambert's family and the wives' families was effectively established. But a similarly close family bond was not so keenly felt by Lambert in relation to any of the women who had married into his mother's line. They had obviously been completely absorbed into that house, but that house was of lesser importance from the point of view of the line than that of the father of the genealogy. As for the daughters of the mother's family, they had, by their marriage, been totally removed from their family and for this reason the family remembrance did not even preserve the names of their husbands.

The support of the women introduced from outside into the lineage, however, appeared as a positive and influential relationship. According to the words of the *Annales Cameracenses* it was so from three particular points of view.

In the first place, the brothers of such women exercised a powerful influence over the destiny of their sisters' male children. He became their natural supporter and protector. We can find concrete illustrations of the privileges which the bond between nephew and maternal uncle in the kinship network created. Some historians of feudal society, including Marc Bloch himself, interpreted many of the themes of the literature of knighthood in this sense.[3] There is some direct testimony to corroborate these observations, which reveals clearly that relations of this sort developed without being thwarted by the patrilineal structure of kinship—indeed, quite the contrary. Let us take Lambert's own case. He bore the name of his mother's brother, while another maternal uncle, a churchman who became abbot of Mont-Saint-Eloi, watched over his career, took him into his own monastery, and then appointed him canon, while he had provided for the three sons of his other sisters in the same way. As for Lambert's elder brother, the only one who is mentioned by name and who was dedicated to a military calling, he seems to have followed one of his mother's brothers, himself a knight errant, into the adventurous life of the unmarried warriors known as the 'youths'.

A wife, when she was married, brought to her husband's house material goods, wealth of some kind coming from her own lineage which was intended to be added in the next generation to the part of her children's fortune which came from their father. A significant fact is that in the genealogical tree drawn up by Lambert, the only *cognomena* mentioned, apart from the *cognomen* of his own family and that of the brothers-in-law of his paternal uncles, commemorated the houses of his mother and his two grandmothers. In other words, they recalled parts of the inheritance, property brought into the family patrimony by these women. The maternal grandmother had a large number of brothers and sisters; she had brought no land to her husband, only movables, slaves (*servi et ancillae*), and her grandson still remembered this. On the other hand, the paternal grandmother, probably because she had no brothers, brought with her the fine estate of Néchin where her husband and her children lived and where her grandson was born. In this way, the family of Lambert of Wattrelos exemplifies a phenomenon that seems to me of great significance in the interaction of social relationships within the aristocracy of this epoch. A bride and bridegroom of very unequal wealth were often united by marriage and it seemed to have been quite a common occurrence for the wife to be wealthier than her husband. This was obviously the case for at least three men on Lambert's father's side—one of his uncles, the eldest son of his great uncle, and particularly his grandfather, that *miles casatus* who married the heiress of a rich

---

[3] Marc Bloch, *Feudal Society* (London, 1961), p. 137.

freeholding. And a similar inequality may be the reason why Lambert does not bother to mention his aunts' husbands by name.

This fact leads me to one last consideration: the woman usually brought as a contribution to the family she entered by marriage a good 'name', in other words, nobility. In Lambert's tree, the more honorific side of the family was quite clearly the mother's. Through his mother's father, and the latter's ten brothers who, as he constantly reminds us, were killed on the same day and in the same fight, the family history was worthy of an epic and became part of the *cantilènes* that the bards still sang when the *Annales* were written. But it was especially through his maternal grandmother that Lambert felt himself to be connected with what he calls the *nobilitas*. He employs the adjectives *nobilis*, *nobilior*, exclusively in relation to his maternal grandmother's family, and this was the family he was most proud of and freely spoke of and turned to when he wished to describe the most honourable kin, the most celebrated 'friends' of his own generation. Everything glorious, illustrious and noble emanated from this side of the family.

This raises the thorny problem of the relationship between nobility and knighthood in aristocratic awareness. At the time and in the region when the *Annales Cameracenses* were written, did there exist among the aristocracy a feeling of difference or of a separate identity between the titles *nobilis* and *miles*? At first sight a text like this one, with its revelations of mental attitudes towards kith and kin, might appear to sustain the hypotheses of the historians who consider that in the twelfth century the continuity of nobility in northern France was maintained through the female line. It is, after all, through his maternal grandmother's mother that Lambert is pleased to trace his links with the *nobiles* of Flanders. However, it is possible to reply immediately that if Lambert describes his grandmother as *nobilis*, it is simply because the word *miles* has no feminine form, and he must find another way to indicate that the lady was highly born. But there are, of course, other, more conclusive, arguments. This 'noble' grandmother had sons, heirs to the blood and thus to her nobility. Lambert would not have omitted to describe them also as nobles if such a title had in his view been any different to, or higher than, the title of knight. But he uses the word 'knight' alone to indicate their social rank, thus proving conclusively that already, by the third quarter of the twelfth century in this class of the aristocracy, the sole description to indicate the social superiority of a man was the term *miles*. Moreover, if the nobility had really been transmitted through the female line the family tree would certainly not have been presented by such an obviously masculine and patrilineal framework. In a masculine society of warriors and clergy, family ties, as well as the whole concept of the dignity of a race, the illustriousness of blood, had already acquired a strictly agnatic form, and the idea of nobility had, by the same token, been completely assimilated into the idea of knighthood. This is not to say that, obviously, in Canon Lambert's own opinion, his mother's relations did not shine with greater lustre. But it was the fortuitous consequence of social realities, the frequency of socially unequal marriages, the persistent effort of families to marry their sons into a higher social grade, the intervention of the great lords wishing to settle their domestic vassals, the 'bachelors' of their households, without too great cost to themselves, by providing them with wives who were either widows or wealthy daughters of a vassal. Lastly, there was the inability of aristocratic families with male children enjoying the privileges of successional customs to find husbands not too far down the social scale for their daughters even though they might, in the absence of brothers, be heiresses.

The second example I have chosen for the interpretation of the genealogical literature of northern France is a document of quite different proportions which, instead of fitting into one page of the *Monumenta Germaniae Historica*, as the account of Lambert of Wattrelos does, fills sixty of its pages. Moreover, we have here a work which, on the orders of a lord, was composed by a professional writer using as his evidence not solely what he himself, or members of his family, remembered but also a mass of documentation taken from archives and earlier genealogical writings as well as the testimony of tombs in the family burial place. As a source it is thus infinitely richer and, in addition, it touches innumerable side issues bearing on collective psychology which I must keep for use elsewhere. On the other hand its testimony is much less fresh and spontaneous, much less revealing of the mental viewpoint of one individual. This document upon which I have for so long been working, but am as yet far from having finished exploring, is the *Historia comitum Ghisnensium* written by the priest Lambert of Ardres at the very end of the twelfth century.[4] It is a historical work organized around the personality of Arnould of Ardres, the head of the household in which Lambert himself was employed, who was the eldest son and heir of the count of Guines, and already possessed, through his mother, of the lordship of Ardres. The book is constructed as a genealogy of Arnould, that is to say a castellan, a *sire*, a man belonging to an aristocratic level far above the lineage of the knights of Wattrelos. The contents are consequently concerned with quite another world, one in which the 'nobility' is infinitely more splendid. I am not able to reconstruct here the details of this genealogy, for it is much too complex. It would enormously expand the extent of this article were I to analyse it as minutely as I did the preceding one. I shall therefore limit myself to a few remarks which merely complement the deeper study I have just made of the family tree left by Lambert of Wattrelos.

First, the care taken by Lambert of Ardres when he described the dubbing of his hero lends force to our conviction that the title of knight possessed in this circle and at this time the greatest value, and that even a lord of the highest rank, aware of his connections through remote ancestors with the race of Charlemagne himself, acquired aditional glory by decking himself out in this way.

---

[4] MGH SS xxiv, edited by H. Heller.

Secondly, it is clear that the two tables of kinship, those of Lambert of Wattrelos and of Arnould of Ardres, present many similarities of construction. The castellan's kinship table is merely taken further. In it no less than two hundred individuals are named, and the remembrance reaches back to eight generations, and attempts to penetrate even further. The extension over time is partly due to the technical ability of the author, but mainly to the social rank of the family network, in which not only knightly lineages but also those of castellans, viscounts and counts are woven together. But this said, the recollections which the writing is intended to crystallize are deployed in much the same way: eighty-seven per cent of the named individuals belong to generations one, two, three and four and fifty per cent to generations one and two, but the generation contemporary with Arnould himself is not so fully represented as the one immediately preceding, which contains thirty-seven per cent of the named individuals.

Thirdly, there is the same preponderance of men. Among the individuals actually named, men are exactly twice as numerous as women. The father's side also has the same priority: the history begins with it and the remembrance of it goes back further, by a whole century. Indeed the remembrance goes so far back that in the end it gets lost. In order to continue, the genealogy has to rely on legend, fiction and myth. Having arrived, by passing from sons to their fathers, at the eighth generation, to the year 928, Lambert of Ardres finds it impossible to establish any reliable blood relationships. By a ploy which K. F. Werner has shown was currently used in those days by authors of princely genealogies,[5] Lambert then proceeds to invent an ancestor. At this point he introduces the man he calls *auctor ghisnensis nobilitatis et generis*, a person who seems to be quite mythical and whom he treats as a courtly hero. This *Sifridus* is described as a Scandinavian adventurer, but Lambert nonetheless connects him without any documentary basis to the most anciently known rulers of the country. This he does by an artifice which once more reveals a constant anxiety to represent the family as going back to its most distant origins, in a lineage, a regular succession of heirs who transmit the patrimony from one male to another. Finally, Lambert of Ardres makes this founding hero—and great importance must be attached to this—first the constructor of the castle of Guines, the fortress which was to become the source of the count's power and the physical seat of the line; and second, the seducer of one of the daughters of a neighbouring prince, the count of Flanders. This illicit union makes the man the root of this 'tree of Jesse' that becomes henceforth the *genealogia ghisnensium*. Through the bastard son the family power is legitimized, because his uncle, the new count of Flanders, adopts him as a godson, arms him as a knight (another mythical transfer into the past of the value accorded at the end of the twelfth century to dubbing), raises his lands to the status of county and finally grants it to him as a fief.[6]

[5] K. F. Werner, 'Untersuchungen zur Frühzeit der französischen Fürstentums', *Die Welt als Geschichte* (1960), pp. 116–18.
[6] H Gh, 7–12.

This is the image of their family origins that the counts of Guines had erected at the end of the twelfth century. For them their descent by blood began in the twenties of the tenth century through the union of their ancestor with the daughter of a prince, who was herself descended from the Carolingians through the female line. For them the origins of their lineage coincide exactly with the institution of an autonomous power based on a fortress, a title and the rights which attached to it, and which came to form henceforth the kernel of the family patrimony. If we now look in this context at the lineage of Arnould's mother, that of the lords of Ardres, who were not counts but merely castellans, we see—and in my opinion this is the essential difference—that the remembrance does not reach equally far into the past: the earliest ancestor quoted lived about 1030. Thus the remembrance of a line of blood relations in the family of counts went back to the first third of the tenth century but, in the castellan's family, only to the first third of the eleventh century. These two chronological dates seem to me worthy of attention.

But in any case, in both paternal and maternal branches the kinship seems, in its various ramifications and ancestral directions, to be strictly agnatic in structure. The author always takes care to present individuals of both sexes in the order of their birth and to distinguish the eldest from the others. The first reference in the *Historia* to a rule of succession through primogeniture is made in connection with the count who died in 1020. The genealogical arrangement according to both the Lamberts is thus similar, except for one particular characteristic in the kinship of Arnould. It seems that the two castles of Ardres and Guines which formed the heart of the ancestral patrimony on one occasion passed into the hands of another, less powerful, line, one in the third generation and the other in the fourth generation, through the extinction of the male heir and through the marriage of the heiress. This is another example of the unequal marriages which I have referred to above, and of the search for rich heiresses that, as I have show elsewhere,[7] played so large a part in the preoccupations and adventurous lives of the *juvenes* of the aristocracy of this region during the eleventh and twelfth centuries. It is from this circumstance that the discontinuities in the genealogical tables spring. Their cause is very significant. The author of the *Historia*, in tracing the father's line, does not pursue very far the ancestry of the heiress's lucky husband; he is probably reluctant to do so since remembrance did not preserve names of ancestors of such a mediocre upstart who had, by his marriage, abruptly brightened the state of his 'nobility'. He was a new man, and Lambert quickly abandons his line and returns to the wife and then develops his account of the ancestry of the lady, her father and the other men who had been owners of the property, castle, title, *cognomen*, in a nutshell, the true ancestors of the house.

This demonstrates again the role of the women. It is true that Lambert of Ardres alludes to marriages which connect his hero three times

[7] See above, chapter 7.

with Carolingian ancestors through the female line, always on the father's side. Here again the most resplendent memory is quite clearly established by the family connections on the mother's side. Nevertheless, the whole history and all the genealogical remembrances of the lord's house in which Lambert lived, and which his work aimed at stabilizing, were organized around the inheritance, the succession to a double title and a double lordship. The patrimony seemed indeed to have been the essential support for the recollection of the forefathers and of the family consciousness. Indeed, so essential was it that the author spreads the family net to include all those who, as contemporaries of his hero, might eventually claim to have some right to the fortune, including among them—a remarkable fact indeed—the bastards and the descendants of bastards of father, great-uncles and great-great-uncle. In the higher aristocracy, among the heads of principalities, the feeling of kinship bears every appearance of attaching itself to a house, to a castle, as the basis of power and of the association of individuals (*collègiale*) with which it was surrounded. This attachment could be reliably traced back to the ancestor, on whichever side it might be, who had built the fortress and by so doing laid the foundations of the power and the glory of his line. Beyond that point all remembrance was lost.

I want to conclude by drawing attention to a point which seems to me essential and by formulating in this connection a hypothesis for research. In this part of western Europe the genealogical recollections of men living at the end of the twelfth century seem, indeed, to reach back according to the rank which they held. At the level of the smaller knights, it goes back towards the mid-eleventh century, in castellan families to the region of the year 1000, in the families of counts as far as the beginning of the tenth century. These thresholds, beyond which the ancestral remembrance was lost, were the more remote the higher placed was the lineage in the political and social hierarchy. This need not surprise us. But it is interesting to observe that the three chronological points appear to be exactly those reached by the researches of present-day scholars trying to reconstruct the real blood relationships of families. Moreover, researches cannot reach any point earlier than these. Thus in the society of the Mâconnais, I have been able to uncover kinships in the lineages of knights up to the first half of the eleventh century, the lineages of castellans to the end of the tenth century, and the lineages of counts down to about 920.[8] Beyond these dates I have found it impossible to discover who was the father of the earliest known ancestor. The obstacle is not in the documentation which changes neither in nature nor quantity. We might therefore think this obstacle (which is similar to the one Lambert of Ardres overcame by inventing the adventurer Sifridus) resulted from the transformation of the very structure of kinship. Indications of patrilineal blood relationships disappear from written sources at the very point at which research, going

[8] G. Duby, *La Société aux XIe et XIIe siècles dans la région mâconnaise* (Paris, 1953), pp. 411ff.

back in time, steps across these chronological thresholds. This reflects a lessening in the importance of these blood relationships in the family consciousness at these dates. In the documents at our disposal it appears as if, at different levels in the aristocracy, the kinship structure was gradually transformed between the beginning of the tenth century and the mid-eleventh century. Before those dates there was no lineage, nor awareness of genealogy properly speaking, and no coherent remembrance of ancestors. A member of the aristocracy considered his family as, if I may use the phrase, a horizontal grouping, spread out in the present, with no precise or fixed limits, made up as much of *propinquii* as of *consanguinei*, of men and women whose bonds were as much the result of marriage alliances as of blood. What in his own eyes was important for success and wealth was not so much his 'ancestors' as those 'close to him' through whom he might approach the sources of power, such as king, duke or local leader, or whoever else was capable of distributing responsibilities, 'benefactions', honours. Everything came from his *senior*: he therefore attempted to attach himself more intimately to a household and to incorporate himself into it by means of alliances of all kinds. He was, in fact, so dependent on this 'patron', that his relations to him were more important than to his forebears. He was a beneficiary rather than an heir. At a later date an individual felt himself, on the contrary, to be part of a family group with a much more rigid structure, centred on agnatic consanguinity and its vertical links. He felt himself to be a member of a lineage, of a race whose inheritance was transmitted from father to son, in which the eldest son took over the direction of the household and whose history could be displayed in the form of a tree rooted in the person of the founding father from whom came all the power and glory of the race. The individual himself became a prince; he was aware of being an inheritor. I should add that in order to feel noble, and therefore to be noble, a man had first to lay claim to known ancestors and to be able to refer to a genealogy.

But, and this is the significant fact, at the three successive moments when, from the highest to the lowest levels of the aristocracy, the remembrance of ancestors in the minds of their own descendants was lost (as for us historians it had already been lost at the end of the twelfth century), important changes affecting political and legal conditions may well have occurred. A coincidence like this merits careful attention. In the kingdom of France the beginning of the tenth century was the exact moment when the counts won their autonomy from the great territorial princes and began henceforth to bestow freely their 'honour', now completely integrated into their patrimony, upon their eldest sons. Around the year one thousand it was the turn of the masters of castles to gain their independence and to appropriate the fortresses which until then they had commanded in the name of another. Finally, in the thirties of the eleventh century we can see two changes occurring. On the one hand, concessions of fiefs multiplied amongst the lesser aristocracy and feudal tenure assumed a more obviously hereditary character, being regularly handed down from father to son according to the rules of primogeniture. On the other hand, the actual position of the lesser aristocracy was crystallizing around privileges attached to a qualification, the title of 'knight' and the special functions which it possessed. At any event, the consciousness of genealogy appeared at the same moment as wealth and power came to count, castellan and knight in turn. It assumed a definitely patrimonial garb when rules of succession began to operate favouring sons at the expense of daughters, the elder brother at the expense of the younger and simultaneously made the paternal connections and the position of the eldest of the family more advantageous. In this respect I freely acknowledge Karl Schmid's conclusions which have so greatly illuminated my researches: 'The house of a noble became a noble house when it became the centre as well as the independent and lasting focus of a race.'[9] But we must stress this idea of independence and associate such a development closely with the degradation of the royal power, the dissemination of authority, and the gradual breakdown of the chain of command which we know as the feudal system. Did not the appearance of new structures of kinship in the aristocracy and the establishment of the feudal system progress at the same pace? There was in any case a close correlation between kinship forms and political forms, a genuinely organic link which expressed itself at the level of ideas through the notion of nobility. The sole aim of this article is to encourage a more profound study of the possibilities which flow from this idea.

[9] 'Zur Problematik von Familie, Sippe und Geschlecht, Haus und Dynastie, beim mittelalterlichen Adel. Vorfragen zum Thema "Adel und Herrschaft im Mittelalter" ', *Zeitschrift für die Geschichte des Oberrheins*, 105 (1957).

10

French genealogical literature

The eleventh and twelfth centuries

It is some years since I began to study the kinship patterns of the French aristocracy in the eleventh and twelfth centuries. These studies have led me to approach anew some central problems of feudal society, such as the relations of nobility and knighthood, the changes in lay estates and the distribution of the powers of command. I have always endeavoured to conduct my research in social history on more than one level—on what I may call the material plane into the biological and economic contributions to family fortunes, as well as on the plane of ideas and notions behind the ties of kinship. The principal tool for investigations of this kind is obviously the study of genealogies. But there are, of course, two sorts of genealogies, approximating to the two approaches I have referred to. There are, on the one hand—and one naturally thinks of them first—the genealogies built up in the course of time by historians and which they are still working on, or at least improving, by adding the references to consanguinity or intermarriage to be found in cartularies, charters or obituaries. For ever incomplete, and often unreliable, genealogies such as these nevertheless provide a concrete picture of the growth and wealth of the families concerned. Much rarer, however, and only coming to our notice when hitherto unknown documents are discovered, are genealogies of the other kind, by which I mean those drawn up in past times by contemporaries. The great value of these, of course, is the light they throw on family psychology and on the mental images lying behind the consciousness of a lineage. It is with reference to this latter kind of document that I should like to summarize the early results of my researches, conducted, I might add, with the invaluable assistance of Mlle de Guilhermier, a technical member of the National Centre of Scientific Research in Paris.

To begin with I have tried to extend to the kingdom of France the sort of enquiry that A. H. Hönger[1] and, more recently, Karl Hauch[2] have

[1] A. H. Hönger, 'Die Entwicklung der literarischen Darstellungsform der Genealogie im deutschen Mittelalter von den Karolinger Zeit bis zu Otto von Freising', *Mitteilungen der Zentralstelle für deutsche Personen- und Familiengeschichte* (1914).

[2] K. Hauck, 'Haus- und Sippengebundene Literatur mittelalterlichen Adelsgeschlechter', *Mitteilungen des Instituts für Österreichische Geschichte* (1954).

carried out for the Empire. This is, primarily, a listing of the sources. Interpreting the sources is, of course, a somewhat more delicate matter, but, taking inspiration from the works of K. F. Werner[3] and Karl Schmidt,[4] one of Gerd Tellenbach's pupils, all published in Germany, I propose to risk a few comments that, I hope, may open up some broad perspectives in political and cultural, as well as social, history.

I intend to confine myself to no more than a part of the literature about families, to genealogical writings in the narrow sense, that is, those that draw up tables of kinship. I shall therefore have to exclude three types of document some of which, although of very great interest for the history of family sentiment, seem to belong to a different category and to merit a separate study. I exclude in the first instance all those histories and chronicles which, like those by Adhemar of Chabannes in the eleventh century and Geoffrey of Vigeois in the twelfth, contain several outline genealogies but were not written primarily to illustrate a family lineage. Next I exclude all the *Vitae* which can be described as either hagiography, eulogy or funeral oration. Lastly, certain lists of counts, often connected with episcopal lists, such as the one to be found in the cartulary of Mâcon Cathedral, which contain no reference to consanguinity. After making this selection (and by so doing excluding all works composed in the eleventh and twelfth centuries in the circle of the dukes of Normandy and, in the eleventh and twelfth centuries, in the circle of the kings of France) there remain, not counting sequels, about twenty texts with dates before the end of the twelfth century. This is, of course, no more than the minute residue of an output that we know for certain, especially from references in other writings which have not disappeared, to have been very abundant. Of those still extant and which can actually be followed from a scholarly edition and in historiographic studies, the following is a brief list:

(a) First of all, unique in the mid-tenth century, we find the genealogy of Arnould the Great, count of Flanders, written by Vuitgerius between 951 and 959 and preserved at the abbey of Saint Bertin.
(b) For the period between the middle of the eleventh century and 1109 there are an account of the ancestry of Arnould the Younger, count of Flanders, drawn up in the monastery of Saint Peter at Mont Blandin; a genealogy of the counts of Vendôme, to be found inserted in the cartulary of Vendôme; and six genealogies of the counts of Anjou which came from Saint Aubin of Angers.
(c) Dating from the very last years of the eleventh century we find the first version of the genealogy of the counts of Boulogne and a fragment of the history of the counts of Anjou. From L. Halphen's critique of the latter, it is possible to attribute the authorship to Count Fulk Réchin.

---

[3] K. F. Werner, 'Untersuchungen zur Frühzeit des französischen Fürstentums, IX bis X. Jahrhundert', *Die Welt als Geschichte* (1960).
[4] K. Schmid, 'Zur Problematik von Familie, Sippe und Geschlecht, Haus und Dynastie beim mittelalterlichen Adel', *Zeitschrift für die Geschichte des Oberrheins*, 105 (1957).

(d) Between 1110 and 1130 two new genealogies of the counts of Flanders appear, one composed at Saint Bertin, and the other inserted by Lambert of Saint Omer into his *Liber Floridus*. There is also the first version to be preserved of the *Geste* of the counts of Anjou, which we owe to Thomas of Loches.

(e) The period around the year 1160 is particularly rich in sources of this kind. While the Flemish and Angevin genealogies were being extensively recast (as in the text known as the *Flandria generosa* and in the new versions of the *Gesta consulum andegavorum* by Breton of Amboise and John of Marmoutier), there appeared simultaneously, in addition to two new genealogical outlines composed at Saint Aubin of Angers, works devoted to the sires of Amboise, the counts of Angoulême and the counts of Nevers. In addition, writings by Wace and Benedict of Saint More date from this period. It is also noticeable that at this same moment authors of regional histories and chronicles gave greater attention to genealogical data (as can be seen, for example, in certain accounts emanating from the abbeys of Anchin in Artois and Foigny in the diocese of Laon).

(f) Lastly, the *Historia comitum Ghisnensium*, written by Lambert of Ardres in 1194, is without doubt the richest and most important of all writings of the kind.

This simple inventory prompts a few preliminary comments which I shall restrict to the more superficial aspects of the texts, and more particularly to their timing and locality.

1   At first sight, it appears as if the kind of literature with which we are concerned was restricted at this period to the northern and western parts of the kingdom of France. And if we leave out of account the duchy of Normandy whose historiography presents different characteristics and does not follow strictly genealogical forms, our documents seem to be mostly connected with the families of the counts of Flanders (where they are the earliest and always the most numerous) and of Anjou. It was not until after 1160 that they spread gradually from these two centres eastwards and southwards.

2   Before the last years of the twelfth century when Philip Augustus's chancellery became a workshop for genealogical writings, there were no genealogies in the strict sense of the term concerning the kings of France. The kind of writings we are interested in might be termed a literature of the nobility or, to adopt Karl Hauck's expression, *Adelsliteratur*. At any rate, it did not flourish at the outset except in the entourage of the very great families immediately below the royal family and belonging to lineages established on great regional principalities. But we can see also that, through a slow process of popularization, it began to permeate the lower ranks of aristocratic society of lesser political importance, such as the earldoms of Angoulême and Guines, or the lordships of Amboise and Ardres. The process was still very slow and cannot be absolutely vouched for before the mid-twelfth century. In this context we must leave out of account the genealogy of the counts of

Boulogne, even though it was drawn up about the year 1100, because two members of the family acquired titles more elevated than that of count, namely the dukedom of Lower Lorraine and the kingship of Jerusalem.

3   Viewed as a whole this evidence is undoubtedly bound up both with the history of political change and with that of literary expression, in other words of culture, and in this connection we can already, at this stage, formulate one or two hypotheses.

(a) First, it must be pointed out that the making of these genealogies often seems to have been prompted by the necessity of legitimizing some power or authority. This might explain the absence of royal genealogies, for the king did not need to proclaim his powers as these already had a legal basis because he was the chosen and anointed one. But in the north of the kingdom and in Anjou, the drawing up of documents of this kind was apparently intended to confirm claims to sovereignty or to prove the rights of heirs after contested successions. This was so in the case of the Flemish genealogies exalting the Carolingian ancestry of the counts composed during the years around 1100; of the account of the earldom of Vendôme justifying the acquisition of the principality by Geoffrey Martel, count of Anjou; and of the tables drawn up at Saint Aubin of Angers after the title of count of Anjou had recently passed to a collateral branch, which were intended to enhance its glory by proving that it was attached through illustrious marriages to the greatest princely houses of the period.

(b) We also have to explain the geographical significance of these documents with reference to the so far unwritten history of literary culture. First of all their place of origin bears evidence of the great activity, we might almost call it pre-eminence, during the eleventh and early twelfth century of certain literary centres with Carolingian roots, some located in the lower Loire, others in Lotharingia, of which the Flemish studios were but a western extension.

Another point worth noting is that this kind of literature became progressively more detailed during the period. The earliest texts are no more than lists; while the later ones take the form of narratives which, little by little, increase in content. Hönger's view that, in the Empire, these catalogues are but later summaries of earlier, fuller, texts, cannot apply to France. It is certain, for example, that the *Gestes* of the counts of Anjou and those of the lords of Amboise which form the *Historia comitum Ghisnensium*, were worked up from much shorter genealogical lists and we can see that in the course of the twelfth century the Flemish genealogies were constantly being added to. In this continuous process two principal stages can be glimpsed—one in the last decade of the eleventh century, and the other around 1160. It might appear worthwhile to place this periodization alongside the timetable established by historians of vernacular literature. However, we may obtain a deeper insight by analysing the actual content of the writings. By doing so we may be able to reconstitute the outline of the family structure and to isolate a model of kinship as it was imprinted upon the minds of contemporaries. Any subsequent changes will then be easier to observe.

These writings all derive from a royal prototype. The earliest to be preserved in the French kingdom, the genealogy of Arnould of Flanders dating from the middle of the tenth century, has two parts. First come funeral prayers, the eulogy of a prince in which his virtues are extolled; then, to show that the natural merits of the hero conform with the nobility of his origins, the author adds a real genealogy, the genealogy of the Carolingian kings. Thus, onto the *sancta prosapia domini Arnulfi*, which does not go further back than Count Baldwin I, Arnould's father's father, a *genealogia nobilissimum Francorum imperatorum et regum* is introduced, for no other reason than that Baldwin's wife, Judith, happened to be Charles the Bald's daughter. The catalogue of ancestors is borrowed quite uncritically from the *scriptoria* of Lotharingia.[5] This habit of annexing a royal tree as a family background for the holders of a principality became quite common; indeed we find it repeated right up to the thirteenth century throughout the society that we are examining, either by William of Malmesbury, by the genealogists of the count of Boulogne, at Foigny, or at Anchin. Thus the upper aristocracy adopted a type of kinship table that we can define as agnatic, a direct line of strictly male descent, with the title—as was the royal title—being transmitted from father to son. But, as it was often the case that the title or the tenure of power was actually acquired by a marriage—the counts of Flanders received their Carolingian blood in this way and so, also, much earlier did Charlemagne's own ancestors come by their Merovingian blood—the genealogical thread connecting with the past was cut and the less illustrious male line was abandoned, so that the thread could be retied through a female ancestor to another line going back from son to father into what was considered to be a more honourable ancestry. It is possible to presume that the attitudes of mind which preferred the memory of more illustrious forebears was borrowed from the royal family and displayed an acquisitiveness similar to the manner by which royal powers were usurped and new dynasties founded. If so, we can extend to France several conclusions about German lands arrived at by historians of the Freiburg school and especially Karl Schmid. According to them, the higher aristocracy began to organize itself into houses and lineages because the royal power was breaking down, and they did so in imitation of what had up to then been the only 'house', or race, or true genealogy known to them—that of the sovereign.

It is not hard to explain why ancestry was restricted to men; why only the male lineage was described; why, after the end of the eleventh century, primogeniture was ever more stridently insisted on; why rules of succession ever more obviously favoured the first born; and why the paternal ancestors were abandoned in favour of the maternal ones if the heritage came through the mother. We see all these things asserted by Fulk Réchin, and after him by other genealogists, including Otto Freis-

[5] PL CCIX, p. 929.

ing in Germany. The reason was simply that the genealogies were concerned, before all else, to show how 'honour' in its primitive, perhaps Carolingian, sense was transmitted. The text attributed to Count Fulk of Anjou begins: 'I, Fulk . . . have desired to write down how my ancestors came by their honour and held it until my own time, and how I myself have held it, by God's grace.'[6] The account of the exploits of the counts of Amboise emphasizes the progressive building up of the patrimony, and the contribution made to it by dowries of wives and inheritances. And the genealogy drawn up by Lambert of Ardres, whose master was heir to both earldom of Guines and lordship of Ardres, took the form of a history of these two estates and their gradual consolidation. Authors of these writings endeavoured to unearth the origin of hereditary ownership from the ever more distant past. This reinforces the hypothesis formulated by Gerd Tellenbach's students: it is precisely at the moment when the members of the higher aristocracy cease to owe their fortune to the temporary favours of a sovereign, or to hold both power and property as a revocable gift for life, and precisely at the moment when power comes to reside in a patrimony freely transmitted from father to son, that kinship groups, until then fluid and formless, rearrange themselves according to a strict pattern of lineage. There were no lineages or noble houses before honour became an indubitably hereditary characteristic. That, for great princes, did not occur before the ninth century, and for lords of lesser rank, not before the tenth century—and, I must add, in France, for mere knights, not before the eleventh century. It is for this reason that none of the texts we are considering bother to describe all relationships in detail, for they are interested only in those that concern the patrimony. In fact the significance of a family has become the significance of its heir.

However, between the genealogies written before the first decade of the twelfth century and the others, one notable difference exists about which I should like to say a few words. The earlier writings remain mere skeletons with little detail to clothe them, even if they were not, as was Fulk Réchin's account, merely catalogues. They are based on memories. Fulk explains this: he relies on his own recollections and on what he has heard from his uncle Geoffrey Martel. There is no sign of his having utilized tables previously drawn up in the monastery of Saint Aubin; he declares he knows nothing of the first counts of Anjou and is not even aware of where they are buried. On the other hand, the twelfth century genealogies were pushing out in every direction filling in each sequel with more detail, adding names of younger sons, daughters and ancestors who had not until then been mentioned, and developing parallel relationships. The family tree whose profile is outlined grows more branches and puts down deeper roots. Cultural, as well as social and political history must surely benefit from a close examination of this new growth, and there are three comments I should like to make on the subject.

[6] *Chroniques des comtes d'Anjou*, edited by L. Halphen and R. Poupardin (Paris, 1913), p. 232.

1   The new material is, first and foremost, evidence of an improvement in literary technique and of a growth of intellectual resources. The first genealogies had been drawn up in monasteries forming part of the estates of the great princely families. The abbeys of Saint Bertin and Saint Aubin of Anger were important because they belonged to the counts of Flanders and Anjou respectively and played the same part in the life of these principalities as did Fleury and Saint Denis in the principality of the Capets. These abbeys were burial places; and there were, it seems, close links between the first genealogical trees of the princes and the epitaphs for dead lords for we know through Raoul Glaber on the eve of the eleventh century that a major part of literary activity was devoted to the composition of epitaphs.[7] By the twelfth century we still find a few monks among the men whose writings I am discussing but, from then on, most of them were secular clergy, particularly domestic clergy, like Thomas of Loches who was chaplain to Fulk the Younger, and the priest Lambert who was a member of the household of the lords of Ardres. In the general movement towards secularizing cultural life, the principal workshops for literature of this kind were transferred from monasteries to the courts of princes. The genealogists could use the resources to be found there, such as the collections of archives and the libraries, as we know from writings about the counts of Guines at the end of the twelfth century. Men engaged in the composition of genealogical texts were educated in the skills of writing; some of them were also experienced in family lore, as is evidenced by the explanatory tree of the various degrees of kinship illustrating folios 126 and 127 of the MS of Lambert of Saint Omer's *Liber Floridus*, preserved in the Bibliothéque National in Paris. Writing to order, they reveal a new attitude towards their task. It is no longer so much a question of reciting a memory as of constructing a genuine history. Starting with a biography of their master, they then go on to try to put together a *vita* of each one of the personalities who finds a place in the lineage being described. For this purpose they assemble a documentation and make use of other texts. They use their skill to fill out the memories, to make them longer and more explicit. From their work we can see how the technique and sense of history gradually improved and how the twelfth century was really a crucial time for the history of history.

2   Genealogical literature as a form of court literature became increasingly secularized in comparison to its liturgical and monastic origins. It also came to be intimately bound up with a parallel development, that of literature written for the purpose of entertainment, which was being composed within the same circle: the group of knights in which, as I have shown elsewhere, the 'youths', the seekers after adventure, were then playing a supremely important cultural role. Here the relationship between genealogical writings of the twelfth century and epic tales is

---

[7] F. Vercauteren has shown that even in the twelfth century Ghislebert de Mons, whose taste for genealogies we know, also wrote epitaphs: 'Gislebert de Mons, auteur des épitaphes des comtes de Hainaut Baudouin IV et Baudouin V', *Bulletin de la Commission royale d'histoire* (1960).

significant. Our authors, indeed, used not only documents, but also drew extensively on the stories told in the halls of the lords. Thus, Thomas of Loches introduced into the narrative of the counts of Anjou legends surrounding the memories of Geoffrey Grisegonelle. As for Lambert of Ardres, he admitted drawing upon tales told to amuse the heir of the count of Guines by three of his friends, 'youths', who had a special talent for story telling. The admission of this link with legend and the world of fantasy is extremely important from two points of view. To begin with, it explains the leading place heroes occupy in the new genealogies where, henceforth, they form a gallery of exemplars, models of virtue. As I have said, in its deepest sense the genealogy traces the transmission of a title and a patrimony. But a secondary characteristic was added after 1110 when, under the influence of the epic narratives and with the introduction of more detailed biographies, genealogies began to sing the praises of a string of individuals. Ancestors thus acquired another aspect in the thoughts of their descendants. They not only passed on political power, but also bequeathed a legacy of glory, of 'honour'—this time using the modern sense of the word—which their heirs had to show themselves worthy of. By providing models to be emulated, the content of the literature fitted in perfectly with the competitive spirit which the circle of 'youths' attendant on princes bred, and helped to codify the peculiar ethic associated with it. Thus a study of these writings can make a useful contribution to the history of chivalry and of the emerging awareness of a separate class, the existence of which at this juncture was fundamental to the development of the whole notion of nobility.

3   However, the interpolation of legends and the adulteration of genealogies by material written to entertain, with the consequent escape into the world of imagination, were responsible for one of the most remarkable changes in genealogical writings in the twelfth century. This was the appearance of the mythical ancestor. As I have said, contemporary authors always endeavoured to push the lineage back ever further into the past. The first Flemish genealogy went back to Baldwin I, that is, to the last third of the ninth century, and to an individual who was perhaps not the first of his line to hold the rank of count, but who was certainly the first whose existence can be verified from documents that are still extant. Drawn up after 1110 the *genealogia bertiniana* pushes this tree back by another three generations and gives Baldwin I three more ancestors of whom scholars can find no trace. Similarly, in Anjou the genealogies of the twelfth century push back the first line of counts two generations earlier into the past than can be verified by facts. There was a new anxiety to link ancestral recollections to the great days of the Carolingian period, the supreme era of the *chansons de gestes*, by reaching back beyond the chronological threshold where memory of ancestors stopped (and thereby producing an insurmountable obstacle for today's scholars). This obviously encouraged domestic historiographers to turn towards mythical material. K. F. Werner has clearly proved this much, and the *Historia comitum Ghisnensium* provides supporting evidence. Lambert of Ardres,

having arrived in his researches at the year 928, produces as *auctor Ghisnensis nobilitatis et generis*, a character strangely resembling the heroes of the new romantic literature. He was an adventurer, a *tiro*, a 'youthful' vagabond, like many men who were, in the period when Lambert was writing, knights errant, companions of the count's heir, nobly born but poor foreigners. This young man, as described by Lambert, seduced the daughter of the count of Flanders, and the son born of the union was later invested with the earldom of Guines, and indeed legitimized his father's fortunate amatory adventure. Thus literary themes had their origin in the surroundings of the court and the social realities of the twelfth century which were the life those young aristocrats hoped for—adventure, errantry, pursuit of a rich heiress and a fruitful marriage that would lead to the possibility of taking over an establishment and a patrimony by which a new lineage could be founded. In short, the kind of profitable alliances that sometimes actually took place as we have already seen in real genealogies. This mixture of wishful thinking and fact was combined into what purported to be history, and the direction thus taken by genealogical literature in the twelfth century shows that it was largely a reflection of ideas current at that period. It might be a rewarding exercise to compare this evidence of writing with what is to be found in the *chansons de gestes* and romances written at the same time and in the same part of northern and western France. The history of tournaments and ceremonies of dubbing, unwritten up to the present, would surely also be highly relevant.

May I in conclusion underline what I believe is the principal contribution that writings on genealogy can make to the kind of social history that does not rely too heavily on economic conditions, but also takes cognizance of political structures and cultural life? It is that the gradual popularization of the royal example of a family lineage caused the fluid nobility of the ninth and tenth centuries to be changed into the rigid nobility of the feudal period. The way in which this change took place was through the strengthening of the consciousness of the family as an entity, primarily because it was attached to a hereditary title and patrimony, but also because it came in time to depend on the honourable estate of the ancestors and the example of their behaviour.

11

The origins of knighthood

Throughout western Europe in the thirteenth century the knighthood formed a clearly defined group at the very heart of the social structure. Its members had by then appropriated the qualities of superiority and excellence which were formerly associated with the concept of nobility and were the essence of its main cultural values. How did the prototype of the knight emerge, and how were the images and ideas formed that gave the group its cohesion and permitted it to play such a dominant role in society? How did the knighthood become aware of itself and mark out its own limits? And how was it that notions of nobility and chivalry finally merged? It is not possible today to give completely satisfactory answers to questions such as these, entwined as they are with some of the most difficult and complex problems presented by the history of medieval society. All we can do is to reflect a little on the subject, offer a few tentative suggestions and adumbrate some hypotheses based on recent enquiries into the nature of nobility and the notion of poverty. The remarks that follow, therefore, mainly concern France, because such personal knowledge of these problems as I have is based on a study of French material, and also because the developments which interest us appear now to have occurred earlier in the various parts of France than they did elsewhere.

Because our task is to define a distinctive social group, to discover how it took its place alongside other groups in society, and then to try to see how contemporaries came to regard its position and its characteristics, it may be useful to start with a study of the relevant terminology. In the thirteenth century a single Latin word, *miles*, was always used to express membership of the coherent group already formed by the knighthood. Exactly when and how was this term introduced? In my opinion an enquiry into this problem is the best way of tackling the origins of knighthood, provided that, to begin with at least, the enquiry is limited to the language of official documents, charters and entries. These texts are particularly revealing because they use a technical vocabulary much more specialized than the language used in literature and also because the function was to define differences of legal status by qualifying them and distinguishing them from each other. Such a vocabulary is obviously stylized, rigid, and highly resistant to change, and we must not therefore ignore the sometimes considerable delay with which it reflected modifications in an individual's condition. But there is no doubt that the moment when a particular word comes finally to be accepted as describing members of a new social category must be that point in time when the existence of such a group is generally recognized and absorbed into the collective consciousness to be passed on to succeeding generations as a part of the established structure of society.

1   To pinpoint the appearance and diffusion of the word *miles* as part of a specialized vocabulary, I shall in the first instance have to rely on my own researches, made nearly twenty years ago, into the archives of the region of Mâcon and, especially, into the cartularies of the abbey of Cluny. Indeed for this key period of history (the years around 1000) the material here available to us is exceptionally rich, and to the best of my knowledge no other enquiry into the vocabulary used to describe the aristocracy has been taken as far as I was able to take it on that occasion. Its results have, I believe, successfully survived the tests of criticism. I need, therefore, do no more than repeat briefly such facts as I have been able to establish which may all be found in my book on the society of the Mâcon region.[1]

(a) In the deeds which have been preserved the word *miles* appears quite precisely in the year 971.[2] In some deeds, in notices which relate to an agreement before a judicial assembly, to concessions of property in *precaria* lease, and to deeds of exchange, we see from that time on the term being gradually substituted for descriptions previously indicating either the subordinate status of vassals, such as *vassus* or *fidelis*, or the distinction of birth, such as *nobilis*. By 1032 the transference had been achieved: the term denoting a knight had replaced other expressions denoting social superiority. Henceforth we find it used in two ways—either individually, by men who displayed it as a personal title in the protocol at the beginning or end of charters, or collectively, to describe the particular rank of certain members of a court of justice or certain witnesses. But in both cases the word *miles* remained for many years unusual and was only irregularly used.

(b) About 1075 a further change took place. The use of the title, which had for some time been incorporated much more intimately into the name of the individuals who bore it, being inserted between their *nomen* and their *cognomen*,[3] suddenly appeared to spread. Scribes acquired the habit of applying it systematically to all men who occupied a certain position. Also, in the cartulary of the monastery of Paray-le-Monial, drawn up between 1080 and 1109, all persons not bearing the title can be seen to belong to social levels clearly separate from the lay aristocracy.

[1] G. Duby, *La Société aux XIe et XIIIe siècles dans la region mâconnaise* (Paris, 1953).
[2] C 1297.   [3] M 483 [1031–60].

(c) Finally, in the last years of the eleventh century, the formulae of the charters reveal three related changes. On the one hand, the very highest lords of the region (such as the sire of Beaujeu) began at that time personally to call themselves knights in the charters which were drawn up in their name.[4] On the other hand, in certain contexts the description comes henceforth to refer not so much to an individual's position as to that of an entire family unit.[5] This implies that the social distinction bestowed by the title was from then onwards considered to be the attribute of a family through whom it could be transmitted from one generation to the next. Lastly, from that time on, scribes, when drawing up lists of witnesses, took care to contrast two groups of laymen—on one side the knights, *milites*, and on the other the peasants, *rustici*.[6] These new uses of the word *miles* lead us to think that the movement set in motion in the region of Mâcon before 980 was completed by the latter end of the eleventh century. Indeed, after that date the language of legal documents treats the knighthood as a coherent body, compact, closely defined by family and hereditary characteristics, and a group which had attached itself to the higher echelons of the nobility and, as a consequence, had identified itself with the entire lay aristocracy.

2   Today it is possible to add to these remarks concerning one small province of central France some other observations, even though these are purely local in scope. Because their documentation is so much thinner, they are not therefore equally well founded or well defined.

(a) In the first instance I shall cite the results of some soundings made in the few available Provençal sources. Here the word *miles*, with its equivalent, *cavallarius*, seems not to have been adopted by those who drew up charters until after 1025; definitely later, therefore, than in the Mâconnais. But on the other hand, there is evidence of two much earlier phenomena—the formal contrast between knights and peasants in the lists of witnesses (the first known instance is in 1035[7]); and the assumption of the knightly description by the very greatest lords. In the preamble to an entry in the cartulary of Lérins in 1035, the mother of two 'princes' of Antibes describes one of them as a bishop and the other as a knight.[8] A. Lewis also finds west of the Rhine in about 975 an increasing number of references to knights in documents and, after 1020, castellans bearing the title of knight.[9]

(b) Detailed research undertaken by J. F. Lemarignier into the records of the first Capets in the Ile de France reveals the word *miles* coming into use in 1022–3, that is at the same time as our first indications proving the existence of independent castellanies; by 1060 the title is borne by castellans.[10]

---

[4] C 3726 [1096].   [5] C 3677 [1094], 3758 [1100], 3822 [1103–4].   [6] M 548 [1074–96].

[7] L. Moris and M. Blanc, *Cartulaire de l'abbaye de Lérins* (Paris, 1883–1906), 74.

[8] *Lérins*, 113.

[9] A. Lewis, 'La Féodalité dans le Toulousain et la France méridionale', *Annales du Midi* (1964).

[10] J.-F. Lemarignier, *Le Gouvernement royal aux premiers temps capétiens (987–1108)* (Paris, 1965), p. 133.

(c) At this point I should like to add to these scattered observations the results of some researches I am conducting at present into the family structure of the aristocracy and the genealogical writings of northern France. I shall extract from my results two comments shown by the sources that complement each other: first, that in Flemish areas, in the last thirty years of the twelfth century at the latest, some of the great magnates attached the highest value to their title of knight; secondly, that the family of a man like Lambert of Wattrelos, author of the *Annales Cameracenses*, who belonged to a very modest level of the aristocracy, had begun by the mid-eleventh century to arrange its lineage in accordance with the possession of knighthood.[11]

It is, of course, important to widen our investigations by extending the regional enquiries. For example, we expect a great deal to come from the researches at present being carried out by Philippe Wolff's students in the southern part of the kingdom of France, in the region of Toulouse and in Catalonia. But the present state of historical studies already allows us to observe changes taking place in the higher levels of lay society, or rather the modification of the views men held at that time of the aristocracy and its legal status. The direction and amplitude of these changes can also be described. Doubtless in some regions the movement was lengthy, since its beginnings can sometimes be placed in the 960s while it was often still continuing in the early twelfth century. It was perhaps most abrupt in the southernmost parts of France where the institution of kingship had weakened earlier. But the moment of decision everywhere could well have been the middle thirty years of the eleventh century. In any event, the common usage of a title, *miles*, and a general participation in the moral values and hereditary superiority that this title expressed, resulted in the different layers of the aristocracy merging and the higher ranks of the nobility, narrowly defined, mixing with other less exalted levels of society.

3   But if, without relinquishing our methods, we transfer our attention to other regions, across the frontiers of the French kingdom in a northerly and easterly direction, we see that the changes which occurred in the Mâconnais about the year 1100 did not reach Lotharingia and the Germanic provinces till another century had passed. Throughout the twelfth century, indeed, legal terminology continued in these countries clearly to distinguish a 'nobility' identified by true freedom, from a knighthood that was considered to be definitely subordinate. Léopold Génicot has shown, for example, that the concluding passages of the charters in the region of Namur, right up to the year 1200, carefully distinguished between witnesses who belonged to the *nobiles* and those who were mere *milites*. The scribes of the duchy of Guelderland did the same right up to 1225,[12] as did that excellent observer of legal realities, Ghislebert of Mons, in his chronicle of Hainault,[13] and a similar enact-

[11] See above, chapter 9.

[12] J. M. Van Winter, *Ministerialiteit en ridderschap in Géldre en Zutphen* (Groningen, 1962).

[13] MGH SS XXI, pp. 571, 578, 584.

ment of Philip of Swabia in 1207.[14] And other sources which are in no way legal show in a striking fashion that a clear distinction existed in people's minds between nobility and knighthood. Honorius Augustodunensis explains in his treatise, *De imagine mundi*, that after the deluge the human race was divided into three social categories, *liberi*, the sons of Shem, *milites*, the sons of Japhet, and *servi*, the sons of Ham.[15] He found an echo a few decades later in the Alsatian chronicle of 1163, quoted by Karl Bosl,[16] where we read that, after the conquest of Gaul, Julius Caesar so firmly established senators as *principes* and plain Roman citizens as *milites* that ever since then the knights, who were above country people but below nobles, helped to keep the peace.

This is what the use of certain words teaches us. We must now interpret what we have learnt by asking ourselves the following questions: why was it that in France at the end of the tenth century scribes began to prefer the word *miles* to other ways of indicating social status? Why was it that the values implied by this term came to be seen as the essence of what one might call class consciousness? Furthermore, why was this movement special to the kingdom of France (for without the relevant studies, of course, we cannot, at the moment fathom what was happening in either Italy, England or Christian Spain)? And lastly why did not the Empire, which had already accepted the idea of knighthood, also proceed to amalgamate it with the notion of nobility?

1   In attempting to answer the first question, our most reliable method is still to return to the word itself. This time, in looking for its significance at a moment when it was adopted by draughtsmen of charters who, at least in France, preferred it to other terms such as *fidelis*, or even *nobilis*, which were in the end abandoned, we must rely on a semantic approach rather than a merely statistical one. What significance or sentimental value, then, is implied by its earlier usage? In this connection it is necessary to turn our attention to another language which I have up to now, so far as France is concerned, purposely left on one side. This is the language of literature.

(a) There is no denying that at the end of the tenth century the word *miles* had a military significance, although we must not forget that, as there is no feminine form of the word, the term *nobilis* which it replaced in charters was retained to describe the wives and daughters of knights. But the word *miles* was used to indicate combatants, or to be more exact, combatants of a special kind, that is horsemen. The use Richer made of the word is evidence of this meaning: in his accounts of fights he contrasts *milites* with *pedites* and he uses the two expressions, *ordo militaris* and *ordo equestris*, indifferently to express the same social

---

[14] MGH, *Constitutiones* II, p. 17.

[15] PL CLXXII, col. 166.

[16] K. Bosl, 'Kasten, Stände, Klassen in Deutschland'. Colloquium organized by the Centre de Recherches sur la civilisation de l'Europe moderne de la Sorbonne in December 1966, *Problems of social stratification: castes, orders and classes*.

reality.[17] Even clearer evidence is to be found in the unquestioned interchangeability of the words *miles* and *caballarius*[18] in charters originating in the French Midi, for this is the region where vernacular words were freely incorporated into the language of the scribes, as is clearly shown by F.-L. Ganshof's researches into the vocabulary of feudalism. In the eleventh century the classical Latin word and the word in the Latinized dialect were, in Provence, Languedoc, Cerdagne and Catalonia, synonymous. Such an equivalence is a clear indication that the only warrior worthy of the name was, in the eyes of his contemporaries, one who rode a horse. Consequently, the success of the word *miles* must be related to the development of special military institutions whose study has been the object of the meeting at which we are now assembled. Acceptance of the word, indeed, reflects an awareness of three complementary facts. In the first place there was the technical fact, the superiority in combat of the horseman. In the second place there was the social fact, the connection between a nobleman's way of life and the use of the horse. This has as yet hardly been studied, but is obviously both intimate and ancient, and any enquiry into it would have to start in Germanic prehistory where chiefs and their horses were buried side by side, and include classical antiquity as well as the social significance of the equestrian art. And thirdly, there was the institutional fact—the restriction of arms-bearing to a small elite. In any event all three facts were very old-established by the year 1000. The most recently established, the third one, probably could already by seen in ninth-century texts, such as *Adnuntiatio Karoli* or the capitulary of Quierzy, in which the obligation to fight, apart from a time of invasion, was reserved to the enfeoffed vassals of princes.[19] But reasons other than recent changes in ways of fighting and the condition of warriors must be found for the appearance of the word for knight in charters about the year 1000.

(b) We can, it is true, easily perceive that the specialist military sense was probably not the most profound meaning with which the word *miles* was charged at that period. At this point I shall have to refer to A. Guilhiermoz's observations which have been somewhat neglected since Marc Bloch's studies. His *Essai sur l'origine de la noblesse en France au moyen-âge*, written in 1906, remains the seminal work for any enquiry of

---

[17] I, 5; I, 7; IV, 11, 18.

[18] *Cavallarius: Lérins* 29 [1038]; B. Guérard, *Cartulaire de Saint-Victor de Marseille* (Paris, 1857) 799 [1042], 438 [1058], 209 [1029]; *cavallaria*: Devic and Vaissette *Histoire du Languedoc* (Toulouse, 1872–1904) v 425 [1105]. The equivalence between the two words is made quite clear in an act of homage made by a castellan of Cerdagne at the end of the eleventh century, cited by A. Guilhiermoz, *Essai sur l'origine de la noblesse en France au moyen-âge* (Paris, 1906), p. 142, note 15.

[19] After the partition of Verdun the Capitulary of Meersen (MGH, *Capitularia* II, 71) authorized vassals to follow their lord if he lived in another kingdom, except in the case of invasion when all men bore an obligation to the *lant weri* in the kingdom where they lived. The Capitulary of Quierzy (MGH, *Capitularia* II, 358) allowed the heirs of a vassal to claim the honour; but if they preferred to live quietly on their lands, nothing was required of them, except again in the case of invasion. From this period, apart from mass levies *pro defensione patriae*, military life was one of service bound up with vassalage and reward.

this kind, mainly because of its critical apparatus and the enormous erudition upon which it is based. Documents quoted by Guilhiermoz lead us to believe that, from the earliest times and through usages which the middle ages inherited from later antiquity, the word *miles* signified, above all else, service. The official language of the later Empire had in fact used this term, its derivatives and metaphorical expressions arising from them, such as the image of the *cingulum militiae*, to describe public service in the household of the Emperor. Henceforth this meaning influenced all interpretations of certain passages in the Vulgate, and especially two of Saint Paul's sayings which all scribes of the year 1000 had read and reread: 'Arma militiae nostrae non carnalia sunt' (2 Corinthians X 4) and 'Labora sicut bonus miles Christi Jesu' (2 Timothy II 3). The semantic importance given to these words explains why the biographers of the Merovingian saints had spoken of their heroes as *milites Dei*. It explains why, in Gregory of Tours as in the Evangelists and the Acts of the Apostles, *miles* describes the subordinate auxiliaries of the public power charged with guarding prisoners and executing criminals. Finally, it explains why, when scholarship was reborn in Carolingian times, and Latin was purified by a return to its classical and palaeo-Christian origins and when, above all, the military life of a mounted man hired for reward against a background of vassalage gradually acquired the form of a specialized service, honourable and private, the term *miles* should often have been chosen. It was now preferred to words deriving from the common tongue, such as *vassus*, to describe either men bearing weapons and serving in the suite of their patron, or else—as is the case in the *De ordine palatii*—young aristocrats maintained in the king's household while serving their apprenticeship. There is no doubt that, for all writers in the year 1000 the expression *militare alicui* could mean nothing else except to serve in vassalage.

(c) But the very quality of subordination implied by the term 'knight' prevented writers, such as Flodoard, Abbon, Richer, Gerbert and Dudon of Saint Quentin, contemporaries of the earliest scribes of the Mâcon region who had used the word *miles* as a social epithet, from applying the vocabulary of the *militia* to all members of the lay aristocracy. Not one of them fails to draw a clear distinction between the nobles, whom they called *principes*, *proceres*, or *optimates*, and the general mass of knights.[20] They all represent the social structure as being on two levels: the 'princes', who were responsible for the public peace either through the delegation of royal powers or through the possession of a charisma given by God to a certain breed of men, were placed well above the auxiliaries who helped them fulfil their mission. These auxiliaries were men-at-arms, too, intimately concerned with the same activities, but they were in a subordinate and dependent position, maintained and rewarded by gifts. In short, the social structure revealed by literature at

[20] Flodoard, MGH SS III, p. 396. When Richer (*Histoires*, edited by R. Latouche, Paris, 1930) wished to indicate that a person was very far below the nobility of 'princes', he said he came *ex equestri ordine* (I, 5) or *de militari ordine* (IV, 11).

the end of the tenth century is the same as that which remained intact in Lotharingia and Germania until 1200. We can thus easily understand how the word *miles* had been able to replace in the vocabulary of the charters of the Mâcon region such words as *vassus* or *fidelis* which similarly evoked submission and service. But it merely adds to the difficulty of another problem lying at the very heart of the matter. How could it have gradually replaced the word *nobilis*, and how could it have been assumed as a title, before the end of the eleventh century, by men like the princes of Antibes, the castellans of the Ile de France and the sires of Beaujeu, who were all indisputably nobles?

2   For my part, I would like to associate this substitution with the gradual maturing of two phenomena, one relating to attitudes and ideas, and the other to public institutions. To understand the first of these phenomena properly, we must start by tracing the germination and gradual development of the theory of the *ordines*, that is, we have to revert to the Carolingian scene. From the moment when churchmen began to reflect on the respective vocations of the different groups in human society and the missions God had assigned to men whom he had placed in different earthly conditions, they discovered that in the world as they knew it there were two different ways to *militare*, two ways of serving God and cooperating for the common good: one was to bear arms and the other was to pray. In a letter to Pepin, dated 747, Pope Zachary, in carefully balanced phrases, contrasted bishops with princes, priests with *saeculares homines* and *Dei servi* with *bellatores*, all of whom were to cooperate in defending their country, each according to his own vocation.[21] Again, in 833, the pen of Agobard pointed to the contrast between two *ordines*, the 'military' and the *sacrum ministerium*.[22] These early writings, it is true, merely underline the deep division in Christian society between the service of God and the lay estate, which were intended, as was recalled by the canons of the Council of Meaux-Paris in 845–6, to be strictly separate.[23] Like all the metaphors portraying the entry into the penitent life of the monastery as the relinquishment of military trappings, these writings merely refer to the 'earthly hosts'—the way of serving in that age—as the carrying of the 'sensual fleshly arms' that Saint Paul speaks of. Meanwhile, in the *Miracles of Saint Bertin*, that is, at the end of the ninth century, another division appeared, this time a threefold one: it separated the *imbelle vulgus* from the *oratores* and *bellatores*,[24] and led quite naturally to the scheme suggested in the 1030s by the bishops of northern France, Gerald of Cambrai (*oratores, agricultores, pugnatores*),[25] and Adalbéron of Laon (*orare, pugnare, laborare*).[26] I should like to make three comments on the appearance and diffusion of this threefold scheme, representing as it

[21] *Codex Carolinus* 3 MGH, *Epistolae Karolini aevi* I, 480.
[22] MGH, *Epistolae Karolini aevi*, pp. 191–2.
[23] 'Non possunt simul Deo et saeculo militari'. MGH, *Capitularia* II, 407.
[24] MGH SS xv, 513.   [25] MGH SS vii, 485.
[26] *Carmen ad Rodbertum regem*, v. 298, edited by G. A. Hückel, 'Les poèmes satiriques d'Adalbéron', *Bib. Fac. des Lettres de l'Université de Paris* xiii (1901) 156.

did a significant turning point in the growth of the ideas from which the notion of knighthood was born.

(a) None of the men of letters of the ninth, tenth or eleventh centuries ever usd the word *miles* to designate the members of the *ordo* dedicated, as they saw it, by the divine plan to the warrior's life. Quite clearly they all felt that the narrowly military meaning of the word was over-shadowed by the notion of service. It was for this reason that scholars chose other words from classical Latin, such as *bellator*, *pugnator*, in which the call to battle was unequivocally expressed. Furthermore, when Adalbéron of Laon developed his ideas, it is clear that in his mind the contrast between 'warriors' and 'workers' took into account the separation between nobility and servitude.[27] To him those 'fighting men, protectors of churches, who defended all the people, great and small', were definitely not *milites*: they were *nobiles*, among whom king and emperor were foremost.

(b) The demarcation on the eve of the eleventh century of a third order of men charged with the special task of labouring, particularly on the land, seems to have come about by the growth of yet another, differing, concept of the social order. This concept is the one recently formulated by Karl Bosl in which the main distinction among God's people was that dividing 'powerful men' from 'poor men'.[28] According to this new scheme, made gradually more popular and more explicit in the course of the tenth century by changes in religious thought, the poor formed a separate class within the laity. They were, like the order of God's servants, unarmed and therefore vulnerable, and for this reason they claimed special protection. While this image was spreading, the bearing of weapons and specifically associated tasks were also coming to occupy a central place in the ideas by which the theory of the *ordines* was carried forward, because actual changes in military institutions made those who bore arms into a separate section of the laity. Thus, in time the social barrier was relocated. Formerly it lay between nobility and servitude, but now each day that passed separated the mass of 'poor men' more distinctly from those who wielded power. This time, those who had power were in truth the entire 'secular host'.

(c) A fundamental shift in ideas probably emerged from this transfer and a new attitude towards the military calling slowly dawned, espe-cially among intellectual leaders like the clergy, men of letters and draughtsmen of charters. For this reason, the life of Saint Geraud of Aurillac written in the 930s by Saint Odon, abbot of Cluny,[29] must be assigned a very special place among those documents which give us a glimpse of the movement of ideas by their use of forms of words. It should be noted that this important document comes from southern France,

---

[27] *Ibid.*, v. 279.

[28] K. Bosl, '*Potens* und *Pauper*. Begriffsgeschichtliche Studien zur gesellschaftlichen Differenzierung im frühem Mittelalter und zum "pauperismus" des Hochmittelalters', *Alteuropa und die moderne Gesellschaft. Festschrift für Otto Brunner* (Gottingen, 1963).

[29] The most recent study is in J. Fechter, *Cluny, Adel und Volk. Studien über das Verhältnis des Klosters zu den Ständen (910–1156)* (Stuttgart, 1966).

from a region which may well have been the melting pot of the new, anti-Carolingian attitudes that helped to create the forms of feudal society. As a source this work is crucial because it is the first of those *Lives* in which the hero was neither king nor prelate but a layman, a prince, an authentic representative of the *nobilitas*. But it is fundamental also because it seeks to show how a 'nobleman', a 'powerful man', can achieve holiness and become a *miles Christi* without laying down his arms. Saint Odon's intention is to portray lay holiness, or more precisely noble holiness; in effect he confers a spiritual value on the military life the specific task of the nobility. Thus he attempts to show that Saint Geraud had succeeded in uniting the exercise of power with the practice of humility especially in the care of the poor, that is, he combined the two special virtues of monasticism.[30] Odon of Cluny is especially clear about the tasks of the man who bore arms. (Note that he does not use the word *miles*, any more than do Adalbéron of Laon or Gerald of Cambrai, to describe the group of men who specialized in fighting. He reserves this word to indicate either, as we shall see, God's servant, or else a 'youth' (an armed follower of a lord). 'Licuit igitur laico homini in ordine pugnatorum posito gladium portare ut inerme vulgus velut innocuum pecus' (the people are both unarmed and innocent) 'a lupis, ut scriptum est, vespertinis defensaret. Et quos ecclesiastica causa subigere nequit, aut bellico aut vi judiciaria compesceret.'[31] Here, then, is a description of the two functions that justify in the strongest terms the carrying of arms—protection of the poor and pursuit of the church's enemies. Saint Odon takes this important idea up again in his *Collationes*,[32] when he declares that powerful men receive their sword from God, not in order to tarnish it, but to pursue those who oppose the church's authority by oppressing the poor.

This may well be the precise point at which the argument about power and poverty entered the theory of the *ordines*. In Aquitaine, where more than anywhere else the king's authority waned, a path to salvation and spiritual perfection was for the first time offered to the holders of secular arms, who would take up the mission which was properly speaking a royal one and assume, in the place of a sovereign henceforth incapable of performing the task, the defence of the church and its poor followers who together formed the two other orders of society. The opportunity was presented to the *bellatores* and obviously, therefore, in the first instance to the *optimates*, the princes and nobles. But of course they were not the only soldiers, and they could not fulfil the role assigned to them without the help of their natural auxiliaries, those specialists in war, the horsemen, to whom they distributed fiefs or who they maintained in their households. In fact the call went out to all who wielded the sword and both *principes* and *milites*, associated by the bonds of feudal vassalage to the holders of 'power' and the military life. By putting a value on the

[30] *Vita Geraldi,* in *Bibliotheca Cluniacensis,* edited by Don M. Marrier and A. Quercatenus (Paris, 1614), 84.
[31] *Ibid.,* 7.   [32] III, 24 in *Bibliotheca Cluniacensis,* 236. [*Ibid.,* 24]

latter, the development of religious thought in the tenth century helped to construct a framework on the spiritual plane within which the *nobilitas* and the *militia* could come together.

3   At this very moment, of course, two institutional changes were being prepared in Aquitaine, Provence and the kingdom of Burgundy. These changes came a little later in the northern part of the French kingdom (and excluded, of course, Lotharingia and the Germanic areas to the north and east). The changes began to be manifest between the end of the tenth century and the 1030s, that is at the exact moment when the word *miles* was substituted for the word *nobilis* in the charters of the Mâcon region, and this time they favoured the union of nobility and knighthood on the temporal rather than the spiritual plane.

(a) The first change concerned the distribution of the powers of command. This power, called in some areas the *ban*, lost its public character at that moment; individual lords appropriated it and used it to impose exactions for themselves in connection with their castellanies. But the manner in which this exploitation of authority was organized acknowledges and makes explicit the cleavage between *potentes* and *pauperes*. It was only the 'poor', that is the labourers, the peasants, the members of Adalbéron's and Gerald of Cambrai's third order, who were subject to the constraints and demands of the lords of the *ban*. The nobles were exempt, and this privilege served to define them in Adalbéron's poem:

> Sunt alii quales constringit nulla potestas
> Crimina si fugiunt quae regum sceptra coercit.[33]

But the *milites* were also all exempt. And it is exactly this exemption that characterizes their legal position and which raises the whole group into a coherent, clearly defined class, and which (at the exact moment when the old ideas about freedom and servitude began to be obliterated within the opposing class of labourers) necessitated the use of a title capable of defining exactly their new personal status. The appearance of the title in legal documents in fact reflects the establishment of precise limits to the aristocracy, encircling it and drawing its separate ranks together in order to share the same rights. The word *miles* was selected in preference to *nobilis* at that time because it was a substantive and probably also because it safeguarded the pedigree of ancient families who did not wish their honourable title to be impugned. But, I suspect, it was chosen mainly because the new line of demarcation was drawn at the bottom of the aristocratic pyramid, below those horsemen who were indeed its most lowly members, and who had to be clearly set apart from ordinary folk. It was thus that the social barrier, henceforth to prove so fundamental, was set up between *milites* and *rustici* and referred to in the concluding formulae of Provençal charters from the year 1035 and in the charters of the Mâcon area from about 1080.

(b) But the establishment of independent castellanies and the installation of the customs of the *ban* were closely bound up with another

---

[33] *Carmen ad Rodbertum regem* v. 282–3.

innovation—the setting up of the institutions of the peace of God. It is most certainly in the documents concerning those institutions,[34] the canons of the councils convened to establish them, that we can see the earliest and clearest statement of the differences between knights and peasants. I have tried to show elsewhere[35] that this movement, which began in the south of the kingdom of France in the provinces where the Carolingian influence was lightest and the collapse of royal power most cruelly felt, represented the church's own attempt to promote, with the help of princes but using what were essentially spiritual weapons, the defence of those poor men, described as peasants even at the first council of peace at Charroux in 989. The church's efforts were conducted within the mental climate created by the theory of the *ordines*, and it thereby helped considerably to crystallize the theory, while at the same time providing a justification for the establishment and redistribution of the exactions of the *ban*. From the year 990 onwards and throughout the whole of the eleventh century the activity of the *reformatio pacis*, the vocabulary of its orders, the decisions that upheld it, all its forms of words and the idealistic sentiments enshrined in them, helped in a positive way to reinforce the idea that the knighthood formed a coherent social group. Primarily this was because it enveloped the *militia* and all the *caballarii*[36] in a common aura of disapproval; because, for protective purposes, it organized a system of interdicts against the whole body; and because it put everyone in it, as Bishop Jordan of Limoges did in 1031, under the same curse.[37] But in a second phase, and without dissipating the churchmen's distrust and condemnation of the knights, the ideal propagated by the movement of peace combined with the models proposed a hundred years earlier by Odon of Cluny; this time the peace of God exalted the military function and associated it with the building of the kingdom of God. Through the prescriptions of what was known as the 'truce', through the movement of the peace culminating in the Crusade, the knighthood in France between 1030 and 1095 became even more clearly one of the paths of the *militia Dei*, fully equal to the priesthood and the monastic calling. In the process, it acquired so many spiritual values that soon members of the very highest nobility ceased to scorn the name of knight.

It is true that the aristocracy was not uniform all over France. And on this point, as I conclude, I shall return to the linguistic basis which has formed the backbone of my argument. I should like to point out some very significant changes affecting vocabulary during the last thirty years of the eleventh century. The word *nobilis* and its equivalents

[34] Brought together in L. Huberti, *Studien zur Rechtsgeschichte der Gottesfrieden und Landesfrieden* (Ansbach, 1892).

[35] See above, chapter 8.

[36] This term, contrasted with *villani*, is the one contained in the Latin text of the vows of peace taken at Verdun-sur-le-Doubs and afterwards at the instigation of the bishop of Beauvais, in the canons of the Council of Narbonne in 1054 (Huberti, *Studien* I, pp. 167, 320).

[37] Huberti, *Studien* I, p. 214.

reappear in the language of the French charters: this time, however, they are honorific epithets applied to the substantive *miles* in order to underline the particular splendour of some knight, whose ownership of a castle or control of a *ban* placed him at the summit of the local aristocracy.[38] With a similar attention to detail, and in order to underline the economic and social heterogeneity of knighthood, the authors of literary works about the year 1100 took good care to distinguish between *milites gregarii* and *milites primi* or *mediae nobilitatis*. However, and this is what really matters, by the end of the eleventh century the French aristocracy formed a single whole, despite diversity and the fact that it was divided into several ranks by the inequitable distribution of wealth and power. It identified itself with the old *ordo pugnatorum*, which had without any doubt become the *ordo militum*. It was united now by certain ceremonies, and in this connection the, up to now, unwritten history of the dubbing of knights must be mentioned, for it would probably reveal quite clearly how class consciousness had gradually hardened. These rituals clustered around the attributes of chivalry; they had their own liturgy devised by the church to consecrate the *miles Christi*, and a common ethic which gradually acquired the form originally sketched out by Odon of Cluny.

Lotharingia and the Germanic regions probably absorbed both the ethic and the ritual, together with everything else that infused the military calling with its new spiritual values. We can be sure of this when we note the importance that twelfth-century chroniclers in these areas accorded to the *militia* of the greatest princes.[39] Nevertheless, the propagators of the *reformatio pacis* did not cross the frontier separating the kingdom of France from the Empire, whose sovereign, as the bishop of Cambrai affirmed in 1025, was alone in retaining sufficient power to keep the peace by himself. In fact, royal power stood firm here and lost none of the full exercise of public authority. It was not much influenced by the twofold change—the establishment of the peace of God and the appearance of independent castellanies—through which the fusion of the values of chivalry and nobility had been accomplished in the French and Burgundian kingdoms. This was the principal reason why—and here, in conclusion, we may be allowed one hypothesis at least— throughout the twelfth century right up to the delayed victory of the cultural models transmitted by French courtliness, the survival of the old political structure, Carolingian and royal, retained in the German and Lotharingian provinces in a lively and realistic fashion the ancient distinction between knights and their princes, who had the exclusive right to liberty and were alone considered to be truly noble.

[38] In the Mâcon region, for instance. See C 3438 [about 1070].

[39] In this connection see the texts collected by Guilhiermoz, *Origine de la noblesse*, pp. 400–401, note 19.

12

The diffusion of cultural patterns in feudal society*

I begin with a very ordinary idea, a simple statement of a known fact. This is that the cultural patterns of the upper classes in society tend to become popularized, to spread and to move down, step by step, to the most deprived social groups. If we take the word 'culture' in its narrowest sense, beginning, that is, in the realm of literary or artistic creation, of religious knowledge, belief and attitudes, it is very easy to discern this phenomenon of popularization. Hence, I shall confine myself to illustrating this theme with two linked and parallel examples taken from fourteenth-century Europe.

As is well known, in the fourteenth century, at least in the towns, and owing to the propaganda of the mendicant orders, Christianity began to be, what it had not been for some centuries, a popular religion. Sermons in the popular tongue, theatrical representations of holy scenes, the singing of the *laudes*, gradually revealed to the laity some of the precepts of the Gospels and characteristics of Christ which had not hitherto reached them. Nor was it simply a question of the diffusion, outside the narrow confines of the clerical order, of certain texts and mental images. This period was one in which forms of piety which had previously been limited to a small number of churchmen and to monks and canons, were introduced to all strata of urban society—the practices of collective chant, solitary meditation and, at least for some of the laity, the regular reading of books of hours. During the same period, laymen, in family groups and fraternities, lower and lower down the social scale, appropriated forms of artistic expression formerly only found among a very restricted elite. In the early middle ages only kings had chapels, ornate tombs and relics. By the end of the fourteenth century, many bourgeois families had private altars, kept chaplains, had tombs and employed artists to decorate altar screens or sculpt funerary effigies. The middling nobility had relics mounted in their personal jewellery. Woodcuts allowed the minor aspects of the art of the upper aristocracy to be

* This chapter, which appeared in *Past & Present* 39 (April 1968), is translated by Professor R. H. Hilton.

diffused among the widest social strata. And there is the striking phenomenon whereby the architectural designs used to frame these pious images made woodcuts, which were essentially popular *objets d'art*, into something in the nature of private chapels for the poor. All this is obvious enough and fairly easy to study,[1] and there is no need to labour the point. I mention these preliminary considerations only in order to present three types of problem.

The first can be expressed as a simple question. Is the movement of popularization quite so straightforward? Did not the descending movement of popularization have a counterpart, a reverse trend? In other words, to what extent, in the middle ages, did aristocratic culture (using the word in its narrowest sense) accept values or forms arising from the lowest social strata? Here it is much more difficult to see just what was happening. On the one hand, the actual mechanics of creative cultural activity are hard to discern in the medieval period. On the other, although historians can detect some aspects of aristocratic culture, since these are embodied in forms which have lasted until our own times, we will always be ignorant of almost the whole of popular culture, and may not even be able to prove its existence. Only three facts, as far as I can see, stand out clearly.

1   In the course of the development of medieval Christianity, culture and propaganda were one: to educate was to convert. The centres of cultural creation were, of course, located in the upper levels of the social structure, among the members of the ecclesiastical *avant-garde*. But since they were consciously working towards a popular audience, they readily accepted some of the diffuse tendencies, general ideas and mental images which were widely spread in lower cultural levels. The intention was to harness these tendencies so that the propaganda, couched in familiar terms, could more easily reach the masses. In other words there was an acceptance of what we would call 'folklore'—and a 'folklore' which, but for this acceptance, would be quite unknown to us. This phenomenon is observable in the Merovingian period (as Le Goff has brilliantly shown),[2] no less than in the thirteenth and fourteenth centuries when the Dominicans and the Franciscans strove to make Christ a living reality in the towns.

2   Aristocratic culture also accepted elements of folklore in a natural and long-lasting fashion as a result of its own leaning towards 'populism'. This leaning is clearly seen, for example, in fifteenth-century princely circles, with their curiosity about shepherds and rustic entertainments. Moreover, some of the decorative motifs in their dwellings and some of the elements in courtly music, though stemming ultimately from aristocratic circles, ecclesiastical and lay, were derived immediately from lower social groups among which they had been simplified (and falsified) during the long period of popularization.

[1] G. Duby, *Fondements d'un nouvel humanisme* (Geneva, 1966).

[2] J. le Goff, 'Culture cléricale et traditions folkloriques dans le civilisation méroving-ienne', *Annales, economic, societé, civilisation* XXII (1967).

3   This leads me to a third fact. In penetrating downwards through successive social levels, the elements of aristocratic culture underwent changes which, generally speaking, as far as form and modes of expression are concerned, are marked by a simplification and progressive schematization. As to content, the characteristic tendency was towards a progressive disintegration of logical structure and a suffusion with emotionalism. These changes mark, for example, the religious art and piety of the fourteenth century, when Christianity was being popularized. But at the same time there seems to have been a rebound, a corresponding change in the elements of culture at the highest social levels. The Christianity of the topmost hierarchy of the church and of the princely courts in the fourteenth century was undoubtedly much enriched by a sensibility that was popular in origin and that found expression as artistic creation and devotional attitudes penetrated more deeply into the mass of the people. We have, therefore, to try to understand (and this could be a primary subject of research) how the popularization of aristocratic models—the essential, determining motive force in cultural history—in effect also established a two-way communication between the cultures of different social levels.

But the ramifications of the problem become much more complex as soon as one extends the enquiry into 'culture' in a broader sense. One sees immediately that the movement of popularization operates over a much wider area, and affects not only beliefs, knowledge, and religious attitudes, but also social consciousness as a whole, individual behaviour and ethical values, in brief the whole mode of life. Here also the phenomenon of popularization is seen in its twin aspects—the acceptance and imitation by lower social groups of models and attitudes put forward by the elites; and conversely, the adoption by the elites themselves of some of the values of the lower social orders. I propose to show this by analysing the 'culture' (in the wider meaning of the word as used by modern ethnologists) of the French aristocracy in the eleventh and twelfth centuries.

Here was a social group which became increasingly coherent and homogeneous by the gradual development of common attitudes, juridical rules, accepted manners, a morality, in short by the evolution of a common culture. This happened in spite of the fact that originally it consisted of nothing more than a number of separate but superimposed elements, and comprised a diverse variety of social types. Socially it ranged from dukes of Normandy to those knights of the Mâconnais that I have written about.[3] It included also all those soldiers of fortune and household knights who were in part emerging from the numerous servitors gathered around noble families in northwestern France. This common culture was essentially forged by the spread to the whole group of habits which at first had been the property of a very small elite only, of the uppermost stratum of the aristocracy, the ancient noble families. And this larger elite was the group which, around the year 1000, was itself

[3] G. Duby, *La Société dans la région mâconnaise aux XIe et XIIe siècles* (Paris, 1953).

achieving definition in the course of that political and social transformation that we know as the establishment of 'feudalism'.

Let us consider two aspects of what is certainly, within the feudal aristocracy, a movement of cultural popularization. First, there is a mental attitude which seems to me to be right at the heart of aristocratic culture. I refer to dynastic feeling, to the veneration of ancestors, to the sense of lineage—a collection of mental images which form the real core of the notion of *nobilitas*. Recent research has led me to the conclusion that the organization of the aristocratic family on the basis of lineage, as a 'house', with a genealogy based on strictly agnatic rules of filiation, strictly patrilineal, together with everything connected with this conception—such as matrimonial customs, primogeniture, patronymic surnames, and heraldic signs—was certainly much later than has generally been thought. In fact, it was a new structure which little by little established itself among the aristocracy until it became its primary principle of organization. But I must add that this establishment of a new structure of family relationships took place progressively from high to low, that is by a process of popularization. These new forms are first to be seen at the highest aristocratic level, that of the territorial princes and comital families in the middle of the tenth century; they appear among the castellan families about the year 1000, and among the ordinary knights some fifty years later.[4] A process of popularization is also to be seen taking place, but more slowly, in the case of certain attributes originally reserved for the highest ranks of the aristocracy. I am thinking, for instance, of the castle keep, which was thought of as the symbol of sovereign power and military and jurisdictional dominance. To begin with it was a royal monopoly, kept by the sovereign himself and by his agents and servants, his counts and bishops. Round about 1000 it became a more common possession, having fallen into the hands of certain private families, as yet small in number. Then, during the twelfth century, keeps became less rare; some passed to collateral branches of the great families, and by the end of the century ordinary knights also began to put up small keeps, to dig moats around their houses and to make their ancestral dwellings into strongholds, replicas in miniature of the great princely fortresses. By similar stages, the exercise of seigneurial power was generalized, as was the use of seals, and of titles. At the beginning of the eleventh century, the titles *dominus, messire* had been strictly reserved to the owners of castles, the holders of real power; by 1200 they were used to qualify all knights and to distir.guish them from other men.[5] Hence by the end of the twelfth century, one can define the aristocracy in France as that group of men which shared the prerogatives, titles and usages which two centuries earlier were the privilege of a few families, the *proceres* or *optimates*, and which two centuries earlier still had been the privilege of one single family, that of the king.

At the same time, an analysis of the culture of the feudal aristocracy is

---

[4] See above, chapters 9 and 10.   [5] Duby, *La Société mâconnaise*.

bound to recognize that one of its principal characteristics was developed by a reverse movement, beginning not at the top of the aristocratic class but at the bottom. Feudal aristocratic culture was organized around two main notions—that of nobility which spread downwards from the small elite of about the year 1000, and the notion of knighthood which undoubtedly spread upwards from a lower level of the aristocracy. In fact, although by the beginning of the eleventh century, *miles* was a title, it was then used only by adventurers and lords of middling wealth, who gravitated towards castles and princes; and *militare* meant not only 'to fight' but also 'to serve'. Gradually, as the values which the title implied—courage, military efficiency, and loyalty —spread and came to occupy for so long such an important place in the aristocratic ethos, so the use of the title itself penetrated into higher and higher social levels. By 1200, the development was complete: the greatest of princes, even kings, were proud to be knights, and the ceremony of the dubbing was one of the most important steps in their lives.[6] One thus arrives at another definition of the French aristocracy at the end of the twelfth century, as valid as that given above: it was that group which shared the virtues, the capacities and the specific duties of the *milites* of the year 1000, those young men, some of low social orgins, who then made up the household and retinue of the great.

The facts I have briefly analysed raise an important general question. What movements contribute to the formation of cultural patterns? Is it not often the case that, as here, these patterns derive from opposite extremes of a single social group? If we could determine this, we would have a much better understanding, as far as both mental imagery and collective psychology are concerned, of the mechanisms which lead gradually to the formation of what we may tentatively call a class.

Finally, I want to direct my last questions at the notion of cultural models, which were, in my view, very important factors in the cohesion of certain groups and in their separation from others. These models of behaviour, exemplary types of human achievement, were first put before the members of one particular social group, but very quickly reached other strata which were dominated by this group. The fascination exercised by these models was one of the most important motive forces in the popularization process which I have described. In western feudal society, there were very few models of this kind. Only two are clear and well defined and, what is more, strictly opposed to each other—the one oriented towards the sacred and the other towards the profane element in aristocratic culture. However, as I see it, they represent the two aspects of a single and doubtless primitive original. This is the royal model, relevant here in so far as the culture of the high middle ages culminates in the person of the sovereign as the image of God, and also in so far as the starting point of the whole process of popularization was the fascination exercised by the example of the

[6] See above, chapter 9 (for example, the place occupied in the *Historia comitum Ghisnensium* of Lambert of Ardres by the description of the initiation cermony of knighthood for Arnulf, son of the count of Guines); and chapter 11.

monarchy. So the two models are on the one hand the man of war, the knight, and on the other, the priest, the cleric. Of the knight I have no more to say. As regards the cleric, we must try to understand better how it was that, during the eleventh century, the clerical ideal progressed towards a different model, superior in the moral hierarchy and nearer to spiritual perfection, namely the monastic; and then how, after 1100, the retreat, whether voluntary or not, of the monastic institution, soon left in the fore the clerical type which specialized as much in intellectual activity as in prayer.

It will, of course, be necessary to analyse carefully the nature of these two models. But other questions also arise of relevance in any consideration of their powers of attraction. I will confine myself here to two aspects of the problem. First, and very important in my view, is the strength and permanence of the two models whose characteristics, already established by 1130, hardly changed in France during the succeeding two and half centuries. As an instance of this stability I quote an example discovered by my pupil, Jacques Paul,[7] who has made a study of the vocabulary and other semantic aspects of the eulogies composed c. 1260 by the Franciscan Salimbene, about men whom he had known. These characterizations, though written by a man with an acute and distinctive capacity for observation, show not the slightest trace of the influence of Franciscan spirituality, nor the least indication of any detachment from the two sociocultural models. All the laymen he has met who are worthy of respect are both 'handsome and noble', two absolutely complementary terms; they are *docti ad proelium*, courteous, generous and rich (poverty being, for this Franciscan, a defect), and they are deft in the composition of songs. In other words, what is praiseworthy about them corresponds exactly to the knightly model. On the other hand, all praiseworthy churchmen are for Salimbene both holy and learned, corresponding exactly to the clerical model. When it was, and under what influences, that these models disintegrated is something that remains to be investigated from the literature and iconography of the later middle ages.

As far as concerns their origins, their place of birth, and the factors involved in spreading their influence, I believe that attention could be most usefully concentrated, to begin with at any rate, on that social *milieu* which I believe to have been the point of crystallization of this collective imagery—the princely courts. It was around the prince and sustained by his gifts that the representatives of the two social elites were gathered—the religious and the lay. Within this grouping, within the princely court, did not the dynamic element come from the 'young', the *juvenes*? I have already discussed elsewhere[8] the importance in feudal society of this group of young men already famed for the accomplishment of their military or religious mission, already educated, already ceremonially initiated into adult society, but as yet neither established in their own households nor in religious benefices—men,

---

[7] 'L'éloge des personnes et l'idéal humaine au XIIIe siècle, d'après la chronique de Fra Salimbene', *Le Moyen Age* (1967).   [8] See above, chapter 7.

that is, who were still seeking their fortune. In my article I was only concerned with the young men of the knightly class. But I am convinced that one could easily find similar groups among the clerics with similar attitudes and frustrations.[9] This clerical and military group of the 'young men' in the prince's entourage was the focal point of rivalry and emulation. The concept of the prize to be gained in military or oratorical competition is fundamental here; and the types of perfection whose characteristics were determined by this emulation were natural points of reference which had to be accepted by all. The court, that is its most youthful members, seems to me to have been the fire in which the models were forged and where the exemplary figures of the perfect knight and the perfect clerk were created. In those competitions between young knights and young clerks, the contrasts between the two models were accentuated and fixed: at the end of the twelfth century, for example, one of the major themes of the games played in the ladies' quarters was, whom was it best to love, clerk or knight? At the same time, within these gatherings and as part of the permanent contact between clerk and knight, the two exemplary types occasionally came up against one another. It was in the princely courts, therefore, that, in the eleventh century, holiness gradually took on a colouring of heroism while later, during the twelfth century, the knights themselves were inclined to become *litterati*. The point of creation therefore was also the source of diffusion. At every stage along those routes which converged and crossed in princely courts, these models were propagated and may therefore properly be termed 'courtly', *courtois*. Eventually they reached the furthest limits of aristocratic society, and then spread even more widely among men who were not themselves noble but who were fascinated by the glamour of the court. On the one side was the prince (that is, the king) and near him, the clerk and the knight; on the other, the masses, admiring these models of human perfection: this was the general framework of feudal society. This too was the framework for the currents of popularization and the complex phenomena of borrowings and exchanges at all levels of what, for want of a better word, we may call culture.

[9] The young Abelard, for example, behaves in a manner very similar to that of a knight. He thought of his researches in philosophy as conquests; he opposed his masters in the same aggressive way as young knights opposed their *seniores* who were well established in their position and who stood in their way; and finally, Abelard, as is well known, was in no way indifferent to the flattery of fame or to success in love.

13

The transformation of the aristocracy

France at the beginning of the thirteenth century

It seems that the years before and after 1200 were a period in French society when the aristocracy was gradually transformed into a genuine nobility. As detailed studies of the nobility as a social class are still unwritten, I am forced to confine myself to a few reflections that may point the way to further research and indicate how wide the field of study is. I can do no more than pose a problem in social history as seen from a viewpoint in the early thirteenth century. But before the problem itself can be satisfactorily solved it must, of course, be related to contemporary economic conditions and ideas. In my efforts to do this I shall refer to a source of the utmost importance for the better understanding of a period through its collective psychological attitudes. The source I have in mind is contemporary literature.

1   Ever since the beginning of the eleventh century the aristocracy in France had formed a tightly circumscribed group, mainly because its members enjoyed the privilege of avoiding the seigneurial taxes with which all peasants, workers and those described as *laboratores* were burdened. Nevertheless, there were distinctions within this body of people this 'order' (or *ordo* to use the terminology of scholars in the years 1020–30). It was divided into two groups: on the one hand there was a small elite of men who in charters are given the title *dominus* which was the equivalent of the French word *sire*. These men held castles which gave them power to command, punish and exploit the peasants—a power known as the *ban*. On the other hand there were men in a subordinate position who were merely knights, or *milites*, whose social and economic position was much inferior and who were bound by feudal ties obliging them to serve the castellans, to fight for them, and to form their court.

2   What happened on the eve of the thirteenth century—more exactly sometime between 1180 and 1220 to 1230—was that the dividing line between these two ranks of the aristocracy seems to have vanished somewhat abruptly. Castellans and simple knights were no longer separate groups; they fused and became one.

The movement is revealed in several ways. To begin with there was the significance attributed by all, even the greatest lords, to admission into knighthood, to the ceremony of dubbing, and to the taking up of arms. The behaviour and attitudes of the aristocracy during this period can be observed in an extremely important text, *Historia comitum Ghisnensium* (the counts were lords in the north of the kingdom of France on the frontier between Flanders and the county of Boulogne). The history was written in Latin about the year 1195. The author tells the tale of the heir to the title who is the hero of the story. The apogee of his biography is the ceremony of dubbing, the moment when the young man, already a *dominus* and a castellan and soon to be called to succeed his father the count, becomes also a *miles*. This is the moment when, in his own eyes, he acquires a lustre and a distinction that was all-important to him. It was not enough for him to be merely *sire*: it was essential that he should be a knight as well.

There are other signs from the reverse of the medal, revealing that knights of lower degree were beginning to appropriate the distinctions until then reserved solely for owners of castles. In French charters it became customary about the year 1200 to apply the title *dominus* to all knights as a distinctive sign of their estate. This title was rendered into French by the word *messire*. Simultaneously even the humblest knights started to improve their dwellings. These were no more than farm-houses, although perhaps larger and richer than some others, but the knights wanted them to look like castles. They dug moats and raised turrets, thus turning them into what we might call fortified houses. We may well ask ourselves why they did so, for the reason was certainly not security. The times were relatively peaceful and there was no question of any danger. It was for the owners entirely a matter of prestige and of aping the castellans' way of life. At the same time quite humble knights also began to imitate members of the upper aristocracy by taking armor-ial bearings and by adopting successional customs until then practised only by those possessing castles. One such custom favoured the eldest son at the expense of his brothers when the inheritance was divided up. Lastly matrimonial segregation hitherto existing between the upper and the lower levels of the aristocracy was relaxed. Up till then castel-lans had only married among their own kind, but we now see that knights more often found wives for their sons among girls belonging to a hitherto superior social class. In short there was a closing, even a merging, of the ranks. What could have been the cause?

3   It is essential to take account of a political phenomenon occurring at the turn of the twelfth and thirteenth centuries: this was the growing strength of the great regional principalities. It was about this time that the king throughout most of France, and the dukes and counts in other regions (like Flanders, Provence, Savoy, Burgundy and Guienne) found that they were powerful enough to reduce the autonomy of the smaller local areas of power which had been established around each castle at the beginning of the eleventh century, the time of the feudal collapse. These regional princes were now able to crush the local *sires* and to humble them. Their agents claimed the superior power on their mas-

ters' behalf. This meant the power to raise troops for war, and the high justice, in other words all those rights which were formerly the basis of the prestige and wealth of the castellans. As for the lower manorial rights, such as the daily exploitation of the peasants and the policing of the villages, these too began to be fragmented and to pass piecemeal into the hands of simple knights, with the tacit consent of the princes in whose interest it was to break up the castellanies they found irksome. The knights in their dwellings, the fortified manor houses, appropriated judicial and fiscal powers which were very similar to, although more limited than, those which the lords of fortresses had until then monopolized.

In addition the king and the great princes did their best to acquire knights' homage and direct feudal service, to make the attachment a personal one and to sever the dependence of the knights upon the local castellan. In this way the institutions which had up to then kept the two groups of the aristocracy apart were destroyed, the political superiority of the castellans was dissolved, and the diffusion and popularity of the title *dominus*, the fortified manor house and armorial bearings, can be explained.

As for the other aspect of the transformation, the value placed upon the dignity and honour of knighthood by the castellans, the explanation is to be found in a much wider movement, spread over a longer period, but which intimately affected men's ideas and which came to its peak exactly at the time with which I am concerned. Ever since the early eleventh century the church in France had been perfecting a model of ethical behaviour presented to the entire aristocracy as the mission most likely to justify its social privileges and its military vocation. I use the word 'justify' intentionally, because the aim was to give the aristocracy a share in the divine plan for the salvation of the world. The model was the *miles Christi*, Christ's knight. He could be a knight such as the humblest member of the aristocracy was, but he was not to be in the service of a worldly master: he was to be in the service of the Lord himself, fighting for his cause. The ideal eventually resulted in the formation of the military religious orders, the *nova militia* celebrated by Saint Bernard. The greatest lords thus made it a point of honour to be knights as well as lords and to place themselves in the ranks of this *ordo*, the 'order' that little by little became a holy one, since sometime during the eleventh and twelfth centuries the church liturgy took over the ceremony of dubbing and converted it into a real sacrament.

The consciousness of class which gradually caused the French aristocracy to become a homogeneous group was thus crystallized around the knightly ideal, its ethic and the virtues of valour and loyalty. The social group which undoubtedly played a major role in the diffusion of this model of behaviour was obviously the one that I have written about elsewhere.[1] It was, of course, the group of men described in twelfth-century documents by the Latin word *juvenes*, 'youths'. They were

[1] See above, chapter 7.

already knights and adults, but were unmarried. Those among them who were the sons of *sires*, *domini*, who would later succeed their fathers when the time came, assumed leadership. But until then they were all no more than knights, and it was their endeavour to fulfil their role as far as they were able. It was probably to entertain these young men who thronged the courts of the princes that an important class of literature in the vernacular was written. The subject matter of these writings was epic and amatory and the heroes of the stories were all devoted to the practice of chivalry. Thus a French aristocracy of political equals, largely created about the year 1200 by the growth in princely power which eliminated the castellans, was also based on the recognition in men's minds of an image of the perfect knight. It finally found concrete actuality in the pursuit of the ideal of chivalry.

Several pieces written at the turn of the twelfth and thirteenth centuries for an aristocratic public show clear evidence of such cohesiveness. Firstly, there were some moralistic writings—we might almost call them sociological to the extent that they laid down an ethic fitted to the 'states of the world', the different classes of which society was formed. One of the oldest of these writings is the *Livre des Manières*, written about 1175 by Stephen of Fougères, former chaplain to Henry, a king of England but also, and primarily, a French prince—count of Anjou, duke of Normandy and Aquitaine. Stephen identified the entire aristocracy with the knighthood which, in his eyes, unmistakably formed a single group. It had a single economic purpose: God had placed the knight above labourers in order that they might support him. It had a single mission: the knight had to wield his sword to defend the weak and to perpetrate justice. Above all, it had a single moral purpose: the knight must follow the duties of the *miles Christi* which were to be brave, to be loyal and to submit to the church. If he performed these duties he was a 'man of honour' (*prud'homme*) and as such he was the equal of all other 'men of honour' who were his peers. It was, indeed, mainly the exercise of these virtues that bound the aristocracy into one homogeneous body. Finally, for Stephen of Fougères, who was himself a member of the group even though he belonged to the church, a knight's superiority was inborn, hereditary, the legacy of his forebears. The knighthood brought together men of breeding, 'gentlemen', as they were to be called in French a little later. It was in fact this latter characteristic which made them into a true nobility.

The theme was taken up and developed endlessly in other writings of a similar nature. As, for instance, in the treatise written by Robert of Blois in the mid-thirteenth century, the *Enseignement des princes*, where precepts of correct behaviour were set out for the instruction of nobles. They were to be courteous and to practise the Christian virtues, and it was this ethical rule which set them apart from others and also united them to each other. They were to revere all other 'men of honour' (*prud'hommes*) even if they should be poor, but, on the other hand, they were enjoined to despise all those men, known collectively and pejoratively as 'serfs', who did not belong to the knighthood. This was a class rule intended to segregate its members and to exclude non-members.

The same ideas can be traced in another kind of literature composed at the beginning of the thirteenth century; this was the romance with a realistic intention. The most interesting of these romances are those written by Jean Renart, as in them the nobility is presented as having a special life style, as being the product of a special sort of education. Furthermore, they reveal another, and fundamental, characteristic to which I should now like to draw the reader's attention. Although in the early thirteenth century the French nobility formed a united and homogeneous group, linked by a feeling of inborn and hereditary superiority and by a common respect for the ideals of chivalry, as a class it also felt itself to be threatened. In face of the threat it closed its ranks and strengthened the bonds which held it together.

At this period, indeed, the theme giving expression to this sentiment in literature was a common one. It was the theme of the *vilain* upstart. The word *villanus* originally meant peasant: thus he was a person belonging to a group in the heart of lay society which was the very antithesis of knighthood. But the word came to assume a pejorative meaning in a moral sense which it has kept in modern French. The person appearing in the romances and tales of about the year 1200 is a base-born man, badly educated, who has enriched himself and raised himself to economic equality with the knights; he is a man who has taken the knight's place, become a lord, usurped the noble's position, his house, his lands, and who apes his manners in a way that is both uncouth and unattractive. He is a grotesque and disreputable personage, but a very real one. The bad prince who tolerates such an intruder and encourages a non-noble to rise in the social scale, by admitting such a person into his counsel or army, also behaves in a scandalous way. He is denounced in moralistic literature, such as, for example, the *Enseignement des princes* quoted above, where great lords are exhorted to mistrust 'serfs', men who cannot be brave or loyal because they are not wellbred. The upstart's assault on social position provokes a defensive reaction. The reaction of a nobility dimly aware of impending economic difficulties is also one of anxiety. In fact there is much evidence of economic problems in the literature of the late twelfth and early thirteenth centuries, especially of the indebtedness of aristocratic families. In the eleventh and twelfth centuries it had been a chronic state, but what changed the situation was that about the year 1200 knights were no longer able to find anyone among their relations and friends, among lords, or even amongst other knights, who was prepared to lend them money. They were forced to apply to business men in the towns, in other words, to 'villeins'. They were hard put to it to repay their debts, too, so that after about the year 1200 they were forced to sell—a sign of an even more profound difficulty. First of all they had to sell their homage to a prince, receiving back the estate that their ancestors had owned in complete independence as a fief. Then they had to sell their lands, portions of their manors—and to whom did they sell? Naturally, to non-nobles who had ready money and who thus became through their purchases the horrible upstarts lampooned in the literature of the time.

Another sign of economic stress was the difficulty aristocratic families had in dubbing their sons when the time came, and in providing them with the arms of a knight, for it was a most costly ceremony needing the expenditure of much money. But if money was lacking, the family had to wait for an opportunity to arise. The son might be old enough to be a knight, but did not become one: he had to wait for something to turn up, a return of capital perhaps, or more often the generosity of a lord who would take over the expenses of the ceremony. The number of knights' sons without arms gradually increased. There were none in the Mâcon region of southern Burgundy before 1200, but by 1250 they formed more than half the aristocracy. The princes were not happy with this situation since the military service they expected of the nobility was likely to be reduced. In 1233 the count of Provence promulgated a statute which distinguished three categories of nobility —*domine*, *milites* and *filii militum*. The latter were enjoined to become knights under penalty of forfeiting the fiscal privileges they enjoyed.

And it was at this very moment that, in order to protect itself against a social decline engendered by its improverishment, the French aristocracy invented as a defensive reaction a particular title to describe the men who by birth could have been knighted, but who, lacking the wherewithal, had not yet been dubbed. The title—*armiger*, *écuyer*, in northern France: *domicellus*, *damoiseau* in southern France (esquire in English)—was really a courtesy title, since it expressed a social superiority which was not attached to a position or a function, like that of a knight, but was solely due to the accident of birth. Its adoption and diffusion on the eve of the thirteenth century marks more clearly than anything that from then on the aristocracy saw itself as the nobility—a caste closed to all who could not claim good breeding.

And what was the reason for this economic embarrassment? According to Marc Bloch the cause was to be sought in changes in the management of aristocratic estates, in the abandonment of direct exploitation of the land, in the lords' transformation into *rentiers* of the soil, at the same time as a depreciating currency was gradually reducing the value of rent from land. I do not myself think that this explanation is a valid one. Such research as I have made into rural economy leads me to believe that the direct exploitation of land had in fact never been given up and that the process of clearing the waste and creating vineyards, together with the general growth of agrarian productivity, had, on the contrary, resulted in an increase in rents from land at the beginning of the thirteenth century. Steadily rising profits from tithes, mills, taxes on change of ownership, the transfer of seigneurial rights, hitherto levied by castellans alone, into the hands of knights, and particularly the incidence of tallage, had all permitted members of the nobility to collect money incomes from the peasantry which were far larger than those in the hands of their ancestors.

In the last analysis the origin of the financial embarrassments of the aristocracy must be seen not as a diminution of their resources but as an increase in their expenses. To lead the life of a noble undoubtedly cost more, much more, in the thirteenth century than it had in the twelfth. Because of improvements in military equipment in particular (progress in material civilization was most rapid in the field of weapons), expenses connected with the ceremony of dubbing were heavier, but there was also the increased burden of the state. Here again we come across the phenomenon referred to earlier, the growth of the princely powers. Kings, dukes and counts were all more demanding than castellans had formerly been, and serving them cost more because within the framework of feudal institutions, apart from personal obligations, service at court and in combat, there were additional taxes. The lord of the fief demanded succession taxes and in some cases he also had to be given 'aid' in the form of money.

Lastly, and above all else, to be noble meant to be extravagant with money: there was an over-riding obligation to appear able to spend money and a noble was condemned to a life of luxury and expense under pain of losing face. I would even say that the tendency to prodigality at the beginning of the thirteenth century was something of a reaction against the social climbing of the newly rich. To set oneself above 'villeins' one had to outclass them by appearing more generous than they were. The literary evidence is quite clear on this point. What was it that set the knight apart from the upstart? The latter was careful over money, but the former was noble because he spent all he had, light-heartedly, and because he was deeply in debt. This attitude is certainly the cause of the dramatic disequilibrium between the noble's income from whatever source and his need for money. At all events it was the main cause of the growing number of poor 'gentlemen'.

What remedy did these men have in their predicament? The most reliable was to serve a prince. One other characteristic of the French nobility from the thirteenth century onwards was its gradual domestication. As a class it was drawn towards the king or the princes of the region who, because of their growing fiscal powers, had considerable monetary resources at their disposal. The nobles aimed to obtain paid employment to save them from their embarrassments. They served in the army, because after the end of the twelfth century military service tended to become mercenary and remunerated. They also served in administrative office, for the reconstruction of the state required many agents. But the knight began to find that he had competitors for these posts—men from nowhere, who were of humble birth, 'villeins', 'serfs', but efficient for all that. It was a vigorous adventurer of this kind whom Philip Augustus engaged to help him in war and who, abler than the knights, made the Château Gaillard his own. It was also a burgess of Paris whom Philip Augustus put in charge of his treasury and who understood more about the conduct of financial affairs than knights did.

This was scandalous and the literature of chivalry denounced the bad princes who surrounded themselves with these men of no account, mere clodhoppers, and who did not keep posts and pensions at court for the gentlemen who so badly needed them to buttress up their economic position. The ancient aristocracy fell back on the only superiority that remained to it, a moral and ethical superiority, a better way of life which became ever more exclusive.

This brings me to my final point. How successful was this aristocratic reaction? Did the nobility effectively succeed in keeping itself to itself? It certainly did not: on the contrary, it seems as if at the beginning of the thirteenth century the barriers that separated it from the lower classes were becoming less impervious. Professor Perroy has in recent years studied in some detail the aristocracy of a small area which he knows so well. This area is the county of Forez which lies west of Lyons. His researches have shown that, in the course of the thirteenth century, a great many noble families of the region became extinct and that the gaps were filled by newcomers, by servants of the great religious establishments or of the county, by burgesses enriched by business activities, or sometimes even by peasants who had assembled parcels of land.

This was renewal through social climbing. 'Villeins' had succeeded in breaching the barriers and infiltrating the nobility. How were they able to do this? It could happen through marriage, as when nobles frequently agreed to give their daughters to a non-noble suitor without a marriage settlement. Of course the husband would remain what he was, a Tony Lumpkin who could be despised. But sons born of these marriages inherited the good breeding of their mothers and were thus able to enter the society of well-born people.

But it could also happen through the agency of the prince who personified the state and whose part reappears in this context. The prince recruited 'villeins' to serve him because they were useful to him, because they had completed the studies, sometimes at Bologna, which improvements in administration had now made essential. But, in order that their services in the positions of power in which they were established should be more efficacious, they had to be able to wield a sword. Therefore the prince, transgressing by means of his own powers the custom which reserved the privilege of dubbing for the sons of the nobility, gave his own servants the arms of knights. Thus he ennobled them through the status which he conferred on them. for, in the heart of the aristocratic structure, the idea of nobility was still enshrined, as it had been in the twelfth and the eleventh centuries, in one pre-eminent, dazzling, glorious, ennobling value, the knighthood.

14

The manor and the peasant economy

The southern Alps in 1338

The study of rural economy in France throughout most of the middle ages is inhibited by the lack of quantitative material. The administrators of the most important manors that were managed in a methodical way very seldom had recourse to writing, and in the few documents which have survived quantitative entries are rare. Officials occasionally went so far as to list the tenants of the manor and to register their dues: 'this or that man on such and such a holding must render on such and such a date so much money or so many measures of grain, etc.' These lists, censuses or custumals were drawn up only in imitation of Carolingian models, and for use in courts of law should there be disputes over services due. It is also possible that a monastic community would think it worthwhile to record the ration allocated to each member of the household—a rudimentary statement of the annual needs of food intended to facilitate the task of distribution. But documents like these are practically the only references found in the records. Prices are hardly ever mentioned, apart from an occasional allusion in a chronicle to unusual prices in times of exceptional abundance or scarcity, or else in a recognizance for debt where a valuation in money and some other standard of value is given: 'I owe this or that sum in cash, or so many cows.' There are no managerial inventories or balance sheets, no attempts to set off the needs of a manor against its resources. Historians are at a loss without such a scaffolding of figures, and this is probably one of the reasons why the history of France's rural economy is so backward when compared to the history of its towns and trade, or to the legal history of the manor.

It should be noted, however, that the indifference to numerical precision in rural circles in France began to dissipate by the second half of the thirteenth century, although, of course, this was well after the use of figures, written accounts and inventories had been adopted by the administrators of the great ecclesiastical estates in England. The change in outlook seems to be of prime importance: the new need to reckon values, to measure profit and loss and the desire to look ahead in fact implies a different attitude towards economic reality, and we might suppose that such an attitude would to some extent have changed the relations between lords and peasants and even the situation of the lord himself in the flow of trade. It is also to be hoped that a detailed and methodical exploration of manorial archives might reveal the stages by which this technique advanced as well as its links with improvements in princely finances and the growing body of professional administrators with accomplishments in writing and accounting. My own research is limited to southeastern France and is based on soundings that are still incomplete. This much, however, is certain. Before the fourteenth century I know of only one document with a certain amount of convergent numerical evidence about the administration of a large-scale agricultural enterprise. It is contained in one of the cartularies of the abbey of Cluny and was drawn up about 1155. The title itself is very revealing—*Constitutio expensae*. It is a list of expenses and a plan for the management of the community's wealth with the aim of provisioning the large number of consumers brought together at that time by the monastery. For this purpose it presents, still only briefly and approximately, on the one hand an estimate of requirements in terms of food and on the other an inventory, manor by manor, of the resources to be drawn upon. This document projects a unique and vivid beam of light on the mid-twelfth century. It comes, of course, from Cluny, a very progressive community. Moreover, the enquiry was undertaken on the initiative of Henry of Blois, bishop of Winchester, the king of England's brother and a magnate in his own country, who was at that time a refugee in Burgundy; and it seems that the influence of English administrative methods was fundamental.[1] In fact, the new practices which prepared the change of attitude were not to show themselves elsewhere for another century.

It was only at this later period that we find the first account books, drawn up for the lord by responsible financiers, such as the exceptional little register known as the *Count of Provence's Victualling Book (Rationnaire)* which contains statements of manorial receipts and expenses for the years 1249–54.[2] But the pages are no more than a jumbled summary of dues and disbursements and the details concerning the rural estates of the lords are inextricably mixed up with information about his other revenues and expenses. There are other texts relating to the proper running of religious communities sponsored by the popes in the thirteenth century. In the autumn of every year daughter houses were inspected. The original intention was to control their moral conduct, but the visitors rightly felt that correct morals depended on material conditions and gradually gave more and more attention to the state of the buildings, the stocks of food, and eventually to the volume of indebtedness, because it was exactly at this period that borrowing was increasing and becoming ever more burdensome. In the end the primary

[1] G. Duby, 'Un inventaire des profits de la seigneurie clunisienne à la mort de Pierre le Vénérable', *Studia Anselmiana* XL (1957), *Petrus Venerabilis*, pp. 128–40.

[2] Departmental Archives of the Bouches-du-Rhône, B 1500.

task of these inquests became the drawing up of a statement of profit and loss.[3]

It is true that the change took place only slowly. To my knowledge the first really explicit document from which it is possible to study the management of a rural manor in the southeast of France in detail (and it is still quite unique for its period) dates from 1338. This document is a register of the visits to dependent houses of the Order of Saint John of Jerusalem attached to the Grand Priory of Saint Gilles. It was part of an official report of a long tour made by two dignitaries, at the end of the summer after the harvest was gathered in and the barns filled, of about thirty-two commanderies and the hundred or so rural manors spread out east of the Rhône around the Great Charterhouses at Carmargue and Embrun near Nice. The exceptionally detailed inquest exactly followed the injunctions of Pope Benedict XII who wanted to reform the religious orders. As a Cistercian he was, to begin with—in 1335—specially interested in the Order of Cîteaux, requiring in particular an exact valuation of the wealth and resources of each of its abbeys in order to fix the number of monks they could decently maintain. In the following year he extended his interest first to the Benedictines and then to other communities. At the end of 1337 and in 1338, therefore, inventories were put in hand everywhere; many are still preserved in the muniment rooms of the establishments concerned.[4] These documents presenting a simultaneous description of income and expenses for a large number of religious communities make possible a comparative study of regional economies across the length and breadth of Christianity. It would indeed be worthwhile if a team of researchers were to set to work to locate them and to explore their contents.

Let us return, however, to the register preserved in the collection of the Order of Malta in the departmental archives of the Bouches-du-Rhône in the shape of three hundred and six folios of elegant writing.[5] Drawn up house by house, the inventory describes little more than their mater-

---

[3] Visits to priories in the Order of Cluny had been instituted at the beginning of the thirteenth century; they then became widespread throughout the monastic world at the instigation of the popes, in particular Gregory IX and Innocent IV. G. de Valous, *Le temporel et la situation financière des établissements de l'Ordre de Cluny du XIIe au XIVe siècle* (Paris, 1935), pp. 95ff; J. Berthold-Mahn, *L'Ordre cistercien et son gouvernement des origines au milieu du XIIIe siècle* (Paris, 1948). The proceedings of the visits to the Cluniac houses are, however, very laconic. A. Bruel, 'Visite des monastères de l'Ordre de Cluny de la province d'Auvergne, 1294', *Bibliothèque de l'Ecole des Chartes* (Paris) LII; U. Chevalier, 'Visites de la province de Lyon de l'ordre de Cluny', P.

[4] The muniment rooms of Normandy have already been explored and used. L. Delisle, 'Enquêtes sur la fortune des établissements de l'Ordre de Saint-Benoît en 1338', *Notices et extraits des manuscrits de la Bibliothèque Nationale* XXXIX (Paris, 1916); Dom J. Laporte, 'L'état des biens de l'abbaye de Jumièges en 1338', *Annales de Normandie* (1959). The inquest into the English Hospitallers, which is much less detailed than the one examined here, was published by the Camden Society in 1857 (*The Knight Hospitallers in England: the Report of Prior Philip de Thame to the Grand Master Elyan de Villanova for AD 1338*, L. B. Larking, introduction by J. M. Kemble).

[5] H (DM) 156. The substance of the document was reported to the Congress of Learned Societies of Toulouse in 1953 by J. A. Durbec, who has been kind enough to put the text of his communication at my disposal.

14.1 Provençal commanderies of the Hospitallers of St John

ial conditions: it is an account of the domestic economy organized according to the interests of those carrying out the inquest, which are in themselves revealing.

In every commandery they begin by listing the lords whose needs came before anything else. The household in its entirety was not included, only the 'family' of masters in strict order of precedence: first came the preceptor, then the chaplains, the knight brothers, the plain serjeants and finally the *donats*, those laymen who were granted a peaceful retreat within the religious fraternity. Next the inquest describes the assets, the property and the resources, also in order of degree. In the first place it records the 'demesne', the land in direct cultivation; then it proceeds to record the arable, the main possession which comes before vineyards, meadows, woods and pasture. Only afterwards come rents and dues of all sorts classified according to their kind. To begin with are all those things that could be eaten and drunk, followed by money in cash. The last section gives details of expenses: here again we see the produce of the earth, the rations of grain and wine distributed in the household to lords and servitors, coming before payments in money, purchases of 'goods', debts or the contribution each house made to the expenses of the Order.

The surveyors had everything drawn up for each house so that the various elements of the inventory could be compared as between one house and another. Everything was very carefully counted. The price of each item was noted so that harvest and consumption could be valued as a whole in money terms. Finally all money values were converted into a comparable unit, a currency in which one 'tournois was worth 16 deniers',[6] and their arithmetic is almost faultless. The accuracy and the competence of men used to handling figures are especially helpful in the interpretation of this huge text. Two points, it is true, are not made entirely clear. The first concerns the quantities of grain and wine. The visitors, familiar as they were with the workings of money exchange, converted money values to common units of account[7] but never reduced to common units the measures which they used thereby to evaluate harvests, product of dues in kind and household consumption and the level of prices. Did they consider that the variations between one place and another were negligible? This is unlikely, since, when the metric system was introduced centuries later the value of the *setier*, the *charge* and the *millerolle*, were quite different at Aix, Orange, Tarascon and Draguignan,[8] and these disparities had obviously existed in the fourteenth century. The fact is that the surveyors spared themselves the

---

[6] Fo 5v. The florin is worth 15 sous 6 deniers of this money of account (fo 7r). The inventory of the commandery of Échirolles is alone in expressing its values in the coinage minted at Vienne. (fos 64–72)

[7] At le Poët Laval rents are expressed in a coinage in which 20 deniers are worth one *tournois*, but total values are expressed in the monetary standard selected for the inventory as a whole. (fo 23v)

[8] E. Nicolas, *Tableau comparatif des poids et mesures anciennes du département des Bouches-du-Rhône* (Aix, 1802); L. Blanchard, *Essai sur les monnaies de Charles 1 ᵉʳ, comte de Provence* (Paris, 1868), pp. 343–50.

bother of conversion: all they considered themselves obliged to do was to assemble the total in local prices and measures in order to establish the aggregate in livres, sous and deniers, which was all they were interested in. But their negligence prevents us from comparing exactly the quantities of grain and wine in one manor with those in another. Moreover the quantitative data has not the accuracy that one might expect from such an inquest. Irrespective of what the point in question was—the yield of seed corn, the ration allocated each year to the domestic servants, the profits of justice, the number of workers engaged by the day, the total of wages distributed, or even the prices of commodities—the quantities registered were always those of 'common' practice. The word *communiter* recurs on every page: 'this land commonly renders,' 'the *charge* of wheat in this town is commonly worth.' The attitude towards figures is worth noting. The officials knew that harvests and prices varied from one year to another but they considered these variations to be accidental and did not think there was any point in registering the current figures for the year 1338 exactly. What counted for them, the really important thing, was what was usual, 'customary'. These prudent administrators, circumspect and careful as they were, had the feeling, and this is particularly significant, that values were stable and ought to be so; they felt there was a fundamental stability underlying changes which they considered to be merely superficial and of no account.

One aspect of this bias is not without its advantage for the historian. It allows him to assess the levels which contemporaries considered to be normal. Nevertheless, such estimates can only be average, subjective, and they therefore impart a certain degree of uncertainty. But if we accept these reservations, the inquest of 1338, because of its truthfulness, detail and the large area it embraces, contains evidence about the manorial economy which is quite exceptionally valuable. What can we deduce from this evidence?

An economy that was essentially domestic in scope provides the background to the inventory. At this period it was the 'household', the 'family' group whose needs and resources had to be ascertained. In this case the manorial 'family' is to some extent peculiar, since it was a religious community, and its way of life and the manner in which it regarded its possessions were determined by the special conditions laid down in the rules of the Order. The discipline[9] imposed a degree of austerity and encouraged limitations on consumption and expense. But in reality the restrictions were not heavy, and commanderies were probably not so very different in social structure or economic needs from other households of rural nobles of middle rank. The commandery was made up of a small number of 'brothers' with military tastes, largely maintained and careful of their retinue: in one commandery there were five brothers, in another thirty, at Manosque, the strongest community, fifty, and on average about twenty. With them lived a number of ser-

[9] See J. Besse, article entitled 'Hospitaliers' in *Dictionnaire de théologie catholique* (1922).

vants 'to cook, knead the dough, wash the linen';[10] there were in addition three or four horses in the stable, a table set for unexpected guests, and the duty of the company's leader to travel properly accoutred. Each house had, of course, its own peculiarly religious function which entailed expense. It had to succour travellers and sick people: that was its specific mission. Three times a week, during the lean months from Michaelmas to Saint John's Day in June, small quantities of grain were distributed to the poor—about two hundred kilos a year of *gros blé* at Saint-Jean de Trièves, eighteen quintals at the very big commandery at Puimoisson near Riez where eighteen hundred quintals were stored in the barns at each harvest; at Bras the weekly dole absorbed less than 0.4 per cent of the total resources available.[11] Lumped together, the costs of hospitality and alms hardly ever amounted to as much as a fifth of the expense of maintaining the lord's household. Cash contributions towards the general needs of the Order had to be added, but these, too, were not heavy. In all probability, these outlays hardly exceeded the value of what a noble family would every year devote as penitences or funeral alms in offerings or annual money payments.[12] Whether large or small, the commandery was thus very similar to the fortified house, and the expenses incurred by the brothers differed little from those of a knight's residence.

The enquiry reveals vividly the nature of the expenses. The primary requirement was for basic foodstuffs. There was the same ration for each 'brother': approximately a kilo of bread a day, which was of course wheat bread;[13] and then wine, in variable quantities, difficult to assign a value for, but served everywhere even if the estate did not produce sufficient and had to beg additional quantities expensively. White bread and good wine were thus the distinctive feature of the lords' household. They would not, of course, have eaten their bread dry, so there was another outlay set aside for the *companagium*. By this was meant the whole cost of additional victuals together with heat and light. According to the inventory of the commandery of Echirolles in the Dauphiné, these other costs were distributed as follows—one fifth for wood and tallow candles, two fifths for meat, fresh or salt, one fifth for eggs, cheese and fish, and the remainder for salt, oil and almonds, onions, garlic and spices.[14] However, the allocation of the 'accompaniment' was not the same for all the 'brothers': although it was 60 sous a year for the master of the commandery, it was 35 sous for a brother and no more than 25 for a *donat*. The hierarchy of this world was consequently primarily manifest

---

[10] Fo 191v.　　[11] Fos 76r, 187r, 175r.

[12] On pious gifts of noble families at this period, cf. R. Boutruche, 'Aux origines d'une crise nobiliaire. Donations pieuses et pratiques successorales en Bordelais du XIIIe au XVIe siècle', *Annales d'histoire sociale* (Paris, 1939).

[13] Except at Lardiers, Roussillon and the three commanderies at Arles where the brothers' wheat was mixed with rye and barley.

[14] Fo 69: 100 livres minted in Vienne for fresh and salted meat; 22 livres for 22 quintals of cheese, 10 livres 10 sous for eggs, 24 livres for fish, 16 livres for oil, 10 livres for salt, 9 livres for spices, one livre for 20 pounds of almonds, 2 livres for garlic and onions, 8 livres for beans and peas, 20 livres for wax and tallow candles.

in the refinements of the table. But it was even more evident in apparel. This is why for the last category of maintenance costs, vestiary expenses, the grades were more numerous and more widely spaced out. The head of the house was allowed 120 sous for clothing, a knight brother 60, the chaplain and the noble *donat* 50, and the serjeant and *donat* of lower birth no more than 40.

The expenses of 'accompaniment' and attire were, in fact, valued in the inventory in money terms. Materials and leather were bought, as were also most of the victuals served at table to go with the round loaves. Consequently the household had two kinds of requirements (and we have seen that the inventory itself was arranged to accord with this distinction): on the one hand there were the requirements for grain and wine and on the other the need for money. They may be compared as follows: at Puimoisson each 'brother' consumed twelve *coupes* of wine, each worth 2 sous, and 18 *setiers* of wheat, at 2 sous each, which added up to 60 sous a year. Money expenses ranged, as in other commanderies, from 95 sous for a knight to 65 sous for a serjeant.[15] Thus for the whole group of brothers, the consumption of 'outside' goods, as they were described in the thirteenth century, those which entailed money drawn from the coffers, was worth—even for those at the bottom of the ladder—at least as much as the victuals which were drawn from cellar or barn. The cost in cash was much higher for the top members of the 'family', especially the head of the community, because the power of the 'house' was through him displayed to the outside world. These, then, were the requirements. Now let us see how the manor succeeded in satisfying them.

In the first place, as lords the Hospitallers of Saint John held the power periodically to draw upon the substance of peasants who were either their men or held land of them. These men, of course inhabited different villages in the vicinity, since the 'manor' was the very opposite of a homogeneous territorial bloc: here one family might be subject to them, and there another patch of ground be held from the commandery, or an *ousteau*, an immigrant, might find himself within the 'empire'. Widely dispersed, the lord's rights were, moreover, very diverse, some being exercised over the land and some over people. The 'exactions' included powers to command, and therefore to judge and impose fines, both high or low; to impose tallage; to protect markets, and therefore to take a portion from all sales; to own the monopoly of a communal oven, a grain or an oil mill, a fulling mill or a hemp mill; to levy dues on houses or land and various taxes on changes of status. These latter could be very lucrative, thus proving how great was the mobility of peasant ownership at this period. Finally, there were tithes and the multitude of profits accruing to the lord of the parish church, such as first fruits, oblations and burial rights. All these appear in the inventory, higgledy-piggledy. In fact, for lords and inquisitors in 1338, as for the

---

[15] Fo 186

historian of the manorial economy today, there was really only one important distinction amongst all the different sources of revenue. Some of the prerogatives authorized a direct levy on the crops of the dependants and resulted in the masters' household acquiring goods, that is wine or wheat, for immediate consumption; others, on the contrary, were indirect claims, providing money; and this meant that small cultivators had to sell their surplus output or a part of their labour in order to fulfil them.

In the manors of Saint John of Jerusalem cash income came almost exclusively from the rights of the *ban*, justice, tallage and funeral taxes.[16] Consequently collection was irregular. One man, it is said, pays when he commits an offence.[17] At Figanières the master exacts fines on five *oustaus* but 'he has not had one for ten years.'[18] Thus the inventory records only an average value for profits as uncertain as these, and because they were variable, these profits were usually small. At Bras, for example, where 140 hearths were listed and where half the *senhoria* belonged to the Hospitallers, the latter levied, in good years and bad, 6 livres 9 sous, that is barely what the preceptor of the commandery expended on his garments alone. The profits of fines on eighteen *oustaus* at Favas were estimated at 10 sous a year; so were the fines on eighteen *oustaus* at Bresc or the liegemen at Clamensane;[19] and the brothers got less than 11 livres in money each year from the thirty-one families at Claret who were subject to their lower justice—4 livres from the church and its tithes, one livre for fines, 30 sous from *bans*, 50 sous from *cens* and *lods*.[20] The yield in cash was thus insufficient, and in normal times it was too low to cover the cost of the lords' food and clothing. Thus at le Poët Laval the forty-eight persons forming the manorial 'family' spent 224 livres each year in money while the manorial rights only brought them in 105; 30 livres were levied in cash at Saint-Jean de Trièves while 64 were expended. Circumstances would have had to be very exceptional for the total money levied on the peasantry in these ways to exceed the cost of maintaining the lords; or else the manor would have to be very large, as it was at Puimoisson (receipts 195 livres, maintenance costs of the group of lords 135), or else it would have had to be near a town. Situated near Arles and leasing out the hunting rights in the Camargue very dearly, the commandery at Sallier collected nearly three times more money than was spent by the little group of six lords. The first conclusion, therefore, is a striking one. In this province and at this period, the country manor yielded very little money. By contrast, whenever the lord could dip his hand into a *bourgade* he could fill it with money. Among the dependencies of the commandery of Comps, Pugnafort in the highlands of Provence yielded the brothers no more than one livre a year, while Draguignan yielded 94.

Profits in kind, and particularly collections of grain, are therefore overwhelmingly predominant in the manorial revenues: at Puimoisson they formed 65 per cent of revenue, at le Poët Laval 80 per cent, and at

---

[16] Fos 11, 19, etc.   [17] Fo 124.   [18] Fo 159.
[19] Fos 171, 156, 171.   [20] Fo 100.

Saint-Jean de Trièves 85 per cent. But this income in kind came neither from the *ban* nor justice; it came mainly from the village oven, the mill, the church, or the tithes. These were the principal sources of dues. The yield was still irregular depending upon the hazards of the village crops, but much more substantial. The single communal oven at Venterol provided the bread ration for eight persons throughout the year;[21] at Lardiers 60 per cent of the rents came from churches; at Puimoisson, oven, mills and tithes together yielded twice as much as rents and eight times as much as the rights of the *ban*.[22] These observations merely confirm the evidence from many other French manorial documents of the thirteenth and fourteenth centuries. The richest lord was not the one who extended his justice and powers of constraint over the largest area of the countryside, nor was he the owner of most holdings: he was the master who controlled millers and levied tithes. And when rents were hard to collect in bad years, and when fines imposed on indigent individuals had to be wholly remitted, it was tithes, multure and oven charges which filled the lord's barns.[23]

Nevertheless, these payments from whatever source, whether they provided returns in corn or money, were in the end of no more than limited profit, since they were only levied at great cost. To begin with there was the cost of overcoming obstacles since they formed the least reliable part of the revenue from the patrimony, the part that was most often questioned by rivals, for the Hospitallers' rights were indeed much entangled with those of other lords. The charges were continually contested by those subject to them who always did their utmost to avoid paying what they owed. It was constantly necessary to go to court and therefore lawyers and attorneys had to be retained, support canvassed and complaisance bought. At Venterol, the inquest noted an annual expenditure of 16 livres on law suits, at Montelier the cost was 10 livres.[24] Moreover the levy itself was expensive. The rent-paying tenants were probably bound to render their dues in person, but the levying of one sou in the livre on all market transactions entailed the permanent presence of an overseer. Similarly, before fines could be collected, sentence had to be passed and thus officers of the court hired. There had to be loyal men on the spot, at the entrance to the oil press, if gross frauds on tithe or tasks were to be avoided. Finally, it was prudent to let these assistants have a share in the profits they were charged with collecting. Thus at Beaulieu d'Orange the tithe collector kept ten per cent of the declared receipts for himself,[25] and the agent installed by the brothers to exploit their rights at Clamensane, a hamlet of twenty houses, received for his own use a salary of 9 livres, one third of all the meagre dues.[26] Here we can see interposed between the lord and those whom he ex-

---

[21] Fo 16v.

[22] At Puimoisson 330 livres as against 150 for rents and 44 for the rights of the *ban*; at le Poët Laval 320 as against 140 and 88.

[23] Cf. Duby, 'Inventaire des profits' and 'La Structure d'une grande seigneurie flamande à la fin du XIIIe siècle', *Bibliothèque de l'École des Chartes* (1956).

[24] Fos 20r, 46v.   [25] Fo 9v.   [26] Fo 101.

ploited a small group of middlemen, lawyers or collectors, who lived
wholly or in part at the expense of the manor.

Finally, the master had to keep up the mill buildings and machinery
which he provided for the peasants in return for their dues. At the mill of
Saint Michael of Manosque, for instance, the millstones, costing 100
sous, had to be changed every four years,[27] and the upkeep of the great
mill and the mill race at Vinon cost 30 livres every year.[28] The lord
provided lighting oil, wax candles and incense for the churches on his
estate. Above all, he had to feed, clothe and remunerate the priest in
charge. It is true these expenses were relatively modest, since the men
who performed religious duties usually received a small salary in kind
as well as the 'accompaniment' and the allocation of clothing accorded to
the humblest members of the household. But they were given the same
ration of wine and grain as was due to a knight brother. The servants of
God ate the white bread of the masters. Thus the expenses and cares of
management were burdensome; moreover, to be free of these burdens
while assuring themselves a more regular income, the Hospitallers
frequently granted ovens, mills, tithes and churches to farmers—more
middlemen whose share had to be deducted. When the final sums were
done the returns from lords' prerogatives were greatly reduced. Here is
the balance sheet of le Poët Laval, one of the larger manors owning three
mills, two ovens, three churches, rents, justice and the *ban* in seven
villages. The receipts were considerable—540 livres in kind and in cash.
But out of this income a clerk, three bakers, two bailiffs, a dozen
serjeants, as well as haywards and collectors, had to be supported and
this ate up nearly 100 livres. So much was devoured that the innumerable small exactions levied over an entire peasant district no longer
sufficed to procure the 520 livres that were needed every year for the
expenses of the 43 brothers, their servants and their guests.

In the first place the inventory reveals the insufficiency of manorial
renders. The low level can probably be explained by the poverty of the
population. We do not have any direct information about the possessions
of the peasants which greatly reduces the significance of what we can
learn from the inquest, since we cannot even remotely appreciate what
was the real weight of the lords' demands or the relative volume of their
deductions. We can guess, however, that in many districts the country
folk subject to the Hospitallers were very poor people. Densely settled,
the countryside was perhaps even overpopulated and reduced to destitution: there were 140 households at Bras which now has less than 700
inhabitants, and 18 families at Favas and 40 at Esparel—places which,
lying as they do in the midst of stony wastelands, are today practically
deserted. Of 28 subject households at la Roque-Esclapon, only 12 owned
any farm animals; at Clamensane, out of 20 homes only one possessed
an ox and another a donkey. At Bresc the 18 dependent families never
killed more than three pigs each year for themselves.[29] Consequently
although the lord might well hold in his hands all the powers to con-

[27] Fo 213.   [28] Fo 279v.   [29] Fos 149, 101, 184.

strain and collect, he could hope to extort little from such miserable wretches, especially as they were frequently subject to demands from other directions, from the Dauphin, the count of Provence, the heads of those principalities whose fiscal powers were so rapidly growing and who helped themselves first. The masters perhaps succeeded in extracting from the peasant all or nearly all the money that passed through his hands: but very little did. How many villagers, liable to heavy fines, were not given their release in return for a few small coins, because the lord's judges had no hope of extracting any more? Wherever the district was less proverty-stricken, as in the countryside around Arles or in the valley of the Argens, the amount of manorial income rose dramatically. But prosperous zones like these were exceptional and were usually confined to the neighbourhood of the *bourgades*. As a rule nature was unproductive, the peasants half starved and the income accruing to the manorial household very scanty.

Even though the manorial household possessed the higher justice as well as tithes and mills, income from these sources could not satisfy its needs. But it also had its close connection with the direct exploitation of the soil. In 1338 the Hospitallers of Saint John owned a huge 'demesne' in this part of Provence. The woodlands were few and very poor, there were some almond orchards, walnut and olive groves, some meadows and enclosed vineyards: by far the largest part was made up of arable land (*labours*). The cornlands of the Order were spread over nearly 7,000 hectares in plots of variable size, unequally divided between the different houses, although some of the latter were well provided for, as for instance on the demesnes at Manosque and Vinon which extended over 300 hectares of fields.[30] I have been astonished to find in the inventory so little evidence of a pastoral economy. Almost everywhere draught animals are the only ones to be mentioned: here and there twenty or thirty sheep are listed, but where are the huge flocks which are referred to at this period in the accounts of some commanderies, such as Manosque?[31] At the time of the year when the inquest was conducted they were certainly away in transhumance. But how could such a detailed statement of domestic resources have remained silent about animal husbandry in a region where it constituted the main wealth? If we follow the text we see that the officials who drew up the inquest presented the demesne as being totally directed towards cereal production. For them the arable lands formed the solid foundation of the possessions, the part that was the real support of the manor. In most of the houses of Saint John the gross returns from the demesnes, expressed in money terms,

[30] The area of the arable is estimated in *séterées*. The area that can take one *setier* of seed varies considerably according to the quality of the soil and the capacity of the measure. The average sowing in traditional Provençal agriculture is 20 litres of seed per hectare, and most *setiers* contain about 40 litres. I have, therefore, taken one hectare of five *séterées* as my estimate of value.

[31] F. Reynaud, 'L'Organisation et le domaine de la commanderie de Manosque', *Provence Historique* (1956 Mélange Busquet); T. Sclafert, *Cultures en Haute-Provence. Déboisement et pâturage au Moyen Age* (Paris, 1959).

accounted for a large part of the combined revenues. I shall take as an example the commandery of Comps, to which were attached nine manorial units dispersed over the high Verdon and the slopes of the mountains of the Maures. Two of these units, Esparel and Favas, were purely collecting centres without a demesne: manorial dues—55 and 50 livres respectively—formed the sole income. At Draguignan, a manor that was more urban than rural, highly profitable taxes produced 104 livres, exactly double what usually came from the vineyard, the meadows and a piece of fertile ground 6 hectares in area. But everywhere else the really large profits came from the master's land, 38 livres as against 23 at Roque-Esclapon, 334 against 56 at Roquebrune, 6 livres against 1 at Riufre, 58 against 3 at la Faye, 144 against 74 at Comps, and 144 against 3 at Pugnafort.

But even on these lands which were well cared for and benefited from frequent long periods of fallow,[32] yields were very low. The inventory tells us what they were. On 65 demesnes, for every measure of grain sown four were commonly harvested; on 24 others the yield was five to one. But these demesnes were all on good lands situated in the better areas, such as on the plains of the lower Rhône around Arles and at Chateaurenard on the outskirts of Manosque. In only seven cases was there any mention of a higher average yield and these were on the 'ferrages', small, continuously cultivated fields near towns. By contrast, on 21 other demesnes the yield was no more than three to one, and in five mountainous localities a return of only two grains of corn could be expected from every one sown. From these wretched harvests the seed corn had to be deducted as well as the share left to the threshers and winnowers which was a twentieth or even a thirtieth part. This gives us some idea of how precarious the life of a peasant was. How could small cultivators, who probably did not have access to the better soils and whose technical means were very limited wrest tithe, task, multure and oven dues from outputs so derisory, and still have enough left to feed their children? In any event, for the manorial barns to be filled by the huge quantities of cereals listed in the inventory, the demesne had to be vast and hence the labourers engaged on cultivating it had to be numerous. There was thus a labour problem. To harrow, weed and harvest these immense fields, the lord could not rely on labour services alone. It is true he held the right to claim several days' work from men and beasts, though only from a score of the most remote mountain villages. Nor were all these services called upon since those subject to them worked badly and ate too much. It was more satisfactory to remit their labour in exchange for a small money payment. In the inventory these labour services were always listed in the chapter which recorded the income in money. Carting services were the only ones that were effectively performed.[33] Labour, the heavy labour that the frequently infer-

---

[32] G. Duby, 'Techniques et rendements agricoles dans les Alpes du Sud en 1338', *Annales du Midi* (1958).
[33] G. Duby, 'Notes sur les corvées dans les Alpes du Sud en 1338', *Etudes d'histoire du droit privé offertes à Pierre Petot* (Paris, 1959)

tile soils required, had thus to be paid for, and this leads us to ask whether, despite appearances, the cultivation of these huge estates was in fact profitable.

So far as vineyards and meadows were concerned—because wine and hay were both expensive commodities—net yields were high. At la Faye, where two hundred *charges* of hay, worth maybe a score of livres, were carted, the day labourers employed to scythe, toss and bring in the wagons cost only 3 livres 16 sous. At Sallier, 21 livres were spent on working the vineyard, but the 15 *muids* of wine that it yielded in an average year were sold for 45 livres. At the commandery of Bras the cost of cultivating the vineyard was less than 50 per cent of the value of the crop, and the cost of taking hay from the meadows, 35 per cent.[34] but in the case of the arable, the lord's return was much less reliable. Let us look again at the inventory of the commandery of Bras. There the brothers had more than 300 hectares of ploughland. As the soil was left fallow two years out of three, about 100 hectares were sown with winter wheat each year; in addition, there were about 50 hectares of oats, barley and beans—what was called the *restouble*, crops 'stolen' from the stubble. It was a locality where yields were average, that is four to one. Therefore, in good years and bad, about 650 quintals were harvested, approximately half of which was wheat. The crop produced twice as much grain for the lord as did the five mills, the tithe on four parishes and the rents taken together, and was worth 266 livres—a great deal. But twelve ploughs were needed to produce it. To begin with the services of a blacksmith were required, who received, apart from the iron he needed, a stipend of one *setier* of wheat for each ploughshare, which added up to 3 quintals costing 5 livres and a half. Then the plough beasts numbering 48 oxen and 8 other beasts of burden had to be kept all the year round in the stable and they consumed 120 *charges* of hay, plus 24 *setiers* of oats. As the mules had to be shod and worn-out animals replaced from time to time, the annual expenses of maintaining the plough teams amounted to nearly 55 livres.[35] Many servants were occupied in handling the ploughs and caring for the animals—12 ploughmen, 4 grooms, and 4 male farmservants. Their food, clothing and wages absorbed 36 livres in money and nearly 700 *setiers* of rye (nearly as much as the dues produced)—a total of about 115 livres expressed in money values. Moreover the permanent servants could not perform all the tasks; day labourers were hired to help them with the heavy seasonal work. There was the cost of 550 days' weeding by women; of 537 days' harvesting by men; of 190 days binding the sheaves by women; threshing, winnowing and transporting the grain, which required a disbursement of about another 50 livres. Altogether the expense of cultivating cereals alone amounted to 225 livres, which reduced the net profit to about 40 livres, that is not more than 15 per

[34] Fos 147r, 332r, 176r.

[35] The cost of replacing cattle in this commandery was not valued. At la Motte du Caire, which had only 4 oxen, the *renovatio boum* cost 8 livres per annum. We may assume that at Bras this expenditure would have amounted to about 40 livres.

cent of the value of the harvest. This was in an 'ordinary' year. What then could have been the situation in a poor season?

It is true that the profit was higher was higher in the localities where the soil was more fertile and the yield less minuscule, but it was never very much. On 225 of the 400 hectares of the demesne in the commandery of Puimoisson the yield was as much as six to one, quite unusually high; nevertheless, because the price of wheat here was low, the costs of production devoured four fifths of the value of the grain (235 livres out of 300). Cereal growing obviously produced a net deficit in the unproductive disticts where yields were below average. This was the case at Saint Jean de Trièves where, despite the high price of cereals, the harvest was worth no more than 61 livres; upkeep of equipment and plough animals alone (four oxen had to be hired as they could not be fed throughout the year) amounted to 56 livres, nearly as much as the gross value of the crop. The cost of labour, and especially the upkeep of the nine farm servants, amounted to 79 livres, which took the balances well into the red.

In conditions like these would it not have been in the clear interest of the lords to have placed the exploitation of the land in the hands of others, and to have leased out these unproductive fields to sharecroppers? A document like our inventory provides evidence that increasing numbers of French manorial administrators in the thirteenth and fourteenth centuries, who abandoned direct cultivation and put their demesnes out to farm, were impelled to do so by the hard facts of their balance sheets. The Hospitallers themselves had recourse to temporary crop-sharing concessions that were called in this region contracts of *facherie*. In every case it was to their great advantage.[36] One of the manors which had the highest returns—Sallier, near Arles—was profitable precisely because 90 per cent of its 200 hectares of 'demesne' was let out on *métayage*; these fields procured, without any cost, cereals worth 434 livres. Even so, farming out the arable in *facherie* had not gone very far. Out of 7,000 hectares of demesne only 1,200 were under such a system and these were mainly in the valleys of the Rhône, Durance and Argens, that is to say, in the most open countryside, precisely where the soil was most productive, farming was more profitable and economic life most active. Elsewhere, in the manors where direct exploitation yielded less, the brothers of Saint John had few sharecropping tenants. Why should this have been so? Was it from habit? Or was it ignorance of their true interests? It appears that they were frequently obliged to keep their ploughlands in hand because nobody wished to take them on sharecropping agreements, even when five sixths, seven eighths, or eight ninths of the crop was allowed to the cultivator, and even when, as at la Faye or Monfort,[37] all that the peasants still owed in labour and animal services was put at the disposal of the farm. At Saint Auban the 60 *séterées* of the demesne 'remained for

---

[36] L. Caillet, 'Le contrat dit de facherie', *Nouvelle Revue historique de droit français et étranger* (1911).
[37] Fos 147r, 163r.

long without anyone being found who wished to take on the *facherie au tiers*.[38] The reason for this was the great poverty of the peasantry. To undertake the exploitation of such inferior lands and to provide at the outset for the heavy cost of livestock, tools and labour with the prospect of an uncertain profit, required capital and methods of exploitation much superior to those available even to the less famished inhabitants of this countryside. In company probably with many other lords, the Hospitallers of Provence in 1338 were forced in spite of themselves to retain in their own hands the cultivation of most of their lands.

Nevertheless, there is no certainty that the way the domestic economy was organized at this period was solely determined by considerations of maximum profit. In order to explain the tenacious attachment to direct management, we have to look for other motives. Here sentiment undoubtedly played a large part, for to entrust land to sharecroppers was to some degree to lose it. What, after all, was the purpose of amassing more grain? Was it in order to sell it and thus to accumulate capital? Surely it was more important to go on maintaining in the house a larger 'family', made up of farm servants attached to the work on the demesne who would form a devoted and faithful circle around the lords? We can believe that on the eve of the fourteenth century the ideas about the knighthood, shared without doubt by the brothers of the Hospital with the rural aristocracy, still rated the fidelity of a band of household menials more highly than a larger money income produced by better organized sales. This it seems was the reason why the Hospitallers, against what was apparently their best interests, lived surrounded by cowherds and ploughmen and why the 'demesne' always formed the lynchpin of the manorial economy.

In conditions such as these how do we place the manorial economy within the wider economy of the countryside? It appears in the first place that the demands of the master's house stimulated the activity of the smaller peasant cultivators within its dependency. Because it had to pay its tithe and its rent, each household—even if it were miserably equipped to do so—had to produce from its output more than mere subsistance. In localities growing mostly rye, a little of the wheat that the master required had of necessity to be produced.[39] And because they were bound from time to time to find a little cash to pay fines, tallage, funeral or baptismal taxes, even the humblest peasants had to attempt to sell whatever they could. In this way the manor raised an additional obstacle in the way of complete self-sufficiency of peasant cultivation. Merely by being there the manor stimulated a current of exchange. It pushed the circulation of money into the uttermost ends of remote

[38] Fo 147r.

[39] To find out from the manorial inventory how cereal cultivation was distributed it is not necessary to look at total revenues, merely those that come from direct levies on peasant crops—levies on mills, tithes and tasks. At Ginasservis (fo 263v), dues claimed by the lord brought in 164 *setiers* of wheat and 64 of barley; tithes 160 *setiers* of wheat, 238 of rye and 20 of oats. Therefore twice as much rye as wheat was normally grown in the locality, but the wheat was mainly delivered to the lord.

alpine valleys. By this means 10 livres for tallage, 8 sous for rent, 1 livre 10 sous for justice, 8 sous for the *mortelage* of the church, 3 livres for the *ban* and market taxes—in all several thousand small coins of inferior money had, before being collected by the lord's men, to circulate every year among the few inhabitants of Saint Pierre d'Aviez, a wretched village set among stony fields far from the main road.[40]

But the movement of wealth was stimulated by manorial management in an even more direct fashion. The lord's income did not, in fact, correspond exactly to his needs. Broadly speaking, mills, tithes, ovens and especially the demesne, put much more wheat into his barns than he himself, together with his guests, his servants, the poor whom he supported and the animals in his stable could consume; on the other hand his wine casks were not always so full, nor did he ever receive enough money from those holding of him. For example, at Bras the manorial household consumed barely one third of its profits in kind. At

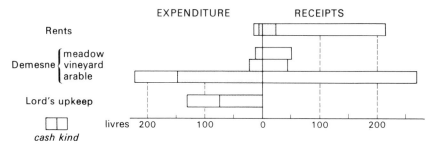

14.2 Budgets of the commandery of Bras

the end of the year a considerable surplus remained: 350 quintals of wheat, 100 quintals of rye, the same amount of barely and oats, as well as hay and 80 hectolitres of wine. But no more than 21 livres in cash was received while about twelve times as much had to be expended on purchases of clothing, meat, salt and spices, on lawsuits, upkeep of buildings, renewal of flocks and the wages of day labourers. A disequilibrium of this kind necessitated the conversion of surplus crops, particularly wheat, into cash. Thus because the cereal demesnes were so extensive and their harvests, in spite of low yields, so large, all the manors in the inventory were centres, and often very large centres, of corn sales. Much of the grain harvested in the mountains probably descended in long mule trains to Avignon, Arles, Fos, Marseilles, Fréjus or Nice. Rigidly enforced labour services provided the transport. But the details of how it was done reveal nothing about the trade itself. Did the Hospitallers deal directly with the great merchants of the ports? Or did they make use of the same small business men in the *bourgades* who provided them with salt, cloth and salt fish? At least one thing is certain and that is that by its sales the manor gave a livelihood to the retailers and brokers who shared in the traffic. They formed another group of

[40] Fo 93.

middlemen and may have been the very same people who, also in the service of the Order, fulfilled the office of notary and held tithes and mills at farm.[41] It is also clear that the men responsible for manorial adminstration who answered the visitors' questions in the summer of 1338 were very well informed about current market prices.

The inquest provides much detailed evidence about these prices, but even so their interpretation is a delicate matter. On the one hand indeed, as I have already said, values were average values, and they provide a subjective estimate of whatever rate was considered to be normal because it was customary; on the other hand the measures of quantity are local and are not the same in all places. In short, our invaluable document gives us less information on this point than we could have hoped for.

Its main interest is to provide, at the same point in time and in the same monetary unit, a very large amount of evidence dispersed over a wide area. It demonstrates that the prices of certain agricultural products were relatively uniform. This was so for hay, for which the *charge* was generally valued at 2 sous. As the price was never more than 2½ sous and never less than 15 deniers the variation was rather limited. On the other hand the price of wine differed a great deal: the price of the *coupe* varied between 1 and 4 sous, although here the disparity between measures makes observation rather uncertain. We shall, therefore, have to limit ourselves to considering the market value of corn, the major food commodity. This varied very much from one village to another.[42] To begin with the relative prices of the different cereals varied very considerably. At Mallemort a measure of rye was worth half of a measure of wheat, but at Puimoisson it was worth four fifths. At la Bordette the price of oats was 80 per cent below that of wheat, but at Fos it was only 25 per cent below.[43] In order to explain such discrepancies one is tempted to connect them with the uneven geographical distribution of different grains. But in fact juxtaposing a list of prices with a list of crops does not reveal any obvious connection. For example, at Puimoisson the parish lands produced half rye and half wheat; at Les Omergues only wheat was grown. But the prices of the two cereals in both places bore the same relationship. Our second observation is that very wide variations affected prices of the same grain equally from one place to another. I shall consider only wheat and, in order to eliminate what in different estimates is due to the disparity between measures of capacity, I shall not take the price of the *setier* as the unit of comparison, but instead the annual allowance given to each brother, because this obviously varied little from one commandery to another. At Mallemort

[41] P. A. Fevrier, 'La Basse Vallée de L'Argens. Quelques aspects de la vie économique de la Provence orientale au XVe et XVIIe siècle', *Provence Historique* (1959); E. Baratier, 'Le notaire Jean Barral, marchand de Riez au début du XVe siècle', *Provence Historique* (1957).

[42] At Lardiers the *setier* of wheat was worth 2 sous and the *setier* of rye 18 deniers; at les Omergues fifteen kilometres away they were worth 20 and 16 deniers per *setier* respectively (fos 221–3).

[43] Fos 320, 181, 285.

350-odd kilos of grain were worth 25 sous per brother, at Puimoisson, Fos, Hyères, and Bras 36 sous, at Saint Pierre d'Aviez, Claret, Manosque 48 sous; at Aix 56, at Avignon 60 and at Saint-Jean de Trièves 80.[44]

Variations of this amplitude are hard to explain. Do prices vary in relation to the yields? Apparently not. It is true the highest price was at Saint-Jean de Trièves, in a locality where the soil was least productive, but at Orange and Sallier, where yields were the same, a *setier* of good grain was worth 38 sous and 54 sous respectively. Similarly, it was worth 48 at both Manosque, where the normal yield of the demesne lands was five to one, and at Saint Pierre d'Aviez, where the yield was no more than three to one. Were not these price differences perhaps more connected with the conditions of sale than with production, that is, were they not connected with a more or less favourable location within the network of trade routes? There is indeed a somewhat clearer geographical link between prices and commercial currents. The places where prices were high—such as Avignon, Arles, Aix, Nice—were almost all large consuming or exporting towns, and wheat was generally much cheaper in the mountains, as at Bras or Puimoisson. Even so, many surprising discrepancies exist. Why should grain have been worth twice as much in the very isolated village of Saint Pierre d'Aviez as it was at Mallemort in the lower valley of the Durance? Why should people have paid less at Fos or Hyères embarkation ports, than they did on the high plateaux of the Verdon?

Variations of this kind are mainly evidence of the isolation of cereal markets. They suggest that the market for basic foodstuffs was not flexible, and that prices in a region at a particular period were to some extent frozen. It is true that price rigidity was probably caused by the natural divisions of a mountainous country, but perhaps the most likely reason was that even 'common' prices were in fact customary prices. Could they have been more the result of habits and traditions than responses to genuine economic factors? In these conditions the relation between the internal workings of the manorial economy and the level of local prices seems a complex one. At Puimoisson wheat was not worth much, while at Arles it was worth a lot. In some places the possessions of Saint John produced enormous amounts of wheat. We might suppose that such a large surplus output at Puimoisson was precisely what kept the price so low, for by attracting buyers from the coast it turned export into a habitual practice which in its turn stimulated further output from the manorial fields. But we could with as much truth claim that the administrators at Arles were encouraged by the high prices to increase cereal farming. It is indeed hard to distinguish, over the whole of the possessions of Saint John, any clear relation between the organization of manorial output and the agricultural price level.

It is obvious however that the economy of these manors was closely linked with trade and the use of money. At the commandery of Bras, for

[44] Fos 181, 223, 320, 285, 312, 170, 92, 104, 195, 262, 245, 73.

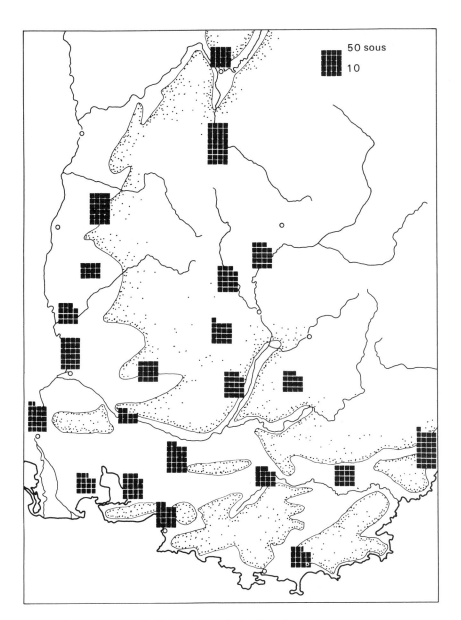

14.3 Value of the annual wheat rations of a brother (in sous)

instance, the balance of receipts and expenses shows that sixty-five per cent of the goods produced or levied had to be sold. Thus, one of the main economic functions of the manor was to inject a proportion of the output of the countryside, both from the demesne and from the peasant lands that were subject to rent and tithe, into commercial circulation and to exchange it for money. What, then, happened to the money that fell into the lords' hands in this way? Some of it was speedily removed from the rural scene by being handed over to the suppliers of merchandise from distant places, by being spent on travel, or by being put into a reserve for the general needs of the Order of Saint John. But not all the money disappeared in this way. Among the expenditure in cash noted by the visitors (*enqueteurs*), much was distributed in the immediate vicinity of the manorial household. The purchase of certain goods for the 'accompaniment' probably profited those peasants of the district who sold pork, eggs or oil. But, more than in any other way, the money was distributed in the form of wages, since an extensive permanent and temporary staff was employed by the commanderies.

First of all there was the team of farm menservants who belonged to the 'family'. The size of this group varied according to the size of the demesne, and its members were placed, according to their qualifications, in an economic hierarchy starting with the *souillard*, the odd job man to whom all the lowly everyday tasks were left, and rising to the master oxherd (*bouvier*), first among the ploughmen and the real chief of the agricultural activities. But these domestic servants lived in an intimate relationship with their lords. It is true that their grain ration, which was the same for each 'member of the family' was not exactly like their masters'; often heavier, it was made up of coarser cereals, rye, maslin or barley, and this put the agricultural servants below the household servants and the clergy. They did not drink the best wine, only wine from the second pressing. Finally the 'accompaniment' with which they were provided cost less—not more than 10 or 15 sous a year, as against 15 or 20 sous for a clerical servant and 35 for a full brother. Within the basic economic cell formed by the 'house', therefore, there existed a clear hierarchy based on material conditions, and the rougher diet they ate, of which bread formed the most important part, erected a barrier between the lords and the demesne labourers and brought the latter closer to the peasants.

Where the farm servants were concerned the inventory listed one other expense expressed in money terms: this was for clothing, described as 'vestment' and 'hose' (*vestiaire* and *chausse*). Sometimes the amount varied slightly according to the job: in some places a few more sous were given to the team leader than to the ordinary manservant.[45] It varied much more between different places—at Marignane an oxherd had the right to 10 sous, at Trinquetaille to 100 sous[46]—but for the

---

[45] At Authon it was 23 sous for the *bovarius* and 18 for the *nuncius* (fo 106); at Luc en Diois it was 50 sous for the former and 30 for the latter (fo 83); at Arles the grades were more numerous: 30 sous for the *souillard*, 60 for the baker, 152 for the ploughwright, 84 for the 'lad', 30 for the servant working in the barns (fo 353).   [46] Fos 296, 342.

members of the seigneurial community of brothers it was the same everywhere. Why should this have been so? Did it depend on direct supplies, with the brothers buying and distributing clothing to the servitors? This could hardly explain the great variations in expenses. Was not the 'vestiary' perhaps more of a cash allowance to the employee who was supposed to clothe himself, in other words a genuine wage? There are some passages in the inventory that make this second hypothesis seem more likely. In the small demesne at Saint Pantaléon in the locality of Apt where four domestics were employed, the 'vestiary' expense was expressed in sous, 8 for each person, but the cost of 'hose' was expressed in wheat: there were 8 measures for the farm menservants and 4 for the kitchen servant[47]—a curious way of valuing something which had to be purchased in cloth or leather. In this case it could not have been anything other than an individual remuneration, a wage supplement. There is evidence of the same kind at Tarascon, where a domestic servant had the right to a global payment of 16 measures of wheat for his vestiary, hose and wage.[48] Indeed apart from victuals and the clothing allowance, the full-time agricultural workers, like the domestic servants, the clergy and the armed followers of the lord's house, received a stipend (*loyer*), a clearly graded salary. At Roquebrune the head oxherd (*maitre bouvier*) was remunerated each year with 25 *setiers* of wheat, the two other oxherds with 16 *setiers*, the groom, the manservant and the baker with 18 *setiers*.[49] The value of the salary was usually above that of the ration of corn consumed in the refectory. It was sometimes paid in money, as at the Col de Menée where the oxherd received 40 sous a year. The wages of domestic servants in all the households of the commanderies of Nice, Beaulieu and Sallier were also valued in money terms.[50] At Comps the wage was paid in grain from Saint John's Day to Michaelmas; but in winter it was paid in money, 35 sous for the head oxherd, 30 for the second oxherd and 25 for each of the others.[51] However, the inventory almost always reports that there was an allowance of corn. What did the beneficiaries do with it? Are we to suppose that they maintained a family outside the lord's household? Or that they exchanged the wheat or barley for other goods? At all events, stipends, those small earnings which were freely disposed of, brought within the 'family' community a group who were to a certain extent economically independent.

However, since many people were perhaps at least partly rewarded in kind, it is by no means certain that the full-time employment of wage-earners transferred very much money into the peasant environment of the Order's manors. The transfer was more likely to have taken place through the distribution of wages to labourers hired for the heavy seasonal work, who were sometimes paid by the season. At both Hos-

[47] Fos 242v, 243r.
[48] Fo 251r; similarly at Manosque the harrower employed from Saint Julian's Day until Christmas received 8 *setiers* of rye 'for his victuals as well as for his tunic and shoes' (fo 215).
[49] Fo 151.   [50] Fos 91, 124, 135, 137, 306, 329.   [51] Fos 143, 146, 148, 149, 154.

pitalet and Granbois 'the man who follows the ploughs to harrow the furrows' is maintained with the other domestic servants during the two autumn months, receiving the same allowance and drawing the same wage.[52] At Saint Michael of Manosque this is what happened to the waterman (*aiguadier*) who regulated the irrigation between Whitsun and Michaelmas.[53] But on some other occasions, during the grape harvest, haymaking, and winnowing, there was piece work and a 'fixed price' contract; the lord made an agreement with a team of seasonal workers, offering the wage in a lump sum, all in money.[54] But in most cases the auxiliary labourers were hired by the day for individual wages. In this way an enormous workforce could be assembled. Every year on the demesne at Bayle, an average sized dependency of the commandery of Aix, 200 days' work by women to weed the cereals were paid for, as well as 200 days' work by harvesters, 66 days' work by women who bound up the sheaves, 12 days' work by men who built the stacks, and 230 more for the various jobs in the vineyard; there were 30 female grape pickers, 18 mowers, 15 haymakers, and 5 men to carry the hay.[55] All these jobs entailed enormous outgoings in cash: 37 livres a year in the commandery at Sallier (where, however, almost all the demesne was in *métayage*); 85 at Bras; and more than 100 at Comps. Everything points to these daily stipends being wholly discharged in cash, quite independently of the supplementary benefits in kind, mainly victuals, which the daily workers could sometimes obtain.[56]

The price of a day's work mentioned in the inventory also differed considerably. Not so much because of sex—the women who bound the sheaves often had the right to the same wage as the harvesters who worked alongside them—but according to the task performed, and apparently even more according to the season, and hence to the length of the day. The really high rewards went to the mowers working at the solstice, who generally earned eight times more than the women who weeded the corn in the early spring. Wages were also very different from one district to another, and from one village to another. To generalizè, we can say that wages were higher in the more favoured regions where agricultural yields were also high. On a map showing day wages of a harvester (figure 14.4) the highest rates are thus clealy localized around Arles, in the valley of the Rhône and in the Aix basin. But a more detailed inspection, more attuned to local variations, reveals that, besides differing between occupations, wages were completely independent of general conditions of economic life and especially of food prices. They cannot be seen to be related, even remotely, to factors influencing the price of corn. To earn the equivalent of a *setier* of wheat a harvester

---

[52] Fos 192, 216.

[53] Fo 212; at Roussillon, 'the man who made the corn stooks' was also maintained for two months.

[54] Fo 59.   [55] Fo 276.

[56] Each of the 48 harvesters at la Roque-Esclapon received a wage of 12 deniers; in addition an outlay of 30 sous was recorded for their victuals (fo 150); similarly at Puimoisson, 510 days of harvesting labour at 12 deniers and 4 livres 10 sous for the labourer's allowance of food (fo 188).

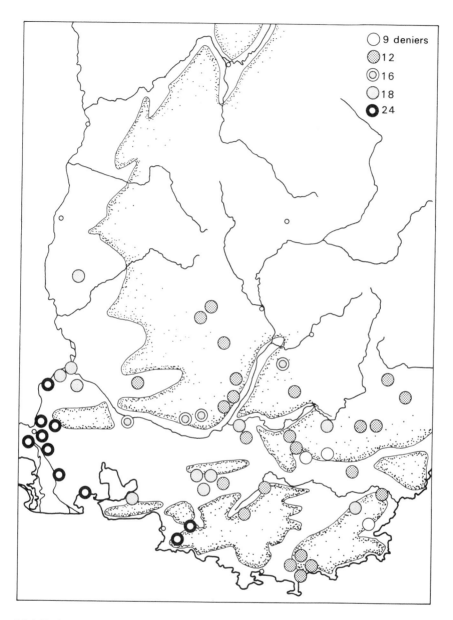

14.4 Daily wage of a harvester

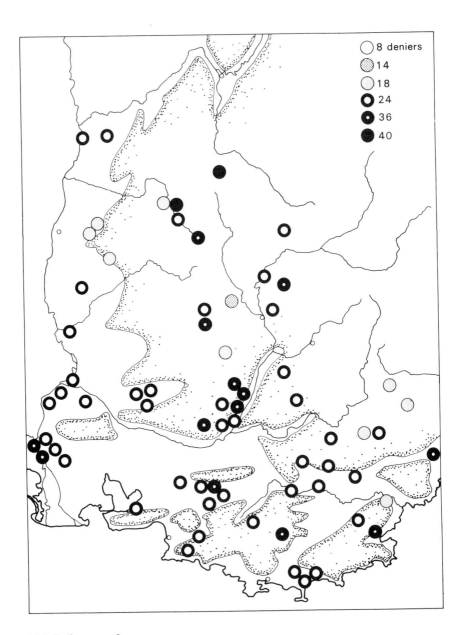

14.5 Daily wage of a mower

would have had to work for 5 days at la Faye, 4 at Draguignan, but only 3 at Bras. The labour market appears, therefore, to have been as localized as the market for cereals. We may see this as another manifestation of the rigidity of prices, whether they were for goods or for human labour, and as probably one more clear proof of the strength of the customs and traditions peculiar to each locality.

All the earnings of labour were very high and this does not accord well with our assumptions about how precarious life was in these apparently overpopulated villages. A labourer working for hire on manorial lands was infinitely better off than a self-employed man on his own small patch of ground. This is a fact that must be brought into the open, and to do so I shall quote some details about the conditions of a farm manservant. To maintain one such man for a complete year cost about 75 sous at Bras, the same sum as the price of about 40 *setiers* of rye in this district. Had a man been an independent cultivator and thus obliged to pay tithes and taxes and to keep back at least a quarter of his harvest for next year's seed, in order to dispose of the same resources he would have had to harvest 80 *setiers* or, in the existing state of technique, to be able to plough 10 or 12 hectares. From this comparison it is clear that the *bovarius*, the ploughman, although dressed in the same rough homespun and eating the same black bread as his peasant neighbour, would nevertheless have been far better off economically. His first advantage, fundamental in such a wretched existence, was that he lived in security. In the manorial house there would always have been enough for him to eat and drink and his wage assured him of a regular surplus. Indeed, everything he earned was free from exactions or tallage; and we must not forget moreover that he shared in the grace flowing from the prayers of the community and that, because he worked for Saint John and for God, his conscience was easy. Furthermore, the menservants of the commandery at Bras in our example were not even the most favoured: at les Omergues, the allowance of a farmservant was worth 90 sous and at Draguignan 170.[57] The material conditions of these servants were thus well above those of the incumbent of a rural parish. Generally speaking, their share of the wealth of the household to which they were attached was the same, or very nearly the same, as a serjeant brother, who was in fact their lord.[58] To enter one of these manorial households as a full-time employee at that period was a genuine improvement in economic status; it meant escape from the cares and privations of country folk and a share in the comforts of the lords.

To the temporary wage-earners the manorial economy also offered important, though less regular, benefits. On countless demesnes of the Hospitallers, to earn the ration of rye consumed by a domestic servant in a month, a mower needed to work no more than a day, a harvester two days, and a vineyard worker three days. And to return to the commandery at Bras which I use as my example, a day labourer could earn a

[57] Fos 230, 154.

[58] In the commandery at Avignon the expenses were 135 sous for a serjeant and 134 for an oxherd (fo 249r).

wage of 75 sous in less than three months by hiring himself out at the times when there was a heavy demand for labour—for a fortnight during haymaking, a fortnight at harvest time, a fortnight pruning the vines and ten days digging them together with a further fortnight's hoeing. This wage was the equivalent of the annual maintenance of a domestic servant, or of the profits from a peasant holding of 12 hectares.

Whether there were in fact many men who were wholly wage-earners like this, living entirely by hiring themselves out, is certainly an open question: perhaps some of the mowers and harvesters working on the demesnes came from distant villages in seasonal parties,[59] a kind of human transhumance. But more likely most of those who did the casual work came from peasant homes in the vicinity and were the same men who had to pay the Hospitallers' *bans* and court dues. For people as poor as they were, such high wages were an important part of their annual income, and an essential defence against destitution. And it was by such activities, the direct farming of its huge cereal estates and the provision of employment, that the manor was able to be the real support of the rural economy, certainly much more than by distributing small amounts of alms to the poor.[60] Similarly, by paying out cash in the form of wages, it largely restored the money it had extracted from the surrounding countryside through tallage, dues and fines. At Puimoisson the earnings received by labourers were equal to half the money the lord had levied from his neighbourhhood. At Comps the figure was two thirds. At Saint-Jean de Trièves, where all the dependants together rendered 30 livres in cash each year, the commandery paid back to the day labourers 35 livres in wages. Finally, at Bras the two thousand days of labour were worth four times as much as the cash receipts from all the lord's rights. Here, by distributing part of its receipts from sales, the manorial house supplied the neighbouring peasant world with money. Through their massive demands for labour, as much as through their levies, the Hospitallers' demesnes were an integral part of the peasant economy.

We should beware of extending the application of these observations too readily. The very diversity of the entries to be found in the inventory calls for prudence. Manors with widely different economic structures are in fact found side by side. What a contrast there is to be seen between le Poët Laval, with little or no demesne and therefore no wage-earners, where the community of brothers found it hard to manage on rents alone; Puimoisson, a vast agricultural undertaking which hired thousands of workers by the day; and Sallier, whose balance sheet was so greatly in surplus and where the widespread resort to sharecropping

[59] In the region of Toulouse harvesters came from the mountains; cf. G. Sicard, 'Le Métayage dans le midi toulousain à la fin du moyen age', *Mémoires de l'académie de législation* II (Toulouse, nd).

[60] At Roussillon the 53 poor people who had the right to weekly alms consumed all together 60 *émines* of rye each year, i.e. no more than two and a half times the ration of one brother (fo 240).

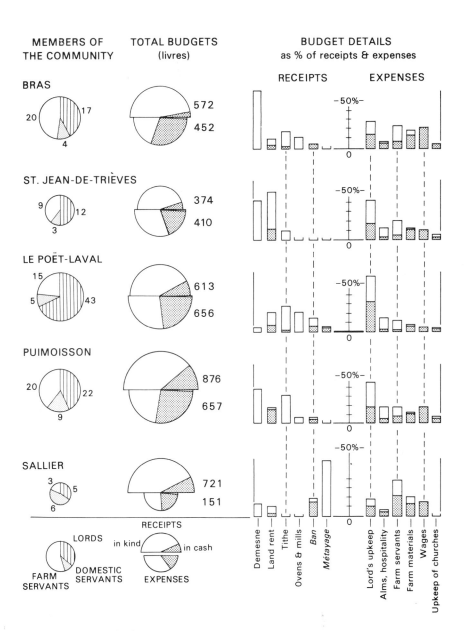

14.6 Commandery budgets

kept the costs of exploitation down to less than fifteen per cent of the gross revenue. We should take warning also from the character of the document: it throws light on the manor only, while the facts it reveals about the peasant economy are no more than uncertain guesses. Nevertheless we must risk a few brief concluding remarks.

The first thing that the document reveals is that in the southern Alps, in order to keep a small group of masters in idleness, the institution of the manor had to send its roots out widely into the thin soil, and to draw its subsistence from an extensive area. Thus the modest requirements of seven brothers and four *donats* at the commandery of Roussillon needed for their fulfilment 350 hectares of arable, rents from nine villages, an oven, a mill, 20 working oxen, 11 farmhands and more than 400 days of labour on piece work. The manorial economy in general had a very low rate of return. This is one reason why so many of the small rural gentry in Haute Provence appear in the documents of the early fourteenth century to be impoverished. Their prerogatives rendered barely enough for them to live on.

It is true, of course, and this is the second lesson to be drawn from the inquest, that the lords were very far from being the only ones to profit from manorial revenues. Many other people took their share, mainly all those middle-men whom we have encountered by the way—men who farmed revenues, tithes, churches and land; the purchasers and suppliers; all the notaries, judges, procurators, people skilled in writing and the ways of bureaucracy; and others too, who were also paid yearly, craftsmen, smiths and ploughwrights who made or repaired the ploughs, farriers, barbers and apothecaries. And because the lords were no mere rentiers, an even greater share of the crops, dues and fruits of sales went to the various household servants or hired labourers.

Was the economy one of sufficiency or was it profitable? In conditions such as these the question has to be expressed in another way. It is obvious that the administrators of the commanderies of Saint John did not to any extent consider whether to invest profits into their enterprises in order to develop them. Indeed, in the inventory drawn up by the visitors, the share reserved for investment was very small, no more than a few livres for the 'repair' of the house or livestock. The manor at the little hamlet of Clamensane brought in 28 livres per annum from which a net return of 19 livres remained; but no more than 10 sous were spent on improving the equipment.[61] In the entire commandery at Claret no more than 4 livres were devoted to general maintenance and 8 livres for the renewal of cattle, while 5 livres were absorbed in legal costs alone.[62] At le Poët Laval the outlay on investment hardly formed one per cent of the gross income: 7 livres out of 613. This does not mean of course that the lords were not at all interested in increasing their profits. Nevertheless, in their view, surplus resources had before all else to allow them to extend the 'family'. Their reluctance to put their demesnes out to farm is one proof of this. For them to be rich meant to recruit new brothers, more

[61] Fo 104v.   [62] Fo 107.

domestic servants, to integrate a larger part of rural society into the household community, to acquire more people in the outside world with obligations—merchants, purchasers, wage-earners. Indeed, by doing so, as by the use to which they put their incomes, each rural manor actively stimulated the exchange of goods and services. The entire village economy was in contact with the manor. But by this very fact, and by the many links which tied it to the currents of trade and to the surrounding peasantry, the manor became a very complicated organism. We can understand why only a few years after 1338 these same manors withstood so badly the disturbances to commerce, the fluctuations in prices and wages, and all those other scourges, pestilences and pillages with which the region, in common with many others in western Europe, was to be afflicted.

15

The history of systems of values

The global history of a civilization is built up from changes arising at different levels, such as ecology, demography, techniques of production and mechanisms of exchange, the distribution of power and the centres of decision-making, or, yet again, mental attitudes, collective behaviour and the vision of the world by which these attitudes are governed or by which these behaviours are dominated. The various movements are linked by close correlations, but each follows, according to its own particular rhythm, a relatively autonomous path. At some levels, especially in political relations, we can observe changes that are sometimes very rapid. My own experience encourages me to think, however, that the history of systems of values does not display sudden changes.

It is true that this kind of history can be disturbed by acculturation. A culture may at a particular moment in its evolution find itself penetrated and dominated by another, outside, culture either through shocks of political origin, such as invasions or colonization, or by the insidious action of infiltration, or by the processes of fascination and conversion, themselves the result of the unequal development of the differing powers of seduction of the civilizations encountered. But even in such cases, the changes appear always to be slow and no more than partial. As a rule, cultures, however simple, obstinately oppose all aggression and all intrusion of allogenous elements and offer continuing resistance.

Very striking, for example, is the slow progress made by Christianity (which is but one of many elements to be imprinted on Roman culture) in the tribes which the great migrations of the early middle ages brought into close contact with less rudimentary civilizations. Archaeology has revealed that Christian symbols were only very gradually insinuated into the graves of Germanic burial grounds, and that pagan beliefs for long persisted under the superficial guise of rites, tales and formulae imposed by force on the rest of the tribe by the converted chiefs. Eleventh-century prelates were still eager to extirpate them, and they had not wholly disappeared, at the very end of the middle ages, even in those provinces of Christianity most securely appropriated by the church. The latter still had to concede a place for several of the most tenacious and probably essential of pagan beliefs, such as the belief in the mysterious survival of dead souls between the funeral rites and the resurrection of the dead. Similarly, when the last years of the eleventh century saw the military expansion of western Christianity, and the scholars accompanying the warriors opened up the overwhelming wealth of Jewish and Graeco-Arab learning at Toledo, Campania and Palermo, intellectuals fell upon it in order to partake of its treasure. But for many decades the system of values of which they themselves were the vehicle held them back from taking over anything more than techniques, applicable either to the art of reasoning, or to the measuring of things, or to the care of the body. Probably repressive efforts on the part of the ecclesiastical powers were soon brought into play to prevent the philosophical and moral content of the translated works being appropriated. But these bans were always evaded; the totalitarian church of the thirteenth century never succeeded at any of the great centres of research in preventing the reading of and commenting on the New Aristotle. Yet even so, two centuries later, the corrosive power of this body of doctrine had still not succeeded to any extent in breaching the coherence of Christian thought.

Movements capable of transforming systems of values proceeded at an even more deliberate pace since they were sheltered from outside pressures. The upward and downward trends in economic activity (medievalists have in fact an advantage in being able to observe the workings of prolonged stagnations and recessions in this field) were themselves closely bound to movements of the demographic curve, and changes in technique brought about corresponding changes in the relations of production and in the distribution of wealth among the different ranks of the social edifice. But these changes themselves appeared spaced out more slowly over time than the economic transformations which caused them: and we may discover that these delays and retardations were in part a result of the strength of the ideological system. They took place within a cultural framework which might bend to receive them, but which was nevertheless little prone to modify itself profoundly and gave way only with the greatest reluctance. The cultural framework was in fact built around a skeleton of traditions which were transmitted from one generation to the next under a multitude of forms and by various systems of education, for which language, ritual and social behaviour formed the most solid supports.

True enough, obstacles to innovations do not reveal themselves with equal vigour in the different cultural milieus which meet and interact in the heart of every society. However, by far the most powerful of these propensities is the one towards conservation. The conservative spirit appears to be particularly vigorous in peasant societies whose long-term survival depends on the highly fragile balance of a coherent and patiently evolved system of agrarian practices which it appears dangerous to disturb. This conservatism shows itself in customs that are respectfully followed, and in the wisdom of the elders which is considered the safest repository. But the same spirit was probably evident in all social elites who were apparently open to the attractions of new ideas, aesthetics and fashions, but were at the same time unconsciously wracked by the fear that less superficial changes might endanger their authority. It was perhaps more alive among clergy of all kinds, dedicated as they were to the upholding of a vision of the world and moral precepts which supported the influence they exercised and the privileges they enjoyed. Resistance of this sort moreover was naturally reinforced by the tendency of all cultural models constructed to support the interests and tastes of the dominant stratum to be gradually vulgarized and, because of the fascination they excited, to be by degrees diffused towards the lower levels of the social edifice. The effect of downward tendencies of this kind was to prolong greatly the vitality of certain ideas and the behaviour which flowed from them and to maintain in contrast to the superficial modernity in which the elites found their satisfactions, a solid foundation of tradition upon which conservative aspirations could find their support.

It is as well, however, to recognize that these aspirations were in fact countered at times when more rapid changes in material structures made internal and external barriers more easily permeated and communication and osmosis was encouraged either by relaxed family solidarity, by providing openings for other cultures, or by disturbing established hierarchies. More direct consequences appear to be changes affecting the political structure to the extent that a new distribution of power could be brought about by the deliberate intention of modifying the system of education. It is at this level that the abruptness of an event—war, revolution, institutional change—can be shown to be to some degree unsettling. It is in any case necessary to distinguish what were the groups of individuals within society which either because of their professional or political position, or because they belonged to a certain age group, found themselves less tied by tradition and more inclined to combat it. It is equally necessary to gauge the power which these agents of innovation effectively disposed of. But whatever their importance or subversive capacity, the cultural system opposed their activities with a rigid framework. It was at the structural points of articulation that the cracks developed, spread outwards and ended by disjointing the whole body, even though the effects of dissolution were nearly always insidious. Despite the illusions which the apparent tumult of superficial agitation generated, the collapse caused by its repercussions never took place except over the long-term, was never anything but partial, and always left irreducible vestiges behind it.

In order to substantiate these general considerations by concrete examples, I propose to describe the circle of scholars who assembled in Paris in the middle years of the middle ages, a milieu which we might think highly likely to accept innovation. Their meeting place was at one of the main crossroads of the world, an urban centre in full growth with a population which found itself more than any other affected by economic currents and, at the heart of the greatest state in the west, by the swings of political activity—in short, the meeting point of all those who, from one end of Latin Christianity to the other, felt most ardently the hunger for knowledge. Their calling, that of teaching, was itself to some extent constricted by routine, all the more because it was a profession aimed at forming eminent members of a clergy. However, by its very nature the profession brought those who practised it face to face with younger persons whose demands encouraged them to go forward (as was so clearly expressed by one of these teachers, Abelard: 'my students demanded human and philosophical reasons; they needed intelligible explanations rather than affirmations.'). Finally the practice of the calling was one of methods of work based on dialogue, dispute and free discussion in a spirit of competitiveness comparable to the spirit which animated knights in the jousts of the period and which invited the same audacities in contests with received ideas. Let us attempt so far as we can (the advantage of historical observation is to be able to cover long periods, but it is also penalized by gaps in information which, when it comes to bygone ages, leaves many questions unanswered) to reconstitute the system of values such as was received, on the one hand, about 1125 by the contemporaries of Abelard, and on the other hand, about 1275, by the contemporaries of Jean de Meung.

One hundred and fifty years apart—one hundred and fifty years filled with a vast activity. A period of expansion comparable in its scale and its repercussions to the one we live in now and, to my mind, equally as unsettling. There were fundamental transformations in the infrastructure. In Abelard's time towns had hardly emerged from their rural background; the circulation of money had recently revived, but the only wealth was still the land and the only labour the labour of the fields. Despite the importance of handicrafts stimulated by the desire for luxurious ostentation of an aristocracy whose economic condition had been relieved by a century of agricultural growth, men's lives were entirely dominated by the pace and pressures of their natural surroundings. On the other hand, by the time Jean de Meung began to write the second part of the *Roman de la Rose*, the population was probably three times greater. The countryside was fully used but henceforth found itself subjugated, economically and politically, by the cities. Within the cities life had been delivered from the tyrannies of nature and had escaped the oppression of hunger, cold and darkness. Money had become the main instrument of power, the mainspring of social movement, and its management enriched beyond measure the Italian business men in the street of the Lombards so close to the schools. Changes on the political front had been hardly less profound. At the beginning of the twelfth century political actions were entirely ordered in the framework of the *seigneurie*. For the mass of labourers this meant complete subjection to the lords of castles and chiefs of villages; for the richer man it meant military specialization, profits from expeditions of pillage and freedom from all constraints except those arising from homage, feudal concessions or submission to the ties of lineage. A hundred and fifty years later there emerged a genuine state built upon an administrative framework sufficiently perfected for an abstract notion of authority to be reborn and for the personalities of sovereigns to be overshadowed by those of their servants. The period was to witness the assuaging of discords, which ritualized the art of war and bestowed upon combat the air of a sporting event. Judicial rules were now fixed by being written down and were operated by professionals of procedure. There grew up habits of debate. A feeling of liberty was strengthened by associations of equals into groupings of mutual interest binding people together at various levels of society, and which were vigorous enough in the suburbs of the towns to encourage the first attempts at strikes. A century and a half had seen the rise of the adventure of the Crusades, and its check—the pillaging in Spain, Sicily and Constantinople, with their superior cultures whose splendour had in the past made the countrified Carolingian civilization appear even more derisory. There was an astonishing retreat of the outermost limits of the universe, an overflow from Mongol Asia, Marco Polo's journey to Peking, the penetration of the African and Asian fringes, no longer by warriors but by traders and missionaries, who now became accustomed to speak in other tongues and to use novel weights and measures. A century and a half which had seen the growth of a many-headed heresy and had then seen it contained and dismantled by the repressive drill that the church succeeded in imposing all over Christian society. The heresy was now yoked and partially assimilated into orthodoxy at the cost even of distortion, as is shown by the fate of the Franciscan message. A century and a half sufficed to enable aesthetics to cover the distance from the tympanum of Autun to Cimabue and the pulpit of Pisa, from the vaulted roofs of Vézelay to those of the Sainte Chapelle, from Gregorian plainsong to the polyphonics of Nôtre Dame.

But in a cultural milieu such as this, so full of the striving after truth, the thirst for understanding and the taste for what was modern, it does not seem as if such upheavals had modified the system of values to any great extent. Without doubt the primacy of reason was, about 1275, more deliberately exalted: and we know from the second *Roman de la Rose* how insistently. But two generations before Abelard, Berenger of Tours proclaimed reason to be 'the honour of man'; and the lucid vision of things that Jean de Meung's contemporaries attempted to attain by logical tools derived in fact from the patient use of logical mechanisms which the masters of the school of Paris had learned to use in the first years of the twelfth century in order to resolve the ambiguity of the signs of truth in the sacred texts and in the spectacle of the visible world. Meanwhile, these processes became more subtle and more efficient, but they did not change their nature nor their objective. The spirit of criticism in 1275 probably challenged audaciously everything that the intellectuals of that time called the sham, the hypocrisies, of religious observances, the submission of the sanctimonious to pontifical orders. But the challenge was also directed against the privileges of noble blood that Abelard, perfectly at home in that social category, had never denied and had never thought of questioning; it was also directed against the extravagances of the game of courtesy which the same Abelard had attempted to practise to the best of his ability and also against the sophistications of the worldly ethic. But there too we can divine a similar attitude, a similar inclination for the contest of argument, a similar aspiration to honesty to the extent to which it already existed among the masters of Paris in the first quarter of the twelfth century. If they did not aim at the same targets it was only because the problems posed by the social, political and moral environment did not present themselves in the same terms. As for the more sustained attention devoted in the last thirty years of the thirteenth century to nature, that 'art of God', and as for the will to discover its laws, to achieve a clear understanding of a natural order 'from which flow honest ways' and to attain there the solid foundations of an ethic and a faith, we can observe these already present: more timid it is true, less assured, still unprovided with a conquering weapon but busy forging one, they were there in the spirit of those who a century and a half earlier, in the time of Louis VI and Suger, commented on the Scriptures, studied the course of the heavenly bodies and the manner in which their luminous rays were propagated. In the end we do not see that the corpus of beliefs had been seriously affected. Dante indeed referred to those disciples of Epicurus who believed that the soul died with the body, and he says they were many. But such views had obviously to remain secret, and those who held them, if they were unmasked, escape the historian's eye. But, in reality, for how many Parisian intellectuals did the disquiet and the critical spirit induce anything more than a spirit of raillery? The men I have in mind appear to have adhered well and without effort or dissimulation to the essentials of the Christian dogma. No doubt their Christianity showed a new face; it appeared much more detached from its terrified abasements and enveloping ritualism than it did a hundred and fifty years earlier. It was now oriented towards a suffering and brotherly God, with whom a man might attempt a dialogue; many, like Bonaventure, accordingly took the path of mysticism. But Bernard of Clairvaux had already largely blazed these trails; Abelard had already read the New Testament with an attention sufficient to affirm that the fault was in the intention and not in the act; and Anselm of Canterbury had, before him, concentrated his studies on the problem of the incarnation. What in fact comes out most clearly in all these fields is their enduring consequences—those of analytical techniques, of the desire for understanding sharpened by the methods and objectives of teaching, of the moral exigencies imposed upon men by their situation within society, of a vision of the natural and supernatural universe founded on texts which were increasingly well interpreted.

The only remarkable modulations I can see were on two levels. In the first place they were to found an awareness of the relativity of things and, before all else, the relativity of time. Among thinking men at the end of the thirteenth century, time was no longer thought of as a homogeneous bloc in which the past and the future were coherent with the present, standing in anagogical relations to it. When Humbert of Romano, the Dominican, meditated on the recent history of Christianity, he sought an explanation in a chain of natural causes, and his personal experience of the checks suffered by the church, the decline of imperial dignity, and the retreat of Latin in the east made it impossible for him to continue to believe in the unity and the necessity of the history of God's people. The gradual discovery of the immensity, diversity and complexity of creation, the new awareness that the universe was full of men who refused to listen to the message of Christ, obliged those with the clearest minds to accept that Christianity could not be placed at the heart of the world, or at least that it occupied no more than a limited part of it. In the same way they had to recognize that Christian thought found itself incapable of absorbing or of rejecting the coherent bloc of the Aristotelian system. In the second place, many of the men of whom we are speaking accepted wholeheartedly the taste for worldly happiness, the happiness that was, according to Jean de Meung, offered to man on the morning of creation. It was the joy of living which had been compromised by the offensives of sham and pretence against nature and reason that the philosophers took upon themselves to reinstate. These intellectuals had resolutely repulsed exhortations to the *contemptus mundi* and all models of renunciation and refusal which monks had for so long been, and still were, the triumphant propagandists.

At the level of ideology changes thus appear much less marked than those at the same time affecting economic activity, demography and the cut and thrust of power. But systems of values were not totally immobile; the transformation of material, political and social structures disturbed its foundations and made them move, but this evolution took place without haste and without shocks. This was so even in the cultural *avant-garde* whose special function was to work for the adjustment of the systems. In contrast to the turbulence characterizing the controversies, the diatribes and condemnations, the historian sees the system of values adjusting itself insensibly and with suppleness.

Concerning another major problem, the possibility of forecasting the changes I have discussed, I shall only hazard a few comments.

The task of the historian is to propose explanations after the event, that is, to arrange facts which are presented for his observation, to put them into relation with each other and in this way to introduce a logic into the unfolding of linear time. The historian is led by this very process to attempt to show himself more aware of novelties, to run them to earth and, in order to display them, to abstract them artificially from the full stream of customs and routines by which they are enveloped in the web of life. He is led, moreover, when he wishes to give an account of these novelties and especially when they occur on the plane not of events but of structures, to give preference to necessity rather than to chance. The historian can thus succeed in re-establishing satisfactory correlations between the affirmation at the end of the thirteenth century of the notions which the words nature and reason were then meant to express, between the growth of enjoyment in life, between the discovery of relativity and moreover the forward leap in urban prosperity, the unlocking of the western world, the rise of certain social groups, the slow fading of the mirages of the New Jerusalem and the perfecting of the syllogistic tool. He can do this in the same way in which he succeeds in explaining the passage of the religion of the Eternal of Moissac to the religion of the scourged Christ by changes in the environment. But in this way, whether consciously or not, he provides the argument for all systems of hope, all ideas that the succession of the ages of mankind are established on a chain of determining causes—systems which lay claim to prevision and which set out to build on an experience of the past a vector which they assume will extend its relevance into the future.

For example, the convictions of the eleventh-century monks whose periodical processions were meant to enact the march of man towards the ineffable light rest on an interpretation of history. The same is true of the Eternal Evangelist of Joachim de Fiore who gave 1260 as the precise date of the advent of the reign of the Holy Spirit. Marxist thought is based on an interpretation of history and takes up, with regard to forecasting the future, a position that demands detailed consideration.

As Antonio Labriola writes:

> Historical foresight, which lies at the base of the doctrine of the *Communist Manifesto* implies neither a chronological point of time nor an anticipated description of a social configuration. It is society as a whole which, at a moment in its evolution, discovers the cause of its predestined march, and at a salient moment of its evolutionary trajectory itself sheds the light which illuminates the laws of its movement. [This prevision] belongs neither to chronology, nor to forecasts, nor to promise; it is, to put it in one word, which in my view expresses everything, 'morphological'.[1]

Let this be understood: what is considered to be foreseeable is society's progress towards new forms; this phenomenon can be foreseen to the extent to which the recurrence of certain relationships and their regular subordination to determined laws can be solidly established. But since Marxist analysis strives to be rigorously scientific, it cannot claim to establish these relations and their subordination solidly except on the level of the material foundations to the social edifice. In dealing with what he calls 'ideological social relations', Lenin ('Who are the friends of the people?') in fact holds back, whereas the major objective upon which, in my view, present research in social history has to fix itself is precisely how the discordant movements which animate changes in the infra- and superstructure move, and how they react upon each other. If the dissolution of the relations of personal dependence within the medieval *seigneurie* seems indeed directly the result of the action of long-term trends—the perfecting of agricultural techniques, the growth of population and the spread of the use of money—then supposing that men at that time had the same means of analysis as we can use nowadays, it would have been possible, to the extent that the extrapolations were not mostly misleading, to foresee the dissolution as it would have been. On

---

[1] A. Labriola, 'In memoria del Manifesto dei communisti', *Saggi nel materialismo* (Rome, 1964).

the other hand, who could have predicted the sudden advent, in the buildings undertaken at Saint Denis by Abbot Suger, of an aesthetic of light? Or the appearance of rituals of courtly love as counterpoint to developments in the structure of the aristocratic family and the conjugal ethic proposed by the church? Or, indeed, the Vaudois heresy and the forms that Franciscan devotion took on when it was domesticated by the authority of the pope? In the present state reached by the science of man, it seems indeed that 'morphological' forecasting of the future of a civilization could not, without being excessively rash, know how to allow, among other things, for the probable course of the deep tendencies which propelled economic history (such as population, technology and perhaps scientific knowledge), without concealing the fact that it could at any moment change direction under the influence of movements of opinion, propaganda or decisions of authority.

All this does not mean that the historian cannot offer the futurologist certain propositions of method which would apply to the observation of systems of values. If we admit that the ideological envelope (which was, as we have seen, extremely flexible and did not easily split like a chrysalis) is obviously affected by movements in the infrastructure, but tends to respond to them rather slowly, we must look first of all into the massive trends of the present day, such as demographic change and the transformation of economic relations. It is these that are apt to cause adjustments in the envelope by unsettling systems of thought, by encouraging or impeding communication between groups and by favouring transfers, uprootings, exchanges and fusions. In the second place, we can pick out the points where resistance to tradition appear most fragile: we can test the rigidity of educational systems, within the family, at school and in all the centres of initiation and apprenticeship, we can measure their capacity to receive external stimuli and also the inherent capacity for assimilation of a particular view of the world in the face of a possible assault by elements from external cultures. But it is also necessary to take the historical event into consideration. The latter acts mainly at the political level. No doubt it can be taken to be a mere surface effervescence, largely determined by the disposition of more fundamental structures. However, to the historian who has already noted how narrow are the limits of foresight in relation to long-term trends of demographic or economic changes the event will appear, by its very nature, to be fortuitous. Its development, at least even if not its initial occurrence, will reveal itself as specially resistant to forecasting. But in the short term the effects of an event can never be totally negligible. Through the attempts at revolution or reform that it stimulates, and through the transfers of activity that it provokes, it reacts upon the institutions by which the transmission of knowledge, beliefs and ceremonies are framed. In the end the historian must insist on the very importance of history itself as a particularly active constituent in the combination of elements making up a practical ideology. In very large measure the vision that a society forms of its destiny, the direction that it attributes, rightly or wrongly, to its own history, introduces itself as one of the most powerful tools of the forces of conservation or progress. It operates as a support, one of the most effective ever, for the will to safeguard or to destroy a system of values and as a brake or an accelerator on the movement which leads at a variable pace to the transformations of ideas and behaviour.

Sources

The chapters of this book were originally published as follows:
1 'Les Sociétés médiévales: une approche d'ensemble', *Annales. Economie, société, civilisation* I (January–February 1971); an inaugural lecture given at the Collège de France.
2 'Recherches sur l'évolution des institutions judiciaires pendant le Xe et le XIe siècle dans le sud de la Bourgogne', *Le Moyen Age* II–IV (1946), I–II (1947).
3 'Lignage, noblesse et chevalerie au XIIe siècle dans la région mâconnaise: une révision', *Annales. Economie, société, civilisation* (July–October 1972).
4 'Histoire et sociologie de l'occident médiéval: résultats et recherches', *Revue roumaine d'histoire* III (1970).
5 'Aux origines d'un système de classification sociale', *Mélange F. Braudel* (Toulouse 1972).
6 'Une Enquête à poursuivre: la noblesse dans la France médiévale', *Revue Historique* 226 (1961).
7 'Au XIIe siècle: les 'jeunes' dans la société aristocratique dans la France du nord-ouest', *Annales. Economie, société, civilisation* V (September–October 1964).
8 'Les Laics et la paix de Dieu', *I laici nella 'societas christiani' dei secoli XI e XII,* Atti della terza settimana internationale di studio della Mendola (21–27 August 1965, Milan 1966).
9 'Structure de parenté et noblesse, France du nord, XIe-XIIe siècles', *Miscellanea mediaevalia in memoriam Jan Frederik Niermeyer* (Groningen 1967).
10 'Remarques sur la littérature généalogique en France aux XIe et XIIe siècles', *Comptes rendus des séances de l'année 1967* (April–June 1967), Académie des Inscriptions et Belles-Lettres (Paris 1967); paper read to the annual meeting of the Academy in Paris.
11 'Les Origines de la chevalerie', *Ordinamenti Militari in Occidente nell 'alto medioevo, Spoleto 30 Marze–15 Aprile 1967* XV (Spoleto 1968); paper read to the Settimane di studio del Centro italiano di studi sull 'alto medioevo.

12 'The Diffusion of Cultural Patterns in Feudal Society', paper given at a conference in May 1966 at the Ecole Normale Superieure in Paris and included among the 'Papers presented to the Past and Present Conference on "Literature and the Historian", 10 July 1967 at University College London'. World copyright The Past & Present Society, Corpus Christi College, Oxford, England. This translation is reprinted with the permission of the Society and the author from *Past & Present*, a journal of historical studies, no. 39 (April 1968).

13 'Situation de la noblesse en France au début du XIIIe siècle', *Tijdschrift voor Geschiedenis* (1969); lecture given at the University of Amsterdam on 6 February 1969.

14 'La Seigneurie et l'économie paysanne: Alpes du Sud, 1338,' *Études rurales* (July–September 1961).

15 'L'Histoire des systèmes de valeurs', *History and Theory, Studies in the Philosophy of History* XI no. 1 (1972).

Subject index

abbeys, *see under individual names*
actores, 40*n*
Acts of the Apostles, 164
Adelsliteratur, 151
  see also Literature
Adnantiato Karoli, 163
advocatus/advocatio, 40, 41*n*
  settlements with ecclesiastical lords, 44
agnatic line (*agnatio*), 101, 102, 139, 140,
    142, 145, 153, 174
  see also Male inheritance, lineage,
    Primogeniture, *etc*
  servile, 103*n*
agricultor(es), 127, 165
  see also Labourers
agriculture, 9
  see also Demesne(s), Cereal cultivation
allodial holdings
  transmission of, 71
  see also Freeholdings
anathema, *see* Excommunication
ancestors
  of Arnould of Ardres, 144–5, 146, 157
  of Lambert of Wattrelos, 136–8
  mythical, 144, 146, 156, 157; nobility of,
    102; search for, 121; *see also* Genea-
    logies
ancestry
  degrees of, 108
  family memory of, 146
animal husbandry, 197
  see also Plough animals
Annales Cameracenses, 99, 116, 120, 135,
    140, 141, 142, 161
  see also Genealogies
anthropology, 2, 84
arbitration
  between lords, 50–51
  see also Courts (of law), Justice
archaeology, medieval, 83–4, 85

aristocracy
  consolidation of, 173–4, 178–85
  family structure of, 68–75
  imperial and regional, 104–5
  lay and church, 8
Aristotelian system, 222
  see also Aristotle, the New
armiger, 183
  see also Esquire
armorial bearings, 101, 103, 179, 180
arms, bearing of, 163, 164, 165, 166, 167,
    178
  see also Dubbing of knights
art, medieval, 171
asylum, 48
  see also Peace, institutions of

bachelor(s), 87, 106, 110, 113*n*, 115, 119,
    140
  see also Celibacy, Youths
ban
  of Cluny, 60
  of Hospitallers, 194, 195
  lordship of, 79, 80, 128; profits of, 66;
    rights and power of, 92, 94, 95, 97, 103,
    106, 107, 108, 111, 168, 169, 170, 178
bannus, area of, 49
barley, *see* Cereals
barons, 12th-century, 105
bastards, 144, 146
bellator(es), 91, 92, 165, 166, 167
birthrate, of aristocracy, 120
births, limitation on, 87
  see also Marriages, limitation on
bishops, 165
  and formation of social structure, 92
  as protectors of poor, 127
  in struggle with monks, 91
  see also under individual names
blacksmiths, 199

Index of proper names

Note: Names of authors and editors cited in the text and notes are given in capitals.

Abbon of Fleury, 89*n*, 164
Abelard, Peter, 114*n*, 177*n*, 219, 220
Adalbéron, bishop of Laon, 89, 90, 91, 92, 107, 128, 165, 166, 167, 168
Adhemar of Chabannes, 130, 150
Aelfric, 90
Africa, 220
Agobard, 165
Aix-la-Chapelle, 6
Aix-en-Provence, commandery of, 190, 204, 208
  Faculty of Letters, 99
  Laboratory of Medieval Archaeology, 83
Alard family, 66
Alemania, 101, 102
  see also Germania
Alfred the Great, 90
Allegret, troubadour, 121
Alps, the knighthood in region of, 98
ALTHOFER, B, 16*n*
Amboise, sires of, 151, 152, 154
  see also Breton of
Ameugny, family of, 67
Anchin, abbey of, 151, 152
Angers, St Aubin of, 150, 151
Angoulême, genealogy of counts of, 100, 151
Anjou, count(s) of, 100
  family of, 121
  genealogies of, 150, 151, 152, 154, 155, 156
  as king of England, 181
  see also Fulk Réchin, Geoffrey Martel
Anjou, 16, 377
Anse, council of (995), 29, 34*n*, 47
Ansould of Maule, 117*n*
Antibes, princes of, 160, 165
Apulia, 119
Aquitaine, duke of, as king of England, 181
  see also William of

Aquitaine, 123, 124, 167, 168
Ardres, *see* Arnould of, Baldwin of, Lambert of, Simon of
Argens, valley of, 200
Aristotle, the New, 217
  see also Aristotelian system
Arles, 108*n*, 123
  commandery of, 192, 194, 196, 198, 201, 204, 206*n*, 208
  council of (1037–41), 131, 132*n*
Arnould of Ardres, count of Guines, 109, 113, 114, 115, 116, 117*n*, 119, 120, 121, 122
  genealogy of, 143–6
Arnould of Ghent, 119*n*
Arnould the Great, count of Flanders, 100, 151, 153
  see also Flanders, counts of
  of Pamele, bishop of Soissons, 114
Arnould the Younger, count of Flanders, 150
  see also Flanders, counts of
Artois, 151
  nobles in, 109
Asia, 220
AUBENAS, R, 34*n*
AULT, W. O, 29*n*, 32*n*
Authon, 21, 42
  pagus of, 35
  tympanum of, 220
Avesnes, sires of, 138
Avignon, 202, 204

Bâgé, Oury of, 34
  sire of, 35
Baldwin of Ardres, count of Guines, 113, 119
Baldwin I, count of Flanders, 153, 156
Baldwin IV and V, counts of Hainault, 155*n*